RICHARD REEVES

SIMON AND SCHUSTER

NEW YORK

PASSAGE
TO
PESHAWAR

PAKISTAN:
BETWEEN THE HINDU KUSH
AND
THE ARABIAN SEA

Copyright © 1984 by Richard Reeves
All rights reserved
including the right of reproduction
in whole or in part in any form
Published by Simon and Schuster
A Division of Simon & Schuster, Inc.
Simon & Schuster Building
Rockefeller Center
1230 Avenue of the Americas
New York, New York 10020
SIMON AND SCHUSTER and colophon
are registered trademarks of Simon & Schuster, Inc.
Designed by Edith Fowler
Manufactured in the United States of America

1 2 3 4 5 6 7 8 9 10

Library of Congress Cataloging in Publication Data

Reeves, Richard.
  Passage to Peshawar.

  Includes index.
  1. Pakistan—Politics and government—1971–
2. Pakistan—Description and travel. 3. Reeves,
Richard. I. Title.
DS384.R44 1984   954.9'105   84-11600
ISBN: 0-671-50842-3

This book is for my traveling companions, Catherine O'Neill, Jeff Reeves, Colin O'Neill and Conor O'Neill—and for the people we met along the way in Pakistan.

The people stared at us everywhere, and we stared at them. We
generally made them feel pretty
small, too, before we got done with
them, because we bore down on
them with America's greatness until
we crushed them. And yet we took
kindly to the manners and the customs. . . .

MARK TWAIN
The Innocents Abroad

CONTENTS

Preface   13

1   Moon Over Gadani   17
2   The Materialism of the Illiterate Masses   24
3   Mister Richard Meets Mister Mister   49
4   Our New Best Friend   62
5   The Refugees From Over the Mountain   71
6   Land of the Pure   90
7   Who Runs Pakistan?   108
8   Donkeys and Suzukis   121
9   The Second English Empire   130
10 Behind the Veil   143
11 To the Khyber Pass   152
12 Bread but No Circuses   163
13 The Police State   172
14 How We Pick Our Friends   187
    Epilogue   205
    Acknowledgments   211
    Index   213

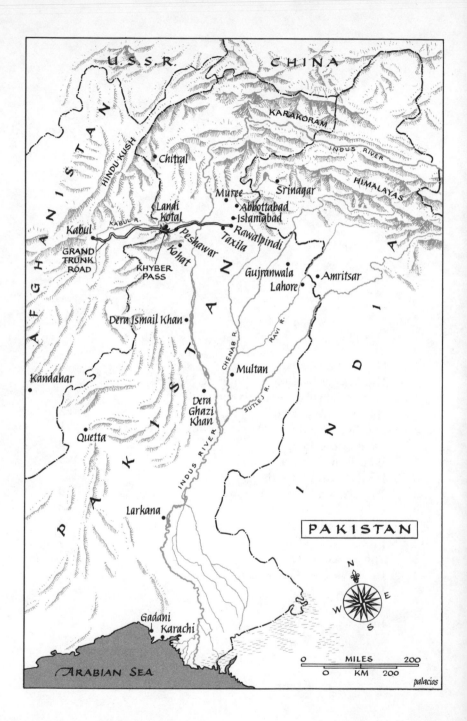

PREFACE

In June of 1983, my family and I moved for a while into a house in Islamabad, Pakistan. We were there because of my wife's work; she was preparing a report on conditions in the camps housing more than two million refugees from war across the border in Afghanistan. As it turned out, we spent very little time in that house, traveling, instead, thousands of miles back and forth across the country.

I knew very little about Pakistan, by population the ninth-largest country in the world, when I arrived. I am an American, rather innocent abroad. Although I had traveled in and reported from many parts of the world, I shared a good deal of the proud provincialism of many of my countrymen. Having left the Old World, in many cases in debt or disrepute, we are generally not much interested in the ways and wonders of far places.

There were many wonders and exotic ways between the Hindu Kush and the Arabian Sea. Pakistan is an exciting place, from the ancient city of Moenjodaro to the ancient ways still practiced in the pagan valleys Rudyard Kipling wrote of in "The Man Who Would Be King." Just to be in the country was an adventure.

But what did all that mean to me? A great deal, I came to believe. This book is about our travels, but it is also an attempt to come to grips with my own relationship to a wondrous place and people living in many centuries at the same time, faithful to a religion foreign and frightening to my part of the world, governed by a military dictatorship backed by the money and might of the United States.

There was certainly a political connection between me and the people I met, whether they knew it or not. I was an American and they were living in a client state of my country. The official term, back home, was "frontline state." The United States government considered Pakistan the front line in a worldwide struggle with Soviet communism—and, in fact, soldiers and airmen of the Soviet Union were in battle (with Afghan *mujahideen*) on the northern and western borders of Pakistan. After years of listening to Presidential proclamations and Congressional debate, I finally saw American foreign policy at its end point—and that was something of a revelation.

But I did not come home as an expert on either foreign policy or South Asia. I was a traveler lucky enough to be carrying credentials of journalism and letters of introduction that might get me in a door or two. I was also carrying a full kit of "Western" prejudices. I say Western because, more often than not outside offices of the government of Pakistan and the homes of friends educated in the United States or Europe, I was constantly reminded of lines written in Lahore by Kipling—"East is East . . . " and I was from the West. In Gadani or Chitral, I didn't think that many people saw much difference between Americans and Frenchmen or Germans; we were all perceived, I suspected, as vaguely British, somehow related to the last White Men to take up residence and local burdens.

If they thought about it at all, the people I met probably figured that I was for modernization and democracy and individual rights, and against public flogging and military regimes and dinners without wine. Also, amazed by *perdah*, polygamy and a month of fasting. Well, all of that was true.

By the time I left Pakistan, at the end of August, I had changed my mind about more than a few things. The country and the people, their faith and their ambitions, did not seem so exotic to me anymore. I still looked at everything as an American, but I hoped that I saw a little deeper than I once did. When I was again in Pakistan, for two weeks in June of 1984, I felt more at home, convinced there had to be some bond between a man who came from a country with the conviction to call itself "The last best hope of mankind" and the people of a country with the faith to name itself Pakistan, "Land of the Pure."

MOON OVER GADANI

1

There was a full moon over Karachi in the early morning hours of April 30, 1983. Muhammad Siddique, the last master of the tanker U.S.S. *Hermitage,* had been waiting for that, the night of the monthly high tide of the Arabian Sea. He was one of only ten crewmen on board the 10,000-ton American-built ship as it sailed northwest from the harbor at just after 5 A.M. Six hours later the *Hermitage* was forty miles from Karachi, three miles off the coast at a place called Gadani Beach. Siddique turned the 661-foot-long ship toward shore, and he ordered full speed ahead. The *Hermitage* was traveling at twelve knots per hour when she hit bottom, slowly sliding to a stop in the huge gash she plowed into the sand a hundred feet from dry land.

There was, for a moment, only a hissing noise as surf surged in around the beached tanker. Then with a yell, barefoot men with loose clothes flapping in the dawn ran into the sea. One of them, a hundred feet below the prow of the ship, jumped onto the lowering anchor and began climbing its chain, wrapping a steel cable into the links. The man below him grabbed the cable and began moving back toward the beach as if he were in a tug-of-war with the ship itself, as if he and the shouting men around him could pull 10,000 tons of ship onto the sand. Which was exactly what they were going to do.

17

Up on the beach, the other end of the cable was attached to a winch powered by an old Bedford truck engine. The *Hermitage* was tied up to this chugging device being run by a man sitting astride the engine as if it were a horse. As the level of the sea was momentarily raised by each surge of the tide, he gunned the engine, straining the cable to pull the ship forward inch by inch. Then, gangs of men carrying tools of destruction—sledgehammers, wrenches, crowbars and portable oxyacetylene cutting torches—climbed aboard the tanker, walking up the anchor chain as if it were a tightrope, or scrambling up monkey style. Then they began the breaking of the *Hermitage*. With clanging and hollow booms sounding small on the beach, the men began nibbling the ship to death. They had no equipment heavier than the old 140-horsepower truck engine attached to a deck winch from another broken ship, and they were taking the ship apart almost by hand—carrying, unbolting, stripping, ripping, draining anything that could be sold anywhere in the world. Engines. Lifeboats. Compasses. Chairs. Toilets. Bottles of whiskey. Portholes. Railings. Pipe. The diesel oil in the crankcases. All of that was done with nothing but the winch and hand tools—and human muscle. The largest pieces of the ship's superstructure—up to twenty tons—were slid off on wires from the deck almost a hundred feet down to the beach, the way children come down a playground slide. It took a week to get all that gear off and into piles on the beach. Then the men, hundreds of them, began cutting up the 661-foot tanker like a salami, into slices weighing ten and twenty tons each.

When I was there, three months later in August, the *Hermitage*, what was left of her, was about 200 feet long. Where her bow had been, where the sea met the shore, was a 60-foot-high rusty wall—it was about 40 feet wide—which had been a bulkhead between two of the tanker's great oil reservoirs. The other 400 feet or so of the *Hermitage* was scattered up the beach—a funnel, the crankcase, the anchor, heaps of steel plate—to be sold as the raw material of new steel. Sparks and glowing chunks of hot metal were raining from the top of the wall as the cutting torches, hand-held by men wearing tanks of mixed oxygen and acetylene, completed another slice. Other men, small silhouettes against the sky, were slowly moving across the top of the wall, straining as against a great wind, pulling the cables from the same old winch. The wires pulled taut against their backs coming over the left shoulder and under the right armpit as they inched toward the high corners of the great wall. The cables were attached. The Bedford engine whined, paused and whined again. The wall finally began to waver. Wiremen and the torchmen leaped back onto the remainder of the ship—flying for a moment like birds, flapping and vulnerable in turbans, sandals and thin flowing cloth. The huge slice of the *Hermitage* tipped away from them and crashed into the wet sand below. Other men rushed forward on the beach, grabbing the cables to help the winch pull the steel wall farther up on the sand. There it was cut again and again by the torchmen, or split by men using wedges and sledgehammers—until eight men, two at each corner, some of them placing a sandal on one shoulder to protect it against the metal heated by the torches and the 100-degree sun, could lift a section, crouching under it and pushing up with a cry of *"Udi!"*

"Lift!"—the word was Pushtu, the language of the Pathans, the people who lived on both sides of the mountain border between Pakistan and Afghanistan. The Pathans, as many as 25,000 at a time, had traveled a thousand miles south to the Arabian Sea to work along the five miles of Gadani Beach, where, at any time, 150 ships were beached and broken. The shipbreakers—their bosses usually did not know their names—were day laborers paid from 30 to 50 rupees for a day that began at 7 A.M. and ended at 7 P.M., seven days a week. That was, roughly, $2.25 to $3.75 a day. If they were killed at Gadani, their families were supposed to receive 15,000 rupees, a little more than $1,000. But I was told by a director of a shipbreaking company that the death fee was rarely paid. It was more economical to scare away survivors with threats or to bribe local officials and the labor brokers who supplied the gangs of nameless workers from the tribes and villages along the country's northwest frontier.

"It's very dangerous there?" I said more as a statement than a question as the director and I watched the men running along the top of the new front of the *Hermitage*. "It's very dangerous right here," he said, looking at the winch cable near us. "Those things snap all the time."

"What do these people think of you?" I said. Another director answered after a quiet moment: "They hate us. You can see the hatred in their eyes if you come upon them suddenly. But they need cash because Pakistan is becoming a modern country."

Anyway, the other one said, the beach was getting safer. There had been only a couple of dozen deaths so far in the year, he said; the actual number, I found, was thirty-four dead during the most recent six months. In most cases they had fallen from the ships or were crushed by falling steel. There were a great many burns, but those were rarely fatal.

"It's a real Pakistani industry. You saw: labor intensive," the older director said later, looking out over the beach from his office, once the captain's quarters of a forgotten ship that had disappeared into scrap steel and then into the furnaces of rolling mills. It was decorated with old calendars, prints of Sweden and New England and a tourist poster of New York City showing the Empire State Building, and a dusty collection of decorated artificial trees from Christmases past at sea. "A few investors get together, usually Karachi businessmen, but also big American companies like American Express, and they buy an old ship. If you can get it here, you don't need anything else. No equipment or anything."

What that meant, among other things, was that there was no water supply or electrical lines at Gadani. All the mechanical equipment used was taken from the ships, and the heaviest thing there was the winch powered by the truck engine. Machinery required fuel and maintenance: men were cheaper. There had been no road to the place for years. The trucks bringing out the steel just bounced away over the rough desert behind the beach. Breaking, at the time I was there, cost out at about $40 a ton. A ship like the *Hermitage*—built in 1956 and relatively inefficient after 1973, when rising fuel costs made many older ships obsolete—could be bought for about $95 a ton. The profits on those investments and costs, at the best of times, were well over 300 percent. The best steel in the ship (about half the tonnage) was selling for $240 a ton. The rest sold for $130 a ton. In addition, the owners also made money from selling the lifeboats, the boilers, the whiskey and anything else on board at the end of a ship's last voyage, plus whatever copper, brass and aluminum could be stripped from the vessel. In all, Gadani was producing one million tons of steel a year, and 10,000 tons of other metal, principally copper and brass.

It added up—to sums large enough during the 1970s to attract a couple of thousand investors, who, through brokers, scouted the ship registry lists of Lloyd's of London for vessels that might be coming up for retirement and a final trip to the Gadani graveyard. There were other bidders, of course. Taiwan has a thriving shipbreaking industry—the difference, though, was that Taiwanese workers were paid twice as much for half as many hours and the process was mechanized, done in drydocks with cranes and the other heavy lifters of modernism. Bangladesh had also recently begun to try shipbreaking on the Pakistani model, often, in fact, financed and managed by Pakistanis. Some of them told me they were concerned that labor costs were getting out of hand at Gadani.

The idea was to buy a ship complete with cargo consigned to a port near the breaking area. For the Gadani breakers that meant Karachi or some other relatively near Asian port. With luck, the investors also made some money on shipping and selling the cargo, before the regular crew was directed to Karachi. On arrival, they would all be dismissed except for a couple of engineers and a cook. Those few waited—for the monthly high tide and for Muhammad Siddique or, sometimes, Hamid Fadoo. Siddique and Fadoo were the two beaching masters of Gadani. Each was paid approximately 20,000 rupees per beaching. Their job was to get the ship to the point where the Pathans could get their hands on the anchor.

The skill of the masters was legendary, and the ships were lined up in amazing precision along the waterline, often only 100 feet or so apart. Next to the *Hermitage* was the British *Dragoon*, or what was left of her after four months: less than 100 feet of the lower stern of what had been a 726-foot, 12,500-ton tanker. Then came the *Nordave*, another British vessel, a 500-foot, 7,500-ton cargo ship. All in a rusty row—along a strip of wide beach that the government of Pakistan once talked about developing as a seaside resort. It had become something far more exotic; Gadani was a place where time rolled backward. Muhammad Siddique brought the modern world, or at least its products, to this strange shore, and people rushed out with little more than their bodies as tools and broke the vessels of modernity down into ever smaller, ever less sophisticated parts until they could lift it and carry it away in pieces, little more than big hunks of mineral, rocks almost. At the edge of the sea were the ships. Then there were large and recognizable parts, products of skilled design and workmanship—the propeller, the crankshaft with cams higher than a man was tall. Farther up were smaller parts—doors and hatches and instrument walls with their dials and gauges removed. Then plates the size of walls, showing rivets and welds and bolts. Finally the smallest piles of steel plate and scrap, almost unrecognizable, just something to lift on a truck headed for a mill furnace somewhere inland.

The Pathans lived behind the last heaps. The beach was bordered by a thin line of housing constructed from the scrap of the sea—flotsam on land, the little of the scrap that couldn't be sold. Broken boards. Torn canvas. Cardboard. Driftwood. The roof line of the shanties was broken occasionally by the towers of small, crudely built mosques. This was, after all, the Islamic Republic of Pakistan—"The Land of the Pure" is the English translation—by population the ninth largest country in the world, more than 90 million people and a growth rate of more than 3 percent each year. The workers seemed to be quite religious—government and peer pressure in the Islamic Republic may produce more religion than meets the soul—and during the Holy Month of Ramazan, when Muslims fasted from sunup to sunset, the men worked at night because they were too weak without food or water to work twelve hours in temperatures above 100 degrees Fahrenheit. The ships were broken then—in part of June and July—by the ancient light of oil-soaked torches in the sand, and a few electric spotlights powered by portable generators.

That was Gadani, and beyond it the desert began and time continued in retreat. Swirling dust rose in plumes and clouds behind the rough shelters of the Pathans. The only life seemed to be nomad families and their animals, camels and goats, dimly seen in the dust. Dimly understood by someone like me. They might have been from Pakistan. But then they could have been from Afghanistan. Or Iran. What country? Just a name. What century? It did not seem to matter in the brown air. The only thing clearly seen on the road from the beach was the white mountain, which was not really a mountain and not really white. It is a conical rock outcropping in the desert flatness. The white was paint, on one side only. What? Perhaps something religious. That would certainly make sense in a country of faith, a land of shrines. It was sort of miraculous, but a miracle that I understood better than the nomads in the haze. The rock had been painted white for a television commercial. The magic of lights and cameras could make it look like the snowy peak of a great mountain, the greatest mountain in Pakistan, the second highest in the world—K-2. The desert rock was being used to film commercials for a popular Pakistani cigarette with that name—K-2. How far were the nomads from the painted rock? How many years or generations would it take them to get to the electronic mountain? But weren't they there already? They could see and touch my world through the dust that was everywhere in Pakistan. What agony there was in that—the agony of an ancient people drawn to miraculous modern mountains.

2

THE
MATERIALISM
OF THE
ILLITERATE MASSES

The road from Chitral south to the valley of Bumburet also ran backward in time.

That was saying something, because Chitral was almost at the edge of Pakistan, which put it at the very edge of the modern world. Guarded against the outside by the peaks of the Hindu Kush and Hindu Raj—one of them, Tirich Mir, is 25,290 feet high—Chitral was closed to land traffic by high snow in the passes from December to June. It was a village of a few dusty (or muddy) streets leading to an old British fort on the Mastuj River and to the polo field. Both were historic. A colonial garrison was besieged inside the fort by Chitralis for three months in the winter of 1895, and the field, long and narrow with four-foot-high stone walls at the boundaries, was one of the first places the game of kings was ever played. Polo came from that part of the world— the British found it there—and men from the mountains and valleys come to Chitral to cheer each other at wild games played to wilder drum beating.

The main street of the town, the Shani Bazaar, was jammed day and night when I was there. Men from the town and outlying settlements shopped and gossiped and promenaded—along with hundreds of men from the Afghan refugee camps built up along the river since late 1979, when the army of the Soviet Union

24

invaded the lands on the other side of the Hindu Kush. Ethnically, Shani was one of the world's great streets. Many of the faces of the world were right there: the Chitralis, an Indo-European people who often had fair hair and, sometimes, blue eyes; Pathans, from Pakistan and Afghanistan, classically handsome with high cheekbones and burning brown eyes; Orientals, with the flat faces of Tibet and southwestern China, which was less than two hundred miles away. They lounged in tiny shops, where merchants, seated cross-legged on the floor among their wares, weighed out a few ounces of tea, or showed off their selection of Chitrali caps, flat woolen hats with rolled bottoms. The Tudor hat, something like the kind Henry VIII usually wore, at least in the pictures I've seen, was the hat usually worn by these mountain tribesmen half the world and more than four centuries distant. But by the middle of 1983, after three years of guerrilla warfare against the Soviets, there were almost as many bulky Afghan turbans in the bazaar, and many of the Afghan men, who crossed back and forth through the passes of the Kush to fight, were wearing blue-gray synthetic fur caps taken from the bodies of Soviet soldiers. They just threw away the Red stars originally on the hats. Many of the Afghans were armed, wearing bandoliers of ammunition over the blankets they used as capes, with Lee-Enfield rifles or Kalashnikov AK 17 submachine guns slung behind their shoulders. It was a street of high colors and high spirits—the people of the bazaar endlessly greeted one another with elaborate ritual embraces and handshakes, bowing slightly and sometimes kissing one another on the cheek or the neck.

All men.

In three days in Shani Bazaar, the only women I saw were four in *burqa*s; they were scurrying down an alley off the main street. I did not really see women; what I saw were four bouncing apparitions, dressed very much the way children at home dressed as ghosts at Halloween. Except that these sheets were colored, usually in shades of brown. The *burqa* was like a small tent, a garment without arms pulled on over the head, fairly tight around the face with a slit of grilled cloth over the eyes. It billowed out to the ground—the fancy ones were pleated from top to bottom. In Chitral, and much of the rest of Pakistan, women were not just veiled, they were hidden; *"chador, chardiwari"* was the phrase in Arabic, the language of Islam, meaning behind the veil and behind four walls. It is the Muslim way. The differences in the protection of women in the Islamic Republic were only differences of degree from the alleys of Chitral to the lobby of the Intercontinental Hotel in Lahore, where elegantly dressed and high-heeled women instinctively reached for their *dupattas* to pull over their lower faces as men passed.

I went through the bazaar in a jeep, a Toyota, one of the few vehicles in the valley, south to a new bridge, built by the Pakistan army, across the river to begin the trip south and back in time to the valley of Bumburet, across and through some middle-level mountains. The roads were built up of scree—fallen rock—and carved into the sides of barren mountains above the rivers and the roaring streams of aquamarine water that divided the peaks and carried the melted snow from their caps down to irrigate the farms of Pakistan. The land outside Chitral, though, was as hard as it was beautiful. This was the territory where snow leopards were found and falcons trained, but there was precious little earth among all the soaring rocky vistas. Mudslides and drifting dirt from the mountains had been trapped over centuries by rock walls to form fan-shaped little terraces where wheat and rice and maize were patiently cultivated with wooden tools. The work of Chitral in the warm months has always been to grow and dry and store enough food for the frightening cold months when the winds come from Tirich Mir. The only contact with the outside comes then if the wind dies down long enough to allow airplanes to fly safely between the peaks that guard the entrance to the valley and the Chitral Aerodrome. Off the floors of the valleys, the houses were built into notches made in the sides of the mountains. Graves were made the same way; the notches, their floors built up with scree, were just smaller, and the bodies were encased in small stones. Families lived in one room, often without windows, keeping animals with them if they were lucky enough to have any. The people lived on roofs or terraces when I was there in good weather—and when it was good, it was magnificent, mocking the word *clear* as used in weather reports where I come from. As we looked down at those houses in July, their terraces were clouded with gold as men with wooden pitchforks threw grain into the air again and again, separating the wheat from the chaff in the old way.

There were also no chimneys in most Chitrali houses; smoke escaped through a sort of skylight. In the winter, people huddled together in hay for warmth at night. Even in the summer, food was short—we were told one morning that we had just eaten the last egg in Chitral—and in the winter there would be no meat or fresh fruits or vegetables. Chronic malnutrition and the fact that the aquamarine water was used for sanitation and for the irrigation of manure-fertilized fields, have made these valleys part of the world where measles and pneumonia are still fatal diseases. Until I spent time in those parts, I had had the vague impression that native populations were somehow immune to problems associated with bad water. "They" were used to it. Only "we" got sick. Ridiculous. Many people in places like the settlements around Chitral are sick all the time; some mountain languages and dialects in that part of the world do not have words for diarrhea or dysentery because such things are normal, too common for special comment.

But it was beautiful. And terrifying. The wobbling passage over a wooden suspension bridge exactly the width of the jeep—with a plaque certifying that it had been built in 1927 by the Bengal Miners and Sappers of the Indian army—offered the choice of gasping in wonder or in terror, after I had controlled fear long enough to open my eyes. A feature of the trip on tracks winding around the mountains toward Bumburet seemed to be that one wheel of the jeep was always riding on sky. The fifteen-mile journey took more than three hours before we passed through a gorge that seemed to be the pass to Shangri-La. It was the entrance to Bumburet and the valleys of the people called the Kalash Kafir, the valleys Rudyard Kipling had written of in "The Man Who Would Be King," a short story of two Englishmen who found a place so remote that they could convince the pagan population that they were gods. But Kipling had never been able to reach Bumburet. He had only heard the stories of light-haired and light-skinned pagans tracing their ancestry (probably inaccurately) back to soldiers of Alexander the Great who had passed their way in the fourth century before Christ.

Kalash Kafir means "black infidel" in the languages of the region. The pagans were obviously infidels to the Muslims of Chitral, and their unveiled women wore black homespun gowns. Pretty women, direct in their gaze, they wore beaded necklaces and elaborate hats of feathers and shells, and danced in the flowered fields of the valley they believe was once paradise, the home of the creator of all life. Their men still sacrificed animals to mysterious gods in secret rites somewhere in the mountains. They buried their dead above ground in rough wooden coffins—a luxury in such fuel-short parts—and eventually the rough boxes rotted and broke open so that the land in the burying places was littered with bones and skulls.

There were only three Kafir valleys left. Somewhere between five hundred and fifteen hundred people were still practicing the old rituals, protected for a while longer by the difficulty of the terrain. The stream we had been following ran twelve miles through the center of the valley, right through many of the houses—primitive indoor plumbing. The sound of the water and the smell of cut pine as men shaved logs with rough adzes to make the timbers of new houses gave the valley a music and perfume of its own. Walnut trees and mulberry trees formed an aisle for the water. A man climbed one and shook some fruit to the ground, and children rushed for the berries while women clapped and laughed at the scrambling boys and girls. It was not hard at that moment to understand why those people believed that Bumburet was the home of *Dezaw*, the Creator, who gave it to them because of the pleadings of the youngest children of the first man and the first woman.

Not a bad story—as good as many a young American Protestant was told growing up. The Kalash have many, more than outsiders know—and all I know are the stories told by Pakistanis who had spent time near the valleys. The Kalash sacrifice goats and bulls on smoky altars in dark huts, I was told. A goat was sacrificed to *Istogosh Deo* the first time a Kafir child wore clothing and the blood of the animal was spread on the child's forehead—baptism. They told their children that the greatest of the gods lived in "Siam," and that earthquakes were caused by flies landing on the nose of the great bull whose two horns held up the earth. They quarantined all women who were menstruating or were pregnant, passing food through the door of a house of confinement called the *Bashaleni*. Any married women who had not become pregnant during the previous year might seek the services of the *Bodolak*, a strong young man who was taken to a hidden mountain place and fed the best milk and meat for months before returning to his valley in September to do his best for the women of the tribe.

Very exotic—to outsiders. "I was told that the Kalash were muttering prayers, but to me it sounded like a confused and gibberish talk," said Lt. Col. Muhammad Afzal Khan, who had commanded Pakistan army troops in the Chitral area for three years in the middle 1970s. "The *shaman* could see invisible gods and communicate with them. He chattered like an ape and foamed at the mouth." One man's opinion. No one, as far as I could tell, had asked the *shamans* (priests) of the Kafirs what they thought of the practices of Colonel Afzal's religion or of mine.

It was a wonderful place to visit, and a few travelers, mostly Pakistanis, did get that far off the tracks beaten around the modern world. The light-skinned, chestnut-haired Kafir women were a staple of Asian travel posters. They painted their faces in intricate mask designs and braided their long hair once every three days in a delightful ritual by the side of the streams—each one hiding her comb under a rock. They seemed gay, calling to us in their language, Kalashwai, and amused at our ignorance of their words. The language provided a clue to their ethnic and geographic origins; it seemed to be a combination of Sanskrit, Persian and Greek.

But the life in this paradise was even harder than among the Chitralis. On the beautiful July day I was there, the Kafirs were doing what they have done all the summers, collecting the mulberries and picking the corn that they dry on rocks in the sun to provide food to survive the winter. The photogenic women and children were filthy. Flies were crawling into the eyes and mouths of babies inside the wood and mud-brick houses—the second-story living quarters were reached by steps notched into walnut logs leaned against outer walls—where cheerful women invited my wife and me to admire their children. The kids were sick—colds, dysentery, ear and eye infections. No one seemed to notice.

And they had begun to charge for those photographs. When the children saw our camera, they ran to pose, holding out their hands for piasters, the pitiful pennies of Pakistan. Cash had begun to mean in Bumburet what it meant at Gadani Beach, or Brighton Beach. The pagans could run, but they couldn't hide. If Bumburet were really another world, I wouldn't have been there.

We're coming. The advance guard of modernization in those valleys, though, wasn't American writers. It was the Chitralis, the Muslim majority, who were beginning to move into the corners of the Kafir valleys, bringing more modern technology with them—innovations like diverting the streams into mud-walled ponds to grow a crop new to Bumburet: rice. The Chitralis even used donkeys; the Kalash carried things themselves. The Muslims we saw on Kalash lands were very ostentatious in their prayers. Groups of them bowed to the East and to Mecca the obligatory five times a day in the fields and on the roofs of their larger homes. They were sending the pagans a very modern message: Your world can't survive inside the world we are making; you must become like us.

It was, I thought, looking out over that valley of the past, the same message that my world was sending to Chitral, to Islam, to the Islamic Republic of Pakistan.

All Pakistan was divided into three parts. Not geographically, because there were four provinces in the country twice the size of California: Punjab, with a majority of the population dominating national life from the sophisticated city of Lahore; Sind, spreading out from and closing in on crowded Karachi; Baluchistan, the hard desert country reaching from Iran to the beach at Gadani; the North-West Frontier Province, including Chitral. The three parts were not ethnic either, because there was no human face or race or style that you could not see in the one thousand miles between Karachi and the Khyber Pass, and there were twenty-four official languages spoken across the country. The division that struck me again and again traveling through Pakistan had to do with time. The question I mentally asked each man and woman I saw was, What century are you living in? The answers, I thought, would have roughly separated them into three groups: the people of the cities; of the towns and the larger villages; and of the small villages, the tribes, the countryside. City, town and rural. Those categories were very far from perfect. If nomads in Baluchistan or peasants in the Sind were living in the Middle Ages (and many were), their views of the world might not be very different from those of the slums of Karachi—and, in fact, it was the peasants migrating from the land that were making new slums as mechanization and cash modernized the agriculture of the water buffalo and the wooden plow. The son of a tribal chieftain in the Khyber region might be a Stanford junior coming home to a mud-walled fortress to tell his people of the wonders of computers, or of the money to be made converting local opium stores to the heroin craved in San Francisco.

There was a confusion of ages in a society where women hidden inside *burqas* waited to pass through metal detectors before boarding a Pakistan International Airlines 747 from Rawalpindi to Karachi. But the divisions in time seemed critical to me in trying to make some sense—Western sense, anyway—of the people and ideas sharing Pakistan.

There was an urbanized elite living in the there and now. A comprehensible, mobile human veneer—people quite a bit like "us." Ph.D.s from Columbia or Oxford, home to teach or to man the federal bureaucracy—perhaps even to stay. Women dermatologists on their way to Baylor University in Waco, Texas, for advanced study. Young Air Force officers, flying General Dynamics F-16s at twice the speed of sound. Newspaper editors, fervent in their commitment to Islam, groping for ideas and movements and men to mold a modern Pakistan that was not Western and not Soviet.

There were the bazaar people, the spiritual core of what middle classes there were in a society that barely has anything or anybody between rich and poor. They looked more ancient than they were, squatting or sitting on rugs in their booths and shops, surrounded by bowls of bright spices and the gossip of street and square. But they had some education and more commercial sophistication— enough to begin thinking about the politics of fundamental Islam or social democracy—and they lived near the fault lines of modernization. Right on those lines was a group that might be called "bazaar graduates," the low-level bureaucrats, hotel clerks and such who lived in one world and worked in another, newer one.

And then there were, everywhere, "the illiterate masses." The phrase was a cliché—I sometimes heard it a dozen times in a day of conversations with Pakistanis and foreigners living among them—but it had real and powerful meaning in a nation where, as far as I could tell, perhaps one person in twenty had ever been inside a school. For a while, they and I were living in the same space, but in different times. I did not know their time. I cannot imagine the thoughts of the Pathans—Aryans so handsome by Western standards they look like actors hired to play poor people—as they walked the Khyber Road past the "Star Trek" video games parlor in Peshawar. The woman carrying twenty-eight bricks on a board on her head at the construction site next to our rented house in Islamabad—what did she imagine I was thinking when she turned and saw me staring? She pulled her veil across her face and went about her business, hod carrying. I looked away and went about mine.

So the twain did meet. East meets West, West meets East, the traditional and the modern fascinated and touched each other, recoiled, cohabited in a place, confused and frightened each other—that was the essence of the tension and the dreams of Pakistan. It was a clumsy ballet, the courtship of and the struggle between the old and the new. The governors of the city of Jhang in the Punjab paid for this half-page advertisement in a national newspaper, *The Pakistan Times:*

"Chairman and Members of Jhang Municipal Council consider themselves dutybound to appeal to the people of Jhang to pledge to keep the City clean and be good citizens.

"1. Pay the Municipal dues in time and cooperate in completing the schemes.

"2. No cattle to be kept in the streets.

"3. No dung to be stuck on the walls.

"4. No litter is to be thrown in the streets.

"5. Not to allow children to use the drains as latrines.

"6. To cooperate with the Municipality to remove encroachments from the city to ensure the smooth flow of traffic."

Another well-meaning appeal to the illiterate masses, who, of course, couldn't read newspapers—and if they ever did, it was almost certainly not going to be the government-owned English-language *Pakistan Times*. But the illiterate masses were like the weather, only more so: everyone talked about them, no one did much of anything for them. But most of the people doing nothing wanted to tell the masses what was good or bad for them. The military rulers of Pakistan, the Westernized elite, the fundamentalist *maulanas* (*mullahs*) and progressive younger Muslim intelligentsia, the Americans and the Soviets and the Saudi Arabians and the Indians, and the politicians who were supposed to keep quiet under the country's martial law—they all had advice and schemes for the illiterate masses. And almost all those willing advisers were troubled and frustrated by the noncooperation of the masses and their "rampant materialism." That was the second recurrent cliché in serious conversation in Pakistan. What disturbed many of those just listed was that when the illiterate masses were given a choice—on a rare day in Pakistan—they seemed to reject appeals to and for Allah and a life of pure Islamic sacrifice, or for capitalism and liberal democracy, or state ownership and regulation. Generally, the masses seemed indifferent to the efficient and orderly procedures of one sort and another favored by their spiritual or intellectual or financial superiors, or those favored by the people who happened to be in charge of things because they had the guns. The better classes on all sides were distressed because when illiterate Pakistanis went to Saudi Arabia and the other oil states to do the dirty work and brought home what for them were enormous amounts of money, they spent that cash on things like television sets and the big portable stereophonic radios called "ghetto blasters" in American cities. And when the masses were allowed to vote—something that hadn't happened in almost seven years—the majority of them seemed unduly attracted to the slogan coined by the late (executed) Prime Minister Zulfiqar Ali Bhutto, *"Roti, Kapra aur Makon"*—that is, "Food. Clothes. House."

So, with some regularity in intellectual Pakistani conversation, mass desire for the things the people in the conversations already had for themselves became "rampant, rampant materialism which just can't be met with our meager resources." That quote was from a young newspaper editor. "Meager resources," by the way, was the last of the three clichés that punctuated many conver-

sations. It meant, I concluded finally, that Pakistan did not seem
to have much oil, which meant much of the sweat of its people
went toward making enough hard currency to buy the stuff from
richer Muslims around the Persian Gulf. It would take a lot of
oil—and sweat—to move a country from Bumburet to 1983.

I occasionally tried to set a date for where Pakistan was on an
American calendar—no easy job in a place where illiterate peasants hooked little transistor radios onto the horns of their water
buffalos—and I usually found myself thinking that maybe the
time, politically and economically, could be compared with the
turn of the century, the eighteenth century, in the United States.
Perhaps it was sometime near the late 1790s—it was much earlier
in many ways—and the people of Pakistan were trying to do what
the people of the young United States did over the next two
centuries. But they had to begin that modernization without the
conditioned reflexes of people who took freedom as their due.
And while the new United States had more or less been left alone
by the (then) more modern world, Pakistan would have to pick
its way among the demands and entreaties of the giants of the
world, the United States and the Soviet Union, and the giant of
their corner of the globe, India. Then there was also the crude
antimodernism of cadres of ignorant *maulanas* who do things
like—this happened in the city of Gujranwala—declaring "kafir"
(we would say "excommunicating") any members of their congregation who believed that Americans had walked on the moon.

But with all the obstacles, the commitment to modernism was
there. Not that there was much choice in a world already opened
to the wonders of 747s, video cassette recorders and antibiotics.
"Solution of the complex developmental problems of our age
requires extensive and sustained application of sophisticated scientific knowledge and technical skills," reads the introduction to
one section of the 486-page Sixth Plan, the latest of Pakistan's
five-year development programs outlining government goals and
budget priorities. "As a poor developing country, our priority
goals include, *inter-alia*, provision of basic necessities like food,
clothing, shelter and health cover to the common man; increase
in industrial/agricultural productivity; modernization of communications, . . . meaningful progress toward attainment of these
objectives cannot be achieved rapidly until effectiveness of the

relevant development programmes is appropriately enhanced through regular infusion of basic technical know-how. . . . The Sixth Plan makes many bold departures in its programmes and in its policy prescriptions. Its basic objective is the socio-economic emancipation of the masses."

The plan, like every other public document in the Islamic Republic, was punctuated by inspiration from the Holy Quran. The Health section, for instance, began with this: "If anyone saves a life, it shall be as though he had saved the lives of all mankind" (Holy Quran, V, 32).

Interminable quoting of the Holy Quran is in official deference to the "Islamization" program—a puritanical and cynical attempt to create "Nizam-i-Mustafa," the system of the Prophet, by such Quranic exercises as banning liquor and instituting public flogging—of Gen. Muhammad Zia-ul-Haq, whose titles include Army Chief of Staff, Chief Martial Law Administrator and President. He also had as many uniforms, ranging from the leather, tinkling medals and riding crop of an army that had been defeated every time it had taken to the field, to the simple white cotton gown of the devout, pure and humble Muslim. Watching him for a couple of months, I thought he must have had an exciting time picking his costume each morning and deciding who he was going to be that day. When we talked about modernization one day, sipping tea at a reception in one of the elaborate Victorian government guest houses that are part of the British legacy on the Indian subcontinent, he was wearing a long, form-fitting tunic with a mandarin collar, in light-gray wool, his country's elegant formal dress. "We are totally for modernization of the country," he said. "We want modernization and all the things it can bring to the masses."

"Is there anything," I asked, "that you don't want that could come with modernization?"

"What we don't want is our women forced out of their privacy. That is the thing we don't want. And pop music and jazz, that kind of thing."

"But," I said, "don't modern societies need the brainpower of all their people, of women, to become truly productive? Don't you have to have women engineers and scientists, for instance?"

"We have women engineers. Islam dictates that women cannot

be left out of the mainstream. Islam's respect for women is un-
limited. But we are not going to force our women into the streets.
We encourage women to be active within the parameters of Islam."

There were, I learned later, fewer than 100 women engineers
in Pakistan. The "parameters," as defined by Zia and his Islamic
advisers, who favored the strict puritanical Islam of Saudi Arabia,
provided that the evidence of a woman in court should have half
the legal weight of a man's testimony. In cases of rape, there had
to be four male eyewitnesses to "penetration." Zia ordered that
Pakistani women be withdrawn from international athletic competition because men might see their legs. That manly obsession
for keeping the weaker sex weak, however, was a subject for
another time. Discretion seemed to me the better part of conversation with the Chief Martial Law Administrator.

"You talk of productivity and so do we, but any American, any
Westerner looking at Ramazan"—I was referring to the month
of sunrise-to-sunset fasting in summer's dazzling heat—"would
conclude that almost nothing gets done here during that time."

"Why do you say that?" he said. "Productivity is higher during
Ramazan. I know that. Men work harder! It's amazing, but you
can see it."

What I had seen, described here with controlled hyperbole,
was a country of dazed, irritable men—even in Islamabad, the
Westernized capital city, there were almost no women on the
streets during the Holy Month—squabbling men stumbling into
each other in the midday sun and men curled in the shade, any
bit of shade, sleeping until a mad scramble for food at Ifthar, the
feast each evening after sunset. At the moment the sun set—the
time was announced in advance each day by maulanas—Pakistan
stood still. Cars and trucks did not move. No people could be
seen in the streets—maybe a couple, huddled together, squatting
over a plate with a little rice.

But I did not quite have the courage to argue with a devout—
and he is apparently very devout—Chief Martial Law Administrator. I saved my skepticism for a conversation with a young
Oxford-educated administrator in the Federal Planning Bureau,
asking him whether there were studies of the relative productivity of Pakistan when its people were going without food or

water fifteen hours a day. He laughed and said, "We wouldn't dare."

The fabric of the society was being pulled all out of shape by the tugs and tensions between the coming new and the going old. More people than Zia-ul-Haq wanted to have it both ways: to have the miracles of the new world but not giving up the faith and ways of the old. Without consulting the masses, there did seem to be a Pakistani consensus on commitment to both currents, modernization and Islam, contradictions or not. "There is no conflict at all between Holy Quran and science," said Maulana Fazl-ur-Rehman, head of one of the largest congregations in Lahore, during a long conversation. "Muslims once did some of the world's great work in medicine and mathematics. We do not reject modernism. But if you work on a machine, must you become a machine? No! Modernism and materialism has raised your country to great heights, but you pay a price in humanism, in insecurity. We are secure in our ways. We want to keep that security."

The great devotion of Pakistan, it seemed to me, was not so much to the dogma of the religion but to the ways of the past. Islam represented security, the known. It also represented the reason for the existence of the country, created in 1947 as a haven for the Muslim minority of predominantly Hindu India. In the Land of the Pure, the faith claimed the devotion of all but two million Pakistani Christians and other minority believers. "The country is nowhere near as devout as it seems or, perhaps, as the President believes it is," said Altaf Yawar, foreign editor of Associated Press Pakistan, the national (government-owned) press wire service, describing religious attitudes in his country and, I thought, in mine—if I substituted the word Christianity for Islam. We were both from countries bonded internally by an overwhelming majority religion. In his country, though, the faith was the only bond between many of the diverse peoples cartographically thrown together when the British created India and Pakistan in 1947. "Ten or 15 percent, maybe, of the people really believe and practice Islam," he continued. "But another 50 or 60 percent want the society to be based on the old principles, the traditional values. So the country is about 80 percent 'Islamic-thinking.' Conservative."

"What are they most conservative about?" I asked. "What is it they really don't want changed?"

"Women," Yawar said. "Pakistani men are afraid that the place of women in an agricultural society can't be maintained in an industrial society—that women will have to be given more. Why was Bhutto hanged? Really. How could they get away with it? Because he raised women too high. We had one prime minister whose wife traveled the country talking about the liberation of women, not dressing the proper way. He was assassinated."

I assumed there was more than that to that assassination, of Liaquat Ali Khan in 1951, but Yawar was exaggerating to make the point that the old, unquestioned power of men over women was, he thought, at the heart of "Islamic-thinking," and the principal reason that modernization was such agony for the men of Pakistan. It didn't matter what the Holy Quran said; like the Bible it said many things, many ways. Selection was argument; interpretation was power. It was not complicated for most Pakistani men. They wanted the old interpretations and the personal power to treat their women as idols or animals to be worshiped or abused, hidden from view, at the whim of the family chieftain. But not all men. The drafters of the Sixth Plan, modernized men who would change that, like my friend the planner from Oxford, who used their own Quranic verses, including this one at the head of the chapter on women: "To men is allotted what they earn. And to women what they earn" (Holy Quran, VI, 32).

Then the Plan continued:

"In all societies, women's development is a pre-requisite for overall national development; indeed, no society can ever develop half-liberated and half-shackled.

"In Pakistan today, the profile of women is simply shocking. The following cold statistics are a sad commentary on the legacy of neglect. . . . Female literacy is only 14 percent . . . the participation of women in the compensated labour force is only 5 percent . . . less than 3 percent of the civil service jobs . . . crippling handicaps—of illiteracy, constant motherhood, poor health."

And carrying bricks past my house. Or carrying the water in a countryside without aqueducts and pipes: mothers and their daughters were everywhere around farmland and slums, beasts of burden carrying water in pots on their heads, straining, but still able to pull up their veils if men passed. The women worked but were not paid; the reality was far worse than shocking statistics. The numbers were for Western consumption, prepared by Western-educated bureaucrats. Places like Washington can't run without statistical fuel, and places like Pakistan got a lot of money from Washington. So they made up numbers. The one used most often was 25 percent: according to the speeches and reports of the day, about 25 percent of the people of the country had access to potable water, and about 25 percent were literate. In fact, no one knew. Those statistics, as far as I could tell, rose gradually to that pathetic 25 percent level because of the government imperative to show improvement in succeeding five-year plans.

Taking just the literacy statistics and leaving aside the fact that literacy in Pakistan was generally defined as being able to write or recognize one's own name, only 8 percent of Pakistan's children ever went to any school, according to the national Educational Grants Commission. And that was paper, too. Schools in reports did not always exist. The British Council in Islamabad was retained by the federal government to monitor English-language instruction in 350 schools in rural areas of Punjab. There were, it turned out, no schools and no students—only payrolls.

The chief dispenser of statistics in Pakistan and the principal author of the Sixth Plan was the Minister for Planning and Development, Mahbubul Haq. He had come back from Washington, where he had worked twelve years for the World Bank—in fact, he had been a principal assistant to the bank's American president, Robert McNamara. Brilliant. Charming. Persuasive. His office in the Secretariat in Islamabad could have been in Washington, except its occupant was wearing the national costume, the same *shalwar kameez*, the knee-length, light shirt and baggy pants, worn by the shipbreakers at Gadani Beach. "The national per capita income is about $300, compared, of course, with $10,000 or whatever in the United States, but that is a false comparison," he said. "We are, economically, fifty years behind the West. Maybe eighty years in regard to the United States or a little more. But it doesn't take fifty years to catch up fifty years anymore. Chronology is mixed. You have a country still fighting to control tuberculosis and malaria, but it has jet aircraft and satellite television transmission. Direct dialing. People who never could have dreamed of such things as running water have television in their homes. And they want that. People want modernization. In the most remote villages, people are using refrigerators as closets, waiting for the day electrification gets to them. And it will. Look at the plan. In July of 1978, 7,609 villages had electricity, out of 45,000 in the country; that was the beginning of the Fifth Plan, and now about 16,400 are electrified. By the end of the Sixth Plan, that number will be 38,900—95 percent of the rural population will be covered. In terms of catching up, before World War II the growth rate of the Western world was less than 3 percent. Ours is over 6 percent now. Yes, our population growth rate is more than 3 percent, but death rates always fall before birth rates begin to, so . . .

"When I left Pakistan in 1970, the malnutrition rate was 30 percent and the country couldn't afford to import enough grain to feed its people. I came back in 1982 expecting the same absolute poverty, expecting starvation. But the malnutrition rate was below one percent. We were exporting grain. There was no obvious poverty, so . . ."

Haq was glancing at his watch by now—a Washington technique that I had not seen before (or after) in Pakistan—so . . .

I knew my time was up. I asked for a copy of the Sixth Plan and we shook hands. Outside the office, the minister's assistant popped his head inside the next door and said, "Give me one." I had my copy.

I was in the roadway, blinking in the sunlight, almost walking into a donkey loaded with bricks, when I realized what had happened. The minister had slipped me pre-1971 statistics and compared them with 1982 statistics. "When I left Pakistan in 1970 . . ." When he had left in 1970, there was a West Pakistan and an East Pakistan, politically united but geographically separated by one thousand miles of India. In 1971 after a short civil war in which the Pakistani army surrendered 93,000 men and officers when the Indian army intervened on the side of the rebels, East Pakistan seceded and became the new country of Bangladesh. East Pakistan, as it happened, was the poorest part of Pakistan, an abused stepchild, treated as a colony by the bureaucracy of

West Pakistan. So . . . the country's worst malnutrition problems (and statistics) had been shifted to the new country of Bangladesh.

The grass cutters were at work around me as I walked from the Secretariat to my car. On one day in August hundreds of them appeared, moving slowly across the shaggy green growth of the city. Within a couple of days, Islamabad was neat again— as if it had had a haircut. They cut the grass almost blade by blade, squatting in Asian manner, comfortably, with their bodies almost like a backward letter "N," their heads just above their knees and their hands in front of their feet, each man cutting away with a scythe the size of a bread knife. Someone told me that the reasons Asians can squat like that is that the constant repetition of the position as small children, imitating adults, causes their sciatic nerves to follow a different path around their knee-caps. Not all the men I saw squatting were grass cutters, though. Pakistanis, many of them, "go to the bathroom"—to adapt the Western phrase to local custom—in the street, or a field, or wherever they happen to be at the moment. The long top of the *shalwar kameez* covers a man like a small tent, giving him enough privacy. I was surprised by how soon I stopped noticing that as I traveled about, particularly in city slums and the frontier province. Out there, in the land of the Pathans, I asked someone how the men cleaned themselves afterward.

"With rocks" was the answer. Instead of paper or water, men grabbed a chunk of hardened clay off the barren ground.

Anyway, I got used to it—although the squatters did seem out of place and time in Islamabad, one of the most determinedly modern cities in the world. Pakistan had no real capital city after it was hastily partitioned off from India by the British to create a Hindu country and a Muslim country when the old empire, the British Raj, ended on August 14, 1947. The Indians had Delhi; the Pakistanis decided to build a new city, Islamabad. A city plan prepared by Constantine Doxiades, the Greek architect, was laid out on the barren plateau of Potwar, 600,000 trees were planted, and a city began to rise along wide boulevards and around square corners. "A city of airline terminals" was the caustic description of Salman Rushdie, a novelist with ties to Pakistan. Islamabad, with a population approaching 200,000, was built on a scale strange to Westerners. Public buildings were about one and one half times the size they would be anyplace else. The Presidency, Pakistan's White House—unused for years because Gen. Zia-ul-Haq preferred to live with his army down the road in Rawalpindi—looked like the Kennedy Center in Washington, covering, with marble, an area just about the size of a football field. From a distance, an American could hardly tell it wasn't the Kennedy Center: it was designed by the same architect, Edward Durrell Stone. Americans in town were convinced that either he had only one idea or he just hated Pakistan.

It was easy to make fun of Islamabad. Six miles from Rawalpindi and any place else in Pakistan—that was one local joke. But it was quite an achievement and had something of the sterile charm of Washington, including a main boulevard called Constitution Avenue—or, when I was there, "Suspended Constitution Avenue." I, like many other foreigners, lived in a small marble palace—the homes, too, were one-and-a-half scale, built to the taste and needs of wealthy Muslims' extended families—a house I could not have afforded in Los Angeles, where I thought it belonged.

The real Pakistan, a little of it, was actually closer than Rawalpindi, army headquarters before and after the Partition of India, a classic British colonial city of Asian bazaars and a separate "Cantonment," the walled-in once-British area of barracks, drill fields, brick houses, brick churches and brick-walled gardens. Water buffalos still roamed among the embassies and mansions of Islamabad, the people of the place slept outdoors in string beds, and the *katchi abadis*—clusters of houses made of dried mud and dung, mixed with straw—began on the other side of the walls around the marble houses and watered, hand-cut lawns.

The most modern grass-cutting I saw was done with an old-fashioned hand-pushed mower—left over by the British, I guessed—operated by three men. One pushed at the T-shaped handle, while the other two ran along beside the wheels, pushing down on the frame to ensure that the rolling blades cut as closely as the hand-cutters. The lawns, after a cutting, that way or by hand, were beautiful. It took a while, but that didn't matter much. Labor was plentiful and cheap. Before 1981, the day rate for labor in the North-West Frontier Province was 30 rupees a day—about $2.25—but the refugees who came from Afghanistan after the

Soviet invasion were anxious to do the same jobs, road repairs and things like that, for just 20 rupees.

Islamabad, designed so bravely to show how far Pakistan and its people had come along the time scales of progress, really had the opposite effect on me: It had a Holiday Inn and Datsuns and strange, sweet Coca-Cola, but the life of the streets of the city constantly mocked its late-twentieth-century façade. Even in the late nineteenth century, the look of the cities of India (and later Pakistan) was deceiving. Karl Marx was among many who miscalculated the patterns of modernization on the subcontinent. "England has to fulfill a double mission in India: one destructive, the other regenerating—the annihilation of old Asiatic society, and the laying of the material foundations of Western society in Asia," Marx wrote in 1853. "Modern industry, resulting from the railway system, will dissolve the hereditary divisions of labour, upon which rests the Indian castes, those decisive impediments to Indian power and progress."

Not yet.

It was not yet what we would call a modern society. Nothing worked in Pakistan—at least that's what an American found himself thinking day after day after day.

The society had not evolved to the concept of "the line." People did not line up at ticket windows or counters or any place else, they just converged where the action was, avoiding each other's eyes, sliding between, under and over backsides, frontsides, arms, shoulders and heads, thrusting papers or money or whatever was to be taken or processed or, usually, stared at blankly before these dreaded words were spoken: "Not here." With a display of emotion   noise, anger, tears—you might be told where: another window. The windows of bureaucracy were small and built at what I would call waist level. That was on my side. On the other side, the power side, they were at the level of the eyes and ears of a clerk sitting at a desk. To deal with that clerk you had to bend to the window to be heard through the talking slot, assuming the position of a backward number "7," which was also the position for what inevitably happened next.

The society had also not evolved to the concept of "the appointment." It was not only that Pakistanis might or might not have been where you thought they were supposed to be at the appointed hour. It was that you regularly had conversations like the one I had with a Minister of the Islamic Republic:

"I would like to arrange an appointment to speak with you about the work of the Ministry."

"Fine. I am free now. Come over, please."

"Well, I'm afraid I can't do that right now. Perhaps this afternoon? Tomorrow? Anytime this week?"

"But I don't know what I'll be doing then. Call me then. Perhaps I shall be free."

And perhaps the stadium will be finished. On that same day, Islamabad's English-language newspaper, *The Muslim*, ran a photograph with this caption: "A view of the main stadium under construction in the Islamabad Sports Complex. The stadium was supposed to be completed a few years back but it is still unpredictable when it would be available to the sportsmen."

I sometimes thought those things. But I was wrong. Pakistan did work. It just didn't work the way an American thought it should. Modernism as we defined it—and, so far, we in the West have the exclusive franchise—was not a matter of buildings by Edward Durrell Stone and televisions by Hitachi. The difference between the "developed" and "undeveloped" countries of the world, I thought more than a few times while fighting my way to the dispensing windows of Pakistan, was the difference between systematic and individual approaches to handling predictable situations or problems—from distributing food to protecting property, repaving roads or assigning airline seats. In Islamabad or Karachi, you did not find many planned, organized, work-saving, time-saving, sanity-saving procedures. Usually, if you had a problem, you had to find someone, hire someone, or bribe someone who knew how, or was related to someone who knew how, to handle the routine chores of everyday life in any city anywhere. The most welcome words I heard in Karachi were "Come with me!"—the sign that I had finally found the individual who knew enough to return me to my own life.

The old ways, charming or frustrating, usually depended on cheap labor—wealthy Pakistanis hired what amounted to slaves to run errands like throwing themselves at ticket windows—but such charming traditional ways don't come cheap. Food rots. In the Tharparhar district, the government reported, in July of 1983, 30 percent of the vegetables grown were destroyed because they did not get to markets or cold storage in time. The official reason was: transportation problems. When systems broke down or were never really started up, both prices and corruption went up. The United Nations Industrial Development Organization studied transportation problems for the government of Pakistan and discovered that 60 percent of the tires in the country were smuggled in because local manufacturing systems produced on paper but not in factories.

The disorder and inefficiency not only offended "developed" folk like Americans; such things also tended to offer certain opportunities and temptations to any indigenous organizations with internal discipline and certain organizational skills—i.e., the army. The military in Pakistan and other "developing" countries not only had guns, which have always been very helpful in taking over peoples against their will; they had command structures and disciplines, communications systems and, most important, transportation systems. Even the worst of military organizations have some of the strengths of miniature "developed" societies. Armies have trucks, soldiers tend to follow orders. Gen. Zia-ul-Haq, I was told more than once, managed to stay in power year after year—six of them by the time I was there—because he was smart enough to use his troops to maintain reasonably efficient distribution of the necessities of the life of Pakistan's masses—wheat, cooking oil, tea and sugar. It could be that simple for a while, particularly in a society where political systems were among those that had not yet really developed. "These people aren't ready for democracy yet. Sad, isn't it?" said Louis Dupree, an American scholar living in Peshawar. An expert on Afghanistan and the Pathans on both sides of the border, he had been driven out of that country along with millions of others by Soviet invaders. "Democracy is not going to work here for a long time—not what we call democracy now. Our kind of democracy wouldn't have worked in the United States in 1783. Communications were too poor. Loyalties were to regions. People weren't ready then. . . . You and I were serving on committees and voting for things when we were seven years old. There's no history of that around here. People have to learn. It takes time to learn how to deal with things that are new."

To adapt to new things or adapt them to old ways—either is difficult. Maulana Rehman of Lahore, who considered himself very much a modern man, a well-traveled man, argued against American-style liberty for Pakistan. He analyzed our system this way: "Your Constitution, which I have read, emphasizes 'rights.' If you buy a ticket you have the 'right' to a seat on the bus. That is fine, but we emphasize human values. Vacating that seat for an old lady is a human value. Do you understand?"

Almost.

Many things we understand or think we do are almost understood or confusingly new in a place like Peshawar.

That city of more than 300,000 people, the effective capital of the Pathan nation of 17 million people in Pakistan and Afghanistan, just south of the Khyber Pass, the doorway between the countries —its name means "Frontier Town" in the Pathan language, Pushtu—was one of the places in the world where the new and the old bumped into each other every day. The day I arrived in Peshawar, July 1, 1983, local police were confronting a new problem, automobile theft, by going around town letting the air out of car tires. That way thieves couldn't move the cars.

It drives us, "developed folk," crazy.

And we're going to help the underdeveloped whether they want to be helped or not. Two weeks later on July 14, Bastille Day, at the French Embassy in Islamabad—national holidays were wonderful opportunities for Westerners to get together and drink and talk about banging their head against the soft walls of the East—I was talking with a Canadian, a technician in his country's Department of Agriculture. "I'm out at their National Research Center, trying to teach them about better seeds, how to use the rain more efficiently by poking slashes in the earth to form little reservoirs," he said. "We even bought 200 acres next to the center for a demonstration farm, but we can't find out who's supposed to clear off the squatters. They're not like us. We make hay while the sun shines. They disappear for four days for a holiday, or they go at one-thirty in the afternoon during

Ramazan. Gone—you don't know when they're going to come back.

"The average farm here is less than five acres," the Canadian said. "Subsistence farming. We can teach them that with better seed they can have a little left over at the end of each season, to sell. But I'm not sure they want that. They're not like us.

"They're happy, you know. They've been doing it the same way for generations. Thousands of years. They're happy the ways things are. They haven't got a pot to piss in, but they're happy. I wonder sometimes what I'm doing here.

"Jesus!"

Us and "them." How can you deal with people like that? That was our problem. Moving around the country, I felt as if I were spending half my life in PIA offices—Pakistan International Airlines—forever confirming and reconfirming, finding the person who was willing to handle something for me. In Chitral, that meant waiting for an hour for the man who was supposed to open the padlocked ticket cabinet in the corner of the hut with a rough wood table and three low chairs which served as the local PIA office. He came, took out a knife and pried the hinge off the cabinet, pulling out the screws with the slightest flip of the wrist. There was no key to the lock, hadn't been for years. Everyone in the hut knew that but me.

But in the cities they had computers in the offices. I could get out in a couple of minutes after a half-hour or so of fighting the people crowded around the right desk. Computers think like us. We programmed them.

That was a small comfort. So was getting telephone calls from the United States. The first one I had was from Kansas City. Some business. It sounded as if the caller were next door. But he wasn't; in fact, if he had been I probably wouldn't have been able to hear.

"Did you have much trouble getting through?" I asked.

"No," said the voice from Kansas City. "Why would I have trouble? I just dialed the code and your number there. You okay?"

Yeah, fine. He had no trouble dealing with Pakistan. He didn't deal with anyone in Pakistan. Direct dialing. And I had no trouble when I could get to a computer rather than a person.

So, we were using new technologies to get around old ways. We could get around them completely with things like direct dialing—no more Pakistani operators—and get our business done the American way. Computers could go around them or through them, because the Raytheon terminals at PIA brought their systems with them, the quickest and most logical of systems. Western logic. Western systems. That was happening all around me in Pakistan, a kind of new imperialism. Electronic, mostly. But some of it had to do with the rules of internationalized commerce. Pakistan's airplanes were scheduled, maintained and flown under international systems and in the international language, English. Money, with a language of its own, was moved and accounted for in approved internationalized ways, monitored by Western institutions like the International Monetary Fund and Mahbubul Haq's alma mater, the World Bank.

There had been an inconvenient period (for us) in international dealings with this part of the world. Before the independence of British India and its partition into India and Pakistan, the outside world dealt with it through the British-trained and maddeningly British Indian Civil Service. Then, for a while after the British left, we had to deal with the locals. Now, it seemed, an imperious technical relationship, if not a technically imperial one, was being established by modern technology. Very few local people would be required to make Pakistan function relatively smoothly for world purposes.

Inside its own borders, though, and inside the minds and hearts of people, the nation was going to have to suffer the agony of its own modernization. Perhaps it would be better for them and for us if that newest imperialism did isolate them, leave them alone and give them more time and freedom to become whatever kind of modern people they finally decided they wanted to be. Maybe they could actually find a different kind of modernism. Perish the thought—but they might even be able to become modern without becoming like us.

3

MISTER RICHARD
MEETS
MISTER MISTER

"In a few minutes, *Inshallah*, we will be landing at Karachi International Airport. . . ."

I flew Pakistan International Airlines from New York, stopping at Paris, Frankfurt, Dubai and Cairo, but this was the first time the Almighty had been mentioned. *Inshallah.* "God willing." God willing, we'll make it. Until then the only difference between the flight and most any other flight on a Boeing 747 was that no alcohol was served. Liquor, wine and beer had not been offered on PIA since February 9, 1979, when Gen. Zia-ul-Haq had decreed as part of his "Islamization" program that drinking alcohol was a "heinous crime" punishable by public flogging—eighty lashes.

". . . The local temperature is 44 degrees," concluded the stewardess. That was the Centigrade reading. It was 111 degrees Fahrenheit.

Two days later it was a few degrees cooler, but only a few, in the VIP lounge of Islamabad Airport. The air-conditioning had broken down only a few minutes before the arrival of the Secretary of State of the United States, George Shultz, who would be visiting Afghan refugee camps in the North-West Frontier Province and meeting with Gen. Zia-ul-Haq. The Foreign Minister of Pakistan, Sahebzada Yaqub Khan, who was waiting for

Shultz, and other dignitaries passed the time politely apologizing to officials from the American Embassy and a small crowd of reporters. I noticed that one of the other reporters was the man who had sat across the aisle from me on the flight from Cairo to Karachi. We introduced ourselves. He was Altaf Yawar, the foreign editor of Associated Press Pakistan.

"I noticed you also," Yawar said. "I was happy to see you with your wife and the children. A whole family together. I know that in your country the family is collapsing."

The aisle between Yawar and me had been wider than I had realized. In this country there were many things that surprised me and baffled me. The most confusing thing, I'd guess, for any foreigner in Pakistan was this: men shook their heads "No" when they meant "Yes." Instead of nodding in agreement as I would, Yawar showed agreement by turning his head to the right, as if avoiding a light slap. That particular difference between "us" and "them" was a guarantee of continuous low comedy in anyone's passage to Pakistan. But after a while I got it, and I swear, after a few weeks I was doing it myself. I know other Westerners were. When in Pakistan, do as . . . it was "their" country.

"Their" country was different from ours. It was tempting to think that an addiction to Coca-Cola made us all alike, but the Coke tasted very different in Chitral or Kohat. Sweeter. The Pakistanis seemed to make up for the alcohol they were missing by eating enormous amounts of sweets, from good pastries to bad Cokes. Only the name on the bottle was the same. But, later, I began to realize that many names were not the same—that the gap between us and them was wide enough that we didn't even understand each other's names. What made me wonder about names was that time after time, no matter how we were introduced, Pakistanis almost always called me "Mr. Richard"—and then introduced me to others that way. It was quite formal, not the way you would use someone's first name (or Christian name). Then, when I remarked how common the name Khan was in Pakistan, I was told that it wasn't as common as Westerners believed. Often when we called someone "Mr. Khan," we were saying, in effect, "Mr. Mister" or, sometimes, "Mr. California."

Pakistanis were too polite and too used to bowing to Western ways to correct those misunderstandings, but, then, I never corrected anyone about my name. So, there we were, smiling a bit awkwardly at each other, pretty sure we understood each other. They were counting on us to pour billions of dollars into their country to help them modernize Pakistani life, and we thought those billions would persuade them to stand firm as our frontline defense against the spread of Soviet communism—but we couldn't quite get each other's names straight.

After a couple of weeks, I began asking foreigners if they could explain Pakistani names, which were actually Arabic names because almost everyone in the country is Muslim. Without exception, even from people competent in Urdu (the "national language" of Pakistan) or Farsi (the Persian language, which is useful in Pakistan), the reaction was the same—ignorance. "I've never quite gotten it, I'm afraid," said Simon Cole, director of the British Council in Islamabad. "I keep promising myself to ask my Urdu instructor to tell me how it works," said Warren Soiffer, of the United States Information Service in Lahore.

Cole asked one of his assistants, a Pakistani, to join us. "Yes, we tend to accept whatever names you give us," she said. The assistant was a woman, which was very unusual, because the offices of Pakistan usually have the same number of women as the streets of Chitral—none. "And obviously 'Christian names' are not well understood by all of us."

We took a common name, Laeeq Ahmed Khan—"Mr. Khan" to me. Laeeq, she said, was the first name, given to the child by his father. Ahmed was the family name—a "last" name to Westerners. Khan, in this case, was merely the name taken by all Pathans in certain tribal regions. So, I had been saying "Mr. Frontier"—like "Mr. California." Khan, she said, was also sometimes a family name. But more often than that it was a sort of honorarium connoting some family distinction—"Mr. Mister" or "Mr. Sir." Syed, she said, was somewhat similar; that "last" name was not the family name but meant that the family traced its lineage to the Prophet, Muhammad. Many families did. So, I had been calling the editor of *The Muslim* newspaper, Mushahid Hussain Sayed, Mr. Sayed when he was actually Mr. Hussain. (The spellings "Syed" and "Sayed" vary because the Arabic, Urdu and Persian alphabets do not correspond directly to the Roman alphabet and all the spellings in our alphabet are just phonetic representations of the sound of a word or name.)

"What about the President?" I said. Muhammad Zia-ul-Haq. "When we call him Zia, are we calling him by his middle name?" I said. "Like President Delano?" The American joke was lost in translation. "Sometimes," she answered. "His family name is Haq; the 'ul' is a preposition—'of' like the French 'de.' His first name is Muhammad, but that is sometimes merely a way of showing you are a Muslim. His given name was Zia, so perhaps that is a first name or a middle name in your style. His name is Zia-ul-Haq, not Zia, but we use Zia after the first reference. You often begin by saying only Zia."

Perhaps I made too much of this, but after a couple of months the confusion over names—the misunderstanding about who we were, or said we were—struck me as a pretty good microanalysis of relations between the United States and Pakistan. Before I wrote these few paragraphs—back home in New York City—I went to the Pakistan Mission to the United Nations to go over naming once more with Najeeb Butt, the press attaché. "No one really expects Westerners to understand," he told me. His father's name, he said, was Habibur Rehmen Butt, called Rehmen. He was Najeeb ur-Rehmen-Butt, and Westerners had no trouble with the name Mr. Butt. His son was Muhammad Yousef Najeeb Butt. To us, all three were Mr. Butt—the name, luckily, similar to American or English names—but to other Pakistanis they were called in the old way. The boy would be Yousef-ur-Najeeb.

"What a pleasant talk," Mr. Butt said as we walked to the elevator after an hour. "I've never been asked about these things. . . . Oh, here's your elevator. Have a good day, Mr. Richard."

"You know nothing of us," the Commissioner of Refugees back in Peshawar had said to me with surly contempt. "We are forced to study your history, but you are ignorant of ours. You think Islam is a nightmare, because you are ignorant of it. You are afraid of us because of that ignorance." Abdullah Khan, who insisted on being called and written about as only Abdullah, made a sort of hobby of browbeating foreigners. And he saw a lot of them in his position. As the Refugee Commissioner for the North-West Frontier Province, he was responsible for the administration of 280 camps housing about two million men, women and children who had fled or been driven from Afghanistan after the invasion by Soviet troops on December 24, 1979. More than $500,000 a day of Western money, channeled through the United Nations and international relief organizations, was supposed to go through Abdullah's office.

An interesting man. Putting on a bit of the show, but still fundamentally different from me—and, like Maulana Rehman and General Zia, determined to maintain a gap between us. I did not doubt that he knew more about me than I knew about him. He had taught English and English literature before being admitted to the civil service and serving as a political commissioner in tribal areas and as First Secretary of the Pakistani Embassy in Saudi Arabia. He was forty-two years old, bright, attractive, combative, egomaniacal. He meant a great deal when he once wrote: "For strength we must nurture our own roots. Our problems have arisen from foreign imposition. Their solution lies in tapping our inherent strength of character and culture."

He was a fundamentalist Muslim, a zealot. There were many like him in Pakistan—probably including Zia—but they were a minority within the 10 to 15 percent minority of "believers" defined for me by Altaf Yawar. They saw themselves, as Zia had told me, as promodern but not necessarily pro Western. There was another group in Pakistan—smaller than the fundamentalists, I thought—who also saw themselves that way, men like Mushahid Hussain of *The Muslim*, who described himself as a "progressive Muslim." The groups parted company, though, on other issues— they, in fact, despised each other—because there are more interpretations of Islam than there are of Christianity or democracy. And all those interpretations wreaked intellectual and political havoc in the Islamic Republic because as that name implied and Abdullah asserted: "We can't separate God from Caesar. That's something you think you can do."

They saw the world differently; the communication gap is far less complicated than gaps in basic perceptions. Mushahid Hussain, thirty years old with a master's degree in foreign affairs from Georgetown University, told me he once considered himself part of a worldwide youth movement for liberal democracy, but no more: "It began to change in the mid-70s. There were Muslim successes. Oil—the long gas lines in America were a triumph for us. The Palestinians. The October War. Iran—a watershed in Muslim history, in world history. Khomeini told the United States and the Soviet Union both to go to hell. He was a new kind of leader in the Third World; he wasn't afraid of the Americans, he wasn't afraid of the Russians, but most of all, he wasn't afraid of his own people. It wasn't like Egypt telling the Soviets to go to hell and then turning to the Americans. There was something to be proud of, and we began looking inward. We're searching for a way to restructure the social order here without looking east to the Soviet Union or west to the United States."

Progress, a word we both claimed, was obviously in the eye of the beholder. "We want schools and technology," Hussain said. "We don't want miniskirts." In his report on the Kalash of Bumburet Valley, Lt. Col. Afzal Khan, with undisguised condescension, described the housing of the people this way: "These houses express nothing but primitive abundance, security and an enormous zest for living . . . they bear witness to a society that is still isolated in small units, where each has only himself and his own family to think of."

The colonel, looking into the past, had seen us and the way we live. He could have been describing Teaneck, New Jersey. To him, societies inevitably progressed toward the large houses of his people, built for extended families of grandparents, children and grandchildren, in-laws and a few cousins.

We, then, were the society of primitive abundance of people living in isolation. Educated Pakistanis, sometimes impolitely, often let slip their conviction that the West's technological superiority did not translate into cultural superiority. There was in Pakistan, despite its short and depressing modern political history, a long memory. Friends in Lahore taking my family and me through the city's great fort, begun by the Moghul emperor Akbar in the sixteenth century, pointed out that the beautiful central pools and fountains were covered by tennis courts after the British took over in the nineteenth century.

"Always remember, they think we are the barbarians," said Louis Dupree, the American scholar exiled from Afghanistan to Peshawar. "Their cultural heritage is heavy on the Crusades,

when the Christians came killing and looting and destroying."
Commissioner Abdullah, like other Pakistanis I met, had brought
up the Crusades, saying, with what might have been a twinkle
in his dark eyes: "We fought the Christians many times. We
know how to do that." I thought about that when I left his office,
walking into the sunlight and almost colliding with the band of
Pathans lounging in the doorway with their Lee-Enfields and AK-
47s—the old British Army rifle and the newer Soviet submachine
gun—and bandoliers of cartridges draped over their *shalwar kameezes*. "If I were a Russian soldier," said our teenage son, looking at the group, "I would be terrified of those guys."

Me, too.

I went from Abdullah's office to a birthday party—at the home
of the American Consul in Peshawar. It was July 4, 1983. Inside
the walled compound, under the American flag, men and women
were chatting and sipping cans of beer, Budweiser, precious stuff
since drinking it outside the consulate had been declared a "heinous crime." Most of the 140 foreigners living in Peshawar seemed
to be there. Dan Rather was there, too, on videotape, reciting
the CBS Evening News of the week before. The loudspeakers
over the garden were lustily broadcasting "Onward Christian
Soldiers."

A few nights later I was at home with a group of new Pakistani
friends. A lawyer from Lahore idly leafed through the book lying
on a side table, *Asia Overland*, a travel guide published in New
York. "Listen to this," he said, then began to read aloud: " 'As
you wait for the train, don't be alarmed if at least a hundred
Pakistanis come up to stare at you. No one means any harm.' "
There was some nervous laughter, and a university professor said,
"Thank God, the natives aren't dangerous!"

Another lawyer there was talking, later, about his brother, a
thirty-three-year-old businessman. "He's really more conservative than me," he said.

"How's that?" I asked.

"Old-fashioned, you know. He has two wives and . . ."

I was staring more than any Pakistani at a railroad station. It
was one thing to be vaguely aware that the Holy Quran was
generally interpreted to give men the right to have four wives

as the Prophet did, but it was another . . . Sohbat was the first man I had ever met who had one brother and two sisters-in-law living under one roof.

Another night in Lahore, a young woman, studying to be a physician, was talking with my wife about her wedding plans. In two weeks she was going to be married to a Pakistani who was in the United States, a teacher at the University of Southern California. Cathy, my wife, began asking questions about her fiancé. How old was he? How long had he been in the United States? Did he like Los Angeles? Where will you live? Sariah kept answering, "I don't know." Finally she said, "I don't know him. It's an arranged marriage."

"I arranged the marriage with the boy's family," Sariah's mother said. "In your country two young people meet and, when they decide to marry, then they bring in the parents. Here the parents decide, then they bring the children. Which is better? Which marriages are more stable? Are your young people happier in their marriages than ours? I don't think so; they are filled with romantic notions and great expectations that can never be met. I have three daughters, all professional women; I arranged their marriages, and it has worked for us and I think that will continue.

"Touch wood," she said, tapping her knuckles on a table. It was the first thing I could relate to in ten minutes of conversation. I had known there were some arranged marriages. That day's paper in Karachi, *Dawn*, had a half-column of ads like these:

"Proposals are invited for a girl in her early 20's, good-looking college graduate. She is eligible to migrate to the U.S. . . ."

"Match for my son the doctor. MBBS. Sunni, Urdu speaking, age 28, height 5-9, handsome . . ."

"Wanted—suitable match for homely, fair, unmarried girl, 28. B.A., B.-Ed., school teacher, of respectable Sunni family. Contact Mrs. Hafiz. Phone 530349."

What I did not understand was that most marriages were arranged. More than 90 percent, I was told several times. The statistic may be as soft as most numbers in Pakistan, but it certainly gave me some insight into why a world-traveling Pakistani, the foreign editor of APP, would believe that the American family had collapsed. What had things come to if parents couldn't even decide whom their children would marry?

Much of the Westernization of Pakistan was more apparent than real, at least as far as I could tell. I'd pick up *Dawn*, the Karachi English-language daily, and see an advertisement, on July 8, during Ramazan, that said: "This Ramazan take home a pizza for Ifthar"—the feast after sunset when the daily fast is broken. And there was the familiar red roof and the logo: "Pizza Hut." But the extraordinary thing, really, was not that a few people were going to praise the Lord and pass the pizza; it was that tens of millions of people had enough faith or were intimated enough by laws and peer pressure not to eat or drink even a drop of water in 100-degree heat that day from 4:17 A.M. until 7:27 P.M.

That was the twenty-seventh day of Ramazan, the twenty-seventh day of fasting. The next day's edition of *The Muslim* carried a page-one headline saying: "Moon Body Meets Tomorrow." The story began: "The Central Ruet-e-Hilal Committee will meet on July 11 an hour before the sunset at the Pakistan Broadcasting House, Lahore, for the sighting of the moon." When the committee of *maulanas* announced that it had seen the first sliver of the new moon, the Holy Month would be over and the religious men and women of the Islamic Republic—and of the other Muslim nations at slightly different times depending on the phases of the moon—could return to normal life without such self-restraint, or without the fear of public flogging if they were discovered eating or drinking in the daylight.

Only the faithful 10 or 15 percent actually fasted totally, I was told with a tone of disdain by Westernized Pakistanis. Perhaps. But to a foreigner it appeared to be a national fasting; I saw no Pakistani openly violating the law. On the contrary, I saw some of the most sophisticated people in the country bonded in the faith that month with the meanest of their Muslim brothers and sisters—to the point of endangering their health. I knew of a case of a female physician, pregnant, who had fainted on her hospital rounds. Her colleagues discovered that, even though the pregnancy made her exempt from fasting, she was doing it. That was also a common problem among patients, who were also exempt.

It was, in fact, often difficult for nonbelievers to find somewhere or something to eat. Some hotels had small rooms with drawn curtains which would serve foreigners or Pakistanis who swore, in writing, that they were not Muslims; I knew four women who did that, but two of them were turned away, angrily, at the Holiday Inn in Islamabad. Outside the cities, though, hotels were few and far between, and we soon learned the wisdom of carrying, hidden, some boiled water and dried fruits. A little madness agitates behind your eyes when you are thirsty and can't do anything about it.

The sight of hundreds, thousands of men—and the occasional woman—in a daze or sleeping like children in the shade at the end of each day was Islam at its worst—or at its best, depending on your perspective. "Faith at the moment could supply only the simple negatives that answered emotional needs," V. S. Naipaul wrote in his book *Among the Believers* after traveling in Pakistan in 1980. "No alcohol, no feminine immodesty, no interest in the banks" and soon "no political parties, no parliament, no dissent, no law courts."

All of that was still true in Pakistan in 1983. But there was more to it than that, I thought, even under military rule and in the quiet desperation of a mandated Puritan revival. The zeal of the enforcers of faith often played at the borders of fanaticism, but the emphasis on family and responsibility to your own seemed, to me, positive to the point of inspiration. So was a strain of egalitarianism in the faith, not always affirmed in daily life but always there at least as a proclaimed and shared ideal. In the Majlis-e-Shura (Federal Council), an appointed advisory body with the appearance but not the voting power of a parliament— an example of the impotent kind of "National Assembly" favored by dictators everywhere—General Zia's appointees began banging on their desks in approval when an old man named Mahmod Ahmed Minto, who had been a political activist at the creation of Pakistan, rose and said: "In the eyes of God, a *tonga wallah* has the same rights and status as General Zia-ul-Haq." (A *tonga* is a two-wheeled cart; *wallah*, a wonderful and widely used word, means something like "handler of." One man I saw regularly in an Islamabad bazaar was my "Xerox *wallah*.") Another Majlis appointee, Khanzada Taj, jumped up after the old man and said: "This country belongs to the people of Pakistan. The sooner it is handed over to them, the better." There was more clapping on the desks.

I tried to remember moments like that, to remind myself that those ideas have as much claim on Islam and Pakistan as its puritanism and subjugation of women—contradictory claims that gave the faith constant and vigorous intellectual ferment. And in my own ferment over what I was seeing and hearing around me, I had to remind myself again and again that the "subjugation" was in our eyes. That was my judgment. I was sure of what I believed about what we call "equal rights" and "human rights." But they were not us. The man who said that best for me was another foreigner, a Belgian filmmaker, Paul Jacques Callebaut, who had traveled the world doing documentaries on dying religions. We met at the Chitral Aerodrome. His family and mine, a young woman from Michigan and a couple of Christian missionaries from Peshawar on a short holiday seemed to be the only Westerners in town.

"There are no fanatics to me," Callebaut said. "I reject fanaticism. If Muslim mystics get pleasure from driving nails into themselves, that is their concern. If their women cover themselves, that is their concern. If our women wear pants to here"— he drew his hand across the point of his groin—"that is our affair."

"Every time I read or hear about the floggings," said Louis Dupree, the American scholar who said that in his heart he considered himself a Muslim, even as he downed a cold beer in the privacy of his room at Dean's Hotel in Peshawar on a broiling Ramazan afternoon, "I remind myself of what year it really is in this country and that there were years in our history when we used to put people in stocks in the public square of the city of Boston."

(There were indeed floggings in village squares in Pakistan, but the imposition of Islamic punishments under Zia's Islamization decrees was more symbolic than real. The lashes of the whips were padded. There had been no amputations for thievery, up to the time I was there, because the new laws mandated that the amputations must be surgically done and no surgeon in the country had been willing to perform the operation.)

Drinking beer was not the only thing that might make Dupree and me seem a bit strange to a *tonga wallah* in the Rawalpindi bazaar—for instance, keeping dogs in the house, which Muslims consider unsanitary. When I left Pakistan it was to go to a country where the food was better, but in every town, on almost every house sometimes, there were statues and pictures of stripped, bleeding men. Barbaric stuff, to a modern *tonga wallah*. The representations were all of the same person, with blood dripping from a cut in his side. He was actually nailed, through the hands and feet, to crossed boards. The people in the towns would gather together once a week to eat bread and drink wine, repeating that it was the body and the blood of the man hanging from the boards. The country was France; the *tonga wallah* might have thought that it was quite a place and, whatever we might believe, that Christianity was a religion of dark, negative superstitions.

What would they think? What do they know about us? Maulana Fazl-ur-Rehman, in Lahore, told me he had visited San Francisco. "I was amazed at the fanaticism of the belief in democracy," he said. "If the majority of people there say they want to have homosexuality, you have to have it!"

When my wife, who was in Pakistan to prepare a report on the status of Afghan refugees, visited the Majlis-e-Shura, she struck up a conversation with a young guard. He was fluent in English and said that he had graduated from a Christian missionary college—high school in our system—in which English was the medium of instruction.

"The priests," he said, "insisted on English at all times."

"Oh," Cathy said, reacting to the word *priest*. "Was it a Catholic school?"

"What?" he asked in reply.

"Was your college Catholic or Protestant?"

"I don't know."

And most Americans don't have the vaguest notion of the difference between Sunni and Shia Muslims. That difference, though, is essential to even beginning a conversation comparing Pakistan with Iran, or discussing the differing views of Mushahid Hussain, the editor of *The Muslim*, a Shia, and General Zia, a Sunni.

Both of us have a long way to go, the *tonga wallah* and I. But what was an inconvenience for me will be agony for him, because he is the one who has to figure out how to close the gap. I will not change very much, at least not to accommodate illiterate masses. Pakistan will change to be like us in many ways; the struggle I saw going on was over how much of what they were they would give up to have some of what we have. It was very moving sometimes. One night in Lahore, a friend, Anwar Kamal, a thirty-four-year-old attorney, proudly took us to a new park in his city. Thousands of families were roaming great lawns long into the hot night, renting paddleboats and motorboats on an artificial lake, riding a miniature train—a wonderful place. When we praised it, Anwar said, "Yes, but . . ." and began talking about his one long trip outside Pakistan. He had traveled across Europe by train and then across the United States by bus for three weeks, from New York to San Francisco.

"You have created heavens on earth," he said in wonder, with a new perception, at least to me, as he talked of the freedom, the health and the wealth of Europeans and Americans. "I want us to do that for ourselves. We can do that here. I know it and I want to be part of it."

A few nights later, we had dinner with one of the most important spokesmen of fundamental Islam in Pakistan, a man whose name is an important part of his country's history, the son of a man who was spoken of as Americans might speak of Thomas Jefferson. He and I talked on one side of the room while the women congregated on the other. That always happened. Even in the most Westernized groups men pulled me away from conversations with women. His wife would draw her veil self-consciously if I happened to look across. He told me that he thought the Islamization pronounced and promulgated daily by the Zia regime was neither sincere nor sweeping enough. More discipline and more turmoil were needed not only to preserve real Islam but to return the faith to its basic principles. He, however, was going to miss some of the turmoil. His wife was a physician— there were many women doctors in the country because female patients ordinarily do not see male doctors—and he was going to Waco, Texas, with her next year so that she could do advanced study at Baylor University Medical School in her specialty, dermatology.

4

OUR NEW
BEST FRIEND

Three thousand men, fierce-looking Afghans in dirty, flowing robes and turbans with loose ends hanging almost to their waists, sat cross-legged under a tin roof on a hot and dusty plain called Nasir Bagh near Peshawar on the morning of July 2. A handsome young *maulana*, with a sense of drama and gestures and inflections that reminded me of evangelists I had seen in North Carolina and other parts of the American Bible Belt, animatedly recited and interpreted the Holy Quran. But it wasn't North Carolina, and, on cue, a wild-eyed old man in the front would leap to his feet, screaming, and three thousand voices would chant, "*Allah Akbar!*"—"God is great!"

There was great discipline in the scene. The men, their legs pressed against each other, did not move despite the heat that shimmered off the plain in undulating tan waves. At least, not until they heard the noise; then, one by one, they looked away from the *maulana*, staring at three jet helicopters flying in formation. A few bold ones stood to get a better look, then a few more, then many. The Holy Book could not stand up to the spectacle and sense of power as the clattering machines came lower, creating their own weather, a dust storm over the place called Mr. Nasir's Orchard, where 32,000 Afghan men and women were living in tents and mud huts.

The helicopters were bringing the Secretary of State of the United States of America to a refugee camp to have his picture taken for television. That night, back home, Americans—and people in a few other parts of the world—saw images of Secretary George Shultz and were visually reminded, against the background of robes, turbans and *maulanas*, that millions of Afghans had fled their country, most of them to Pakistan, rather than live under the control of invaders from the Union of Soviet Socialist Republics and its chosen government in Kabul. "You fight valiantly, and I want you to know," Shultz said in English, then waited patiently while Commissioner Abdullah translated his words into Pushtu, "you do not fight alone." Cheers. "I come here with a simple message. We are with you."

A *malik*, a tribal chieftain, had spoken before Shultz, pledging that the Afghan *Mujahideen*, the "fighters of the Holy War," would resist the Soviets until death—and, incidentally, added that they were with the United States all the way in our efforts to gain control over left-wing insurgencies and governments in Central America. It seemed to be an across-the-board endorsement of American foreign policy, and the men in the tent cheered each time the *malik* nodded toward them.

"What's his name? Where is he from?" I asked Abdullah later.

"I don't know," he answered.

I persisted, asking for the name again. The commissioner was annoyed with my insistence on things like names and dates. He thought, I was sure, it was a debating trick Westerners used to avoid real discussion of large questions about God and men.

"What does it matter?" he said with contempt in his voice. "He is the man who speaks to the Americans. He knows what they want to hear. We've done this dozens of times."

Everyone did know his part. Sahebzada Yaqub Khan, the Foreign Minister of Pakistan, welcomed Shultz, who would be in his country for less than seventy-two hours, by saying: "With an unparalled record of achievement in the technological and scientific fields . . . with one of the most advanced agriculture and irrigation systems in the world, the United States has much to offer to Pakistan, which has a rich, cultural heritage and ancient civilization."

"We have many things to talk about," Shultz responded, rather indulgently. "First and foremost . . . issues involving the Soviet invasion of Afghanistan."

The United States had become a great friend of Pakistan, a multibillion-dollar friend, since the Soviets moved the first of more than 100,000 troops into Afghanistan on December 24, 1979, to impose a subservient government on the people of that country between the southern border of the Soviet Union and the northern borders of Pakistan.

There is a fictional version of the scene that day in the Army Chief of Staff's house in Rawalpindi. Salman Rushdie, the London-based novelist whose family lived in Pakistan, created, in his 1983 novel *Shame*, a Chief Martial Law Administrator named Raza Hyder, who bears a great resemblance to Gen. Zia-ul-Haq.

"They had just told Raza that the Russians had sent an army into A. across the north-west frontier," Rushdie wrote of three generals going in to see the dictator, "and to their astonishment the President had leapt from his chair, unrolled four prayer-mats on the floor and insisted that they all give thanks, pronto, fut-a-fut, for this blessing that had been bestowed upon them by God. They had been rising and falling for an hour and a half, developing on their foreheads the first traces of this bruise which Raza wore with pride, when he stopped and explained to them that the Russian attack was the final step in God's strategy, because now the stability of his government would have to be ensured by the great powers. General Raddi replied a little too sourly that the Americans' policy was centered on staging a dramatic counter-coup against the Olympic Games, but before Raza could lose his temper Raddi's friends, Phisaddi and Bekar, began to shake each other's hands and congratulate themselves noisily. 'That fat-arsed Yankee,' Phisaddi shouted, referring to the American ambassador, 'he'll have to foot the bills now,' and Bekar began to fantasize about five billion dollars' worth of new military equipment, the latest stuff at least, missiles that could fly sideways without starving their engines of oxygen and tracking systems that could detect an alien anopheles mosquito at a range of ten thousand miles."

The official version of America's new interest in Pakistan—nonfiction—was a little less direct. "The stability and security of Pakistan contribute importantly to meeting U.S. objectives in South and Southwest Asia," the State Department reported to the House Foreign Affairs Committee in closed sessions on March 9, 1983. The briefing was jointly conducted by Howard B. Schaffer, deputy assistant secretary for the Near East and South Asia, and Philip R. Mayhew, director of Near Eastern and South Asian affairs for the International Security Office of the Department of Defense.

"As a frontline state"—that is a new American cliché—"resisting Soviet expansionism, Pakistan has incurred additional security responsibilities. . . . Moreover the Pakistanis have provided refuge to the nearly three million Afghans fleeing the fighting in Afghanistan," their briefing states at the beginning.

"Our commitment to Pakistan's security is given both real and symbolic shape through the existence of our six-year ($3.2 billion) program of security and economic assistance and through our willingness to contribute to Pakistan's military modernization program."

That $3.2 billion—which was supplemented by $200 million a year in direct and indirect U.S. aid to the Pakistani government for refugee programs and a little more for weapons and ammunition for the *Mujahideen*—made Pakistan the second-ranking recipient of American foreign aid. (Egypt, our other client state in the Muslim world, is first.) That is a great deal of money in an economy with a gross national product of less than $25 billion. But the United States didn't make such bad deals for itself. Most of the money, in fact, would be coming right back to the United States, much of it to defense contractors. Among other expensive hardware Pakistan was obligated to buy were forty F-16 fighters from General Dynamics, at something like $20 million each, and one hundred M-48 tanks, also manufactured by General Dynamics, from U.S. Army National Guard stocks at about $1 million each. The local estimate of how much of the American aid would be personally pocketed by Pakistan's military-civil service elite was averaging out at 20 percent. But even some of that would come back to the United States—in tuitions at Stanford and Harvard and for land in places like Sacramento, California, one of the places Pakistani expatriates live in the United States.

It was a tricky business because neither side, neither the Pakistanis nor the Americans, really trusted the other, and both sides seemed highly doubtful that if a crisis comes—i.e., an overt Soviet move from Afghanistan into the North-West Frontier Province or Baluchistan—that the other would actually resist long or effectively.

"The volatile nature of past U.S.–Pakistani relations" was the phrase used in the State Department's briefing for Congress. That referred to the burning of the U.S. Embassy by fundamentalist students in Islamabad back in November 1979, and to the resentment of all Pakistanis—from generals to sporadically jailed dissenters—who believed that the United States abandoned or betrayed Pakistan in its times of greatest need, the 1965 and 1971 wars with India over, respectively, territorial claims to Kashmir and the secession of East Pakistan. The United States, despite a mutual defense cooperation treaty with Pakistan that went back to 1959, cut off military supplies and spare parts to the Pakistan army during those conflicts. I met very few Pakistanis who did not believe the same thing would happen again if there is trouble with India—and almost all Pakistanis always expect trouble with India. Many of the official Americans out there told me they believed that if Pakistan ever did use all the hardware we're selling them, the firepower would probably not be aimed north toward Moscow but south toward Delhi.

Besides that, even the most anti-Soviet American officials— the ones who believed that any negotiations with the Soviets were bargains with devils—had other doubts. For one thing, the Pakistan army had started three wars and lost them all, badly. The only people ever conquered by that impressively medaled bunch under General Zia have been the people of Pakistan. For another, in the 1980s, the country became the most important supply point for narcotics headed for the West; American drug officials in Islamabad told me that 85 percent of the heroin in New York and Los Angeles came through Pakistan, usually following a route from the Khyber Pass to Karachi. And, finally, as far as American intelligence agencies could tell, or would admit, Pakistan was ready or getting ready to build an atomic bomb at a secret installation at Kahuta—in violation of old agreements with the United States and of common sense, because exploding a nuclear device could lead to a fourth and final (losing) war with India. It seemed dangerous for Pakistan—which was traditionally determined to see itself as the military equal of India even though

India was ten times its size in every way—and embarrassing for us because American policy was to prevent proliferation of nuclear weapons, but the Pakistani consensus, at many levels of the society, seemed to be: "If India's got it, we want it!"

"The Chinese gave us a stadium. You give us a museum," said a passionate student leader who had organized demonstrations against martial law. "We don't want stadiums and museums. What are we going to do with stadiums and museums? We want the bomb!"

So, there was a volatile nature, also, to U.S.–Pakistani relationships, depending, as they did, on a not very solid-looking foundation of self-interest—on both sides. The United States wanted its "frontline state," and the Zia government wanted not only U.S. money and expertise but the legitimacy that came with having the most powerful of democracies constantly building up the legitimacy of military rule. "The Soviet entry into Afghanistan provided the Pakistani dictator with a new lease on life," wrote Tariq Ali, a self-exiled Pakistani intellectual. "This could be seen most clearly in the sudden change of attitude displayed by the Western press. The sordid hangman of an elected prime minister"—Zia presided over the execution of Zulfiqar Ali Bhutto on April 4, 1979—"was soon transformed into the plucky defender of the frontiers of the Free World. Prior to the Russian invasion, most Western observers had been in favor of a return to civilian rule, but this theme virtually disappeared in the years that followed."

That analysis from the Left—Ali wrote as a Marxist—may be a little harsh. But at the very least I found ambivalence among official Americans about the return of democracy in Pakistan. "You've got a very complicated situation here . . ." coming from American officials was invariably the signal that a representative of the United States government was about to explain to you—"off the record, please"—that in the real world, dictatorships aren't as bad as we have been teaching our children they are for the past two hundred or so years.

"As these things go, of course, Zia isn't so bad at all. Sort of benevolent . . ." was another opening to the same thoughts.

Or: "There is relatively little brutality here. . . ."

Or: "The alternative is chaos, so . . ."

Or this one: "If you write about the way women are treated in Pakistan, you will only be helping our enemies. Anyway, the women who are complaining are just the middle class. I hear they spend most of their time watching blue movies on their Betamaxes. . . ."

"Our personal views of human rights may be a little too esoteric in this part of the world," said Ronald Spiers, the American ambassador to Pakistan. "As an individual American there are many things I would like to speak out about. But, publicly, as a representative of the United States government, I don't go around lecturing people about the way we do things at home."

I heard that and more from State Department people and others directly or indirectly associated with my government. There was obviously some truth in all of it—except, maybe, the blue movies—but in making my own assessment of the permanence of our self-interested friendship with Pakistan, I couldn't help noticing that two of the three helicopters that brought Secretary Shultz's party to Nasir Bagh were Soviet machines. The Russians provided the Pakistan Air Force's *matériel* for almost ten years after Pakistanis concluded that we had deserted them in the 1971 war that led to the establishment of East Pakistan as the independent country of Bangladesh. Before that, relations between Pakistan and the United States had been very friendly; it was Yahya Khan, the second of the country's military dictators, who used Pakistan's close relations with its neighbor, the People's Republic of China, to help set up the 1972 trip of President Richard Nixon to Peking. (The strong Pakistan-China connection has survived, bonded by fear of the Soviet Union.) Pondering the ups and downs of Pakistan–U.S. relations, I was reminded of something else driving near Peshawar one morning with a Pakistani official. "That's the field where Francis Gary Powers took off," he said, pointing to an airstrip in the distance, "before the Russians shot down his U-2 in 1960."

Airstrips in faraway places are the insignia of superpowers. We are everywhere, or we used to be or will be. We've moved into or been kicked out of—or both—about every place you can send up a plane or put up an antenna pointed toward Moscow. Hope springs eternal in official American breasts, particularly the ones decorated with ribbons and medals. Adm. Thomas Moorer, the retired chairman of the Joint Chiefs of Staff, writing in *Strategic Review* magazine, suggested that the United States utilize Gwadar in Baluchistan as a military port to replace the Iranian military bases and facilities lost when the fundamentalist Muslim (Shia) government took power in 1979. That was a profitable year for the rulers of Pakistan because, even before the Soviets penetrated Afghanistan, the Iranian revolution had left the United States without a geopolitical best friend in that critical area between the Soviet Union and the Persian Gulf. "There is a possibility that the Pakistan army could serve as a proxy fighting in the Gulf," said Francis Fukuyama, a member of the State Department's Policy Planning Staff in 1981 Congressional subcommittee testimony, ". . . provided once again that the United States undertakes to protect Pakistan from the consequences of such a decision."

The people of Pakistan, because of the geopolitical chance that put their lands along invasion routes mapped by strategists from Alexander and Genghis Khan to Leonid Brezhnev, were going to be facing the consequences of many decisions—many of which they never made.

One summer night, in the village of Chitral, I sat with the retired army major who was Pakistan's refugee commissioner for that remote district. There were 25,000 Afghans, much more than the population of the village, living in tents and mud houses on some of the precious flatland in the valley cut by the Mastuj River. Armed men, walking, endlessly it seemed, along the roads and in the bazaars. Washing in rivers and irrigations streams— hundreds splashing around at a time. They seemed to have nothing to do—chewing aimlessly on the shawls many carried on one shoulder, exactly like small children's security blankets. But it was obvious that they were only waiting, resting before going back through the surrounding mountain passes into their own country, to fight for a while and then return again to this sanctuary.

"I am Major Mulk," he said. "Mulk" had great meaning; his family had ruled the Chitral Valley for centuries before it came under the loose control of the British. It was only at the end of the 1960s that the area came under the administrative control of the government of Pakistan, which for many years treated it as tribal territory, within national borders but, effectively, beyond federal law.

"What do you wish to know?" the major said.

"Has there been much trouble with the refugees coming here?" asked my wife.

"For some reason, no," he answered. "I call it a miracle. There has been only a little trouble between the refugees and the local population. Over firewood, usually. There is very little wood here, as you can see."

"Why?" she said.

"The refugees have not faced the reality of their situation. They do not know what is going on in the world. They think they are going back to Afghanistan to live again. Tomorrow or the next day."

"They are all armed. Is that a problem?"

"The government spent a long time persuading the people of Chitral to give up their guns and accept the authority and benefits of central government, and finally they did. Now the Afghans come with guns. But, no, it is not a problem. Not yet, because they are looking that way." He gestured toward the pass into Afghanistan. "But if they lose hope and look inward . . ."

Two shots were fired nearby, but Mulk ignored them for a moment, completing his thought.

"I am in great fear of that."

Then, he looked into the dark and said: "Probably a wedding. They fire their rifles into the air."

And there was another shot.

"It's all very far away from you in America, isn't it? But it is not as far as you think."

There was a burst of several shots, then another.

"I have great fear about what will happen here, in Pakistan," said Major Mulk. "I must go and see about that shooting."

5

THE REFUGEES
FROM OVER
THE MOUNTAIN

The homes of the refugees were hard to see. They blended into the earth because they were made of earth. A few of the more than two million Afghans who crossed the mountains into Pakistan lived in tents supplied by the United Nations, but by the summer of 1983 most of them had been there long enough to construct homes of earth mixed with water, buffalo dung and a little straw.

On the roads and in the bazaars, the Afghans themselves blended into the people and the summer dust of Asia before the monsoons. There were no walls, no fences, no guards around the refugees or their camps. The image I remember of those people coming through the passes of the Hindu Kush with only what they could carry is of men and boys and water buffalos in muddy irrigation canals. The road from Peshawar to Nasir Bagh, where 32,000 Afghans lived, ran along a canal, and sometimes it seemed that I could not see the opposite bank because of the humans and animals finding what coolness they could in the bright heat.

It was, as Major Mulk had said, practically a miracle. One of the poorest countries in the world had absorbed two or three million people: there were elaborate refugee statistics, but no one took them literally. "Within this rough circle live 10,000 people registered (600 families) and 10,000 unregistered," reported an American physician, Dr. John W. Hennessey, to his organization, the International Rescue Committee, after a December 1982 visit to a camp near Kohat. "This figure was arrived at by asking the *Maliks* for their estimate, then dropping a zero. Such is the analytic method in these parts."

Those people, the refugees taken in, were, if anything, even poorer. By the summer of 1983, one out of six or one out of seven people in Pakistan's North-West Frontier Province was a refugee, and there were more in Baluchistan and some in the Punjab. There had been, for all practical purposes, no trouble. Pakistan worked. Not our way, but it got by. People were generous.

Abdullah, the Commissioner of Refugees in the province, told this story: "About two years ago a group of 200 refugee families came to a village because they knew somebody there. The villagers told the refugees that they were poor landless people who earned their livelihood either by working on a government farm or in the city. They had nothing to offer the refugees but their own houses. They literally halved their houses. If someone had two rooms, he built a wall in between and offered one room to a refugee family and kept one for himself. It actually happened.

"It is the way of Islam," he said with great pride. He had reason to be proud of his faith and his people. What would have happened if more than eight million Mexicans came into the United States between Texas and California during an invasion of their country—that would be the proportional equivalent to the Afghan migration—would we, Christians on both sides of the Rio Grande, be as generous? The situations would not have been so different, including the fact many Afghans were unofficially (illegally) in Pakistan's Northwest before the Soviets came, as many Mexicans are illegally among the Mexican-Americans of the American Southwest. But the reaction might be different. One result could be a barbed-wire shortage.

The refugees had begun coming in large numbers, perhaps 100,000 of them, in the spring and summer of 1978 when a new Communist government in Kabul—which took power in a *coup d'état* against other Communists—attempted to impose land reforms, and violence began to erupt in the countryside. Before that exodus began, perhaps 6 million of the 16 million or so Pathans lived on the Afghanistan side of the mountains. Within three years, fewer than 4 million were left there. More and more families and entire villages crossed into Pakistan—the border, the mountains of the Hindu Kush, are cut by more than three hundred passes, some known only to the Pathans—as successive governments (all unelected) harshly escalated the pressure on the countryside to live according to the new dogma of Kabul. By December 1979, there may have been 400,000 Afghans in Pakistan.

Armed resistance, the national sport of the Pathans, continually escalated against the Communists in Kabul. So much that the Soviet Union decided to squash the local rebellions at the end of 1979. Eighty-five thousand Soviet troops invaded Afghanistan that December 24, and the Soviets placed their own man, an Afghan Communist named Babrak Karmal, in power in Kabul. Within twelve months, as many as 2 million more Afghans fled to Pakistan, bringing stories of Soviet terror and brutality. (Smaller numbers of refugees also went to Iran.)

Most came across in groups of fifty or one hundred, villages or nomad clans led by *maliks*, the local tribal chieftains. They brought more than 2 million animals with them—goats, sheep, buffalos and camels. It was a timeless sight. The men in turbans or woolen or embroidered caps, baggy pants and vests or robes like academic gowns, bandoliers of cartridges across their chests, old rifles or new machine guns on one shoulder. Their sons were dressed the same way, miniatures of their fathers. The animals and the women walked behind. When they stopped, they sometimes took the tents offered by the United Nations or, sometimes, just re-created their *katchi* villages on the other side of the mountains. Then the men, many of them, went back to kill Russians.

I saw Afghan women only when I traveled with my wife during her inspections of medical installations, tents set up by such organizations as the International Rescue Committee, the Red Crescent Society and the International Red Cross. The women came to the medical tents with their children—the average refugee family had six children in a society where surviving male children were *de facto* old-age insurance—to what was clearly the social event of the day or the week, literally the only way to get out of the house. Even then, many of the men did not allow their women to speak to male doctors or technicians, instead reciting their wives' real or imagined symptoms.

"I would rather see them die than be corrupted by these males who call themselves doctors," roared Malik Haji Tur Gal, scattering the women waiting at the International Rescue Committee tent at a camp called Lakhti Banda.

He was an important man, a white-haired giant who was the accepted chief of thousands of refugees. He seemed to be over seventy years old—"Wow! He looks like Noah," said Dr. Hennessey, coming out of the tent—although it was impossible to tell because the Afghans did not record birthdays. The wife with him appeared to be about sixteen. It was obvious that part of his rage was at the thought that she might have to wait in line behind the other women.

Dr. Hennessey and Dr. Sayed Abdul Rahman Hashmee, himself an Afghan refugee, tried to calm the old man, explaining that there was a female physician on their team but she was away for a short leave.

"And who are you to decide these things?" the *malik* said. "Two bulls who want to roam among the cows."

It was a scene repeated many times in the camps, sometimes resolved by a *jirga*, a meeting of tribal elders, sometimes by allowing a *malik* to appoint a *chowkidar*, a watchman for the tent. The *chowkidar* was usually a relative and always split his pay with the chief.

The women who made it to the lines outside the medical centers had already broken through one of the walls around their lives. Many more women were behind veils and behind four walls. Afghan society was more fundamentally religious and traditional than Pakistani society, earlier on the calendars of modernity. When Afghan women gave birth to sons, there were feasts and rifle shots into the sky. If the baby was a girl, the event was simply not mentioned. One of the frustrations of the workers of the World Food Program and others distributing food in the camps was that they knew the Afghan men ate first and well, then the boys. What food was left went to the females.

Only a quarter of the people in the camps, though, were men, and a disproportionate number of those were old men like Haji Tur Gal. Yet almost all the patients in refugee hospitals scattered around Peshawar were men between the ages of, say, sixteen to forty. The camps served as the military bases of the *Mujahideen*. So, many of the men who had registered in the camps were actually now in Afghanistan. Others had never crossed the border but sent their women and children to safety in Pakistan. (There were also many working in other parts of Pakistan—as truck drivers in the Punjab, road workers in Sind or shipbreakers at Gadani Beach.)

"We close our eyes to what is really going on," said an official of the Peshawar office of the United Nations High Commissioner for Refugees, an organization obviously pledged to neutrality in such matters as civil wars and resistance movements. He went out the next day with my wife to check out a report that several dozen orphans had arrived the night before at the Wasak camp fifteen miles away. There were, it turned out, 308 "orphans." All boys.

"I take it there are no girl orphans in Afghanistan?" Cathy said.

There were, but they weren't being sent across the border for training to fight the Soviets. That group of future *Mujahideen* seemed to be between the ages of twelve and fourteen and followed the orders of older men who were, or would be, their military superiors. The "orphans" would stay together in the camps, being educated by the United Nations and trained by their elders, until it was time for them to go back and fight the Soviets.

It was already a long war. In one of the Afghan hospitals, Avicenna Balkhi, near Nasir Bagh, there was a poster of a child's crayon drawing of Soviet troops machine-gunning rows of uniformed schoolgirls in Afghanistan in December 1981. Tulips sprouted from the pools of blood. "We will not be defeated by them," said Dr. Mummad Mohmand, a Kabul surgeon who was the director of the hospital, when he saw me looking at the poster. "We fought the British, we fought Genghis Khan, we fought Alexander. They could not defeat us. We will not be defeated, because we will fight to the last blood of a small child."

The hospitals, more than a dozen of them, helped give Peshawar the tension of a city of war. And that is what Peshawar knows best; the frontier town at the beginning of the Khyber Pass has been fought over and in forever, it seems. The old British cemetery on the Khyber Road, near the "Star Trek" video games parlor, was a relic of one round between conquerors and the Pathans.

"In Loving Memory of No. 5345 Cpl. W. M. McCann 1st Bn Royal Scots Fusiliers April 11, 1901."

"In Loving Memory of Capt. Sidney Hartley Killed in Action Peshawar February 22, 1930."

There were even signs among the weeds and the broken headstones that Americans had been here before, trying in their own way to do good. "Rev. Isidore Loewenthal. American. Who first translated the New Testament into Pushtoo was shot by his Chokeydar. April 27, 1864." Shot by his watchman. Must have been a story there.

A city of stories—one of the great bazaar streets of Peshawar was called Qissa Qahani, "The Street of the Storytellers"—and a visiting American must listen. And look. The hospitals of Peshawar were not there only to treat the war wounded of Afghanistan, they were there to impress foreigners, particularly Americans, with the horrors of Soviet tactics in Afghanistan. I was impressed. At the Afghan Surgical Hospital, run by Pakistan's most militant fundamentalist organization, the Jamatt-i-Islami, the "Islamic party," I was not allowed to leave without going from bed to bed. Forty beds. At each one, stumps of arms or legs would be thrust at me, or dressings would be lifted away to show a red hole that had been a face. A young man, what was left of him, held my eyes with his until I cried as the blankets were pulled from his wasting body, most of it scar tissue from burns. The truck he had been riding on was hit by a Soviet mortar shell, exploding into a ball of flame around him. An older man named Abdul Kareem, who said he was a farmer at a place called Bagh Lan, north of Kabul, proudly showed me the foot-long stumps of his legs. "It was the poison gas, I know it," he said through a translator. "A Russian threw it into the room where I was staying; three children were killed."

He was almost certainly wrong about the gas—I could find no evidence to support the many stories any American was quickly told about Soviet toxic weapons—because soldiers do not use poison gas where the fumes would kill or maim them, too.

"How do you know it was a Russian?" I asked.

"I know Russians," he said, making a face. "They have red faces. They look like monkeys."

The maimed men around me burst into laughter. They were broken only in body—and many of their bodies were being patched up so they could fight another day. Readings from the Holy Quran and sermons were broadcast from loudspeakers on each wall of what was once a mansion with a large inner courtyard. The rooms that surrounded the yard were the patients' wards. It was Ramazan and twenty-four of the patients were fasting. The sixteen others were being force-fed by doctors. There were framed sayings from the Holy Book above each door. The one above the room Abdul Kareem shared with five other men said: "Certainly the best people are those whose morals are best."

Most of the injuries were to limbs. Legs and hands and arms. The stumps were usually from land-mine explosions. Not the big mines the Americans bury, but little plastic dirt-colored things about six inches wide that were dropped, from airplanes, along mountain roads. They were almost invisible to a man walking. The hand injuries were mostly to children, from small bombs, dropped from the planes, the Afghans claimed, shaped like ballpoint pens, or watches or small dolls. Toy bombs.

At the International Committee for the Red Cross Surgical Hospital in the center of Peshawar, more than four thousand operations had been performed in the past two years. Almost all were amputations. In another part of the city, the Red Cross operated a prosthesis center, which looked like a combination machine shop and gymnasium. The drill presses, grinding wheels and arc welders were making parts of young men—sturdy artificial arms and legs for people who planned to go back to mountain country and needed wood, leather and iron pipe limbs that could be repaired in the smallest village. Around the shops with their grinding noises and welding sparks, men dragged themselves along parallel bars or stretched painfully, learning to use their new parts or to try to make the old, atrophied ones work again. Along one wall, six young men standing like statues supported themselves against a frame something like a very wide lectern. They were all paralyzed from the neck down. They gossiped cheerfully among themselves. Two were sipping Coca-Cola through straws in bottles held by relatives. In hospitals in that part of the world, a relative was assigned to stay with each patient.

That was all twenty-five miles from the border. The *Mujahideen* wounded, the ones with the best chances of survival, had been carried on the backs of donkeys and men to Peshawar. Few men made it, but the hospitals were still one of the reasons that the Afghans with only light armament could continue their fierce resistance against the more than 100,000 regular Soviet troops occupying Afghanistan. And in case new armaments were needed, there was always Darra, "the town of guns," twenty-five miles in the other direction from Peshawar. The town was off limits to foreigners, but we were issued a pass allowing us to drive through on the way to refugee camps in the Kohat Valley. "Through" meant driving slowly along a dusty main street of more than seventy gun shops. Behind them were warrens of factories where skilled Pathans were making anything and everything from .22-caliber pistols to small antiaircraft guns. The shops displayed copies of just about every rifle and pistol in the world, made in the back, tested in the back: shots were being fired all around. Thirty-eight-caliber pistols started at 800 rupees; a Sten gun was 1,000 rupees. A good copy of a Russian Kalashnikov automatic rifle was 10,000 rupees, the work of one man for a month.

The Soviets obviously knew about all this, and about the medical teams from the Red Cross and other foreign organizations that went up to, and often across, the border to act as the corpsmen of the Afghan resistance. Everyone knew something in Peshawar; everyone seemed to report to someone. The city existed for intrigue. Conspiracy, rebellion, spying, propaganda, arms sales, smuggling—those were the cottage industries of the storytellers' bazaar. If Dean's Hotel, the rambling old resting place for traveling British colonial officials which somehow managed to look like an old American motel out of time and place, did not actually exist, Graham Greene would have invented it. But it existed. Men with submachine guns came there, springing from Datsuns and walking quickly across the fading gardens to step into the midday darkness of the rooms of Americans who said their business was "export-import" or "investments." It was never clear to me what they were investing in or what they were importing. I asked one of the Americans whether he worked for the government. "Everyone works for the government here, don't they?" he said. It was the kind of answer that kept getting you invited places in Peshawar.

The intriguing situation in Peshawar and across the border in Afghanistan seemed acceptable to all concerned in the summer of 1983. The Pakistanis, the Americans, the Russians, the refugees—each had reason to be satisfied with the way things were in that far, violent land of men we called Khan, whether that was their name or not.

For Pakistan, the influx of refugees meant an influx of both foreign aid and foreign sympathy. The aid included hundreds of millions of dollars a year in hard Western currencies—the coin that the world demands for everything from gasoline to make trucks go to tear gas to make mobs go—cash that was critical to a country that spoke, quite accurately, of meager resources. But the sympathy was probably more critical to the people currently running that country, the military. General Zia was certainly one of the few military dictators around the world regularly quoted as a humanitarian. "We are looking after them ungrudgingly purely for the sake of humanitarian grounds and we will continue to do so even if the population increases," the Chief Martial Law Administrator was quoted as saying at the beginning of the United Nations High Commissioner for Refugees January, 1983 report on the status of the Afghan refugees. "But it is a very large burden . . . We are a poor country but we are prepared and we are sharing with our neighbors and friends who may have perhaps less than we have."

The refugee population not only gave the regime respect and legitimacy abroad, but the burden of the Afghans and the threat of the Soviets probably kept Zia in power. Even his worst domestic enemies, lawyers and other Western-educated political activists, sometimes defined the situation on the frontier as a national "emergency"—and emergency has always been the favorite word of military rulers everywhere.

There was one other thing about the Refugees in the North-West Frontier Province. Their labor was needed in Pakistan. As poor as the country was and as low as the cost of a man's day, there was a labor shortage around Peshawar because so many of the local men were working in the Gulf states as laborers in and around the oil fields. The money was much better in Saudi Arabia or the United Arab Emirates, and for the past several years Pakistanis in general—two million at any time—and Pathans in particular had been going to the oil countries to fill three-year and five-year labor contracts at wage levels many times what they could earn at home. Under any circumstances, someone would have been needed to repair the roads and carry the loads of Pakistan—and it turned out to be hundreds of thousands of Afghan someones coming over the mountains.

For the United States, the refugees offered the irresistible chance to embarrass the Soviet Union on a continuing basis. All the Afghans had to do was stand there—preferably in front of cameras—looking displaced and poor. The pictures and their plight provided legitimate commentary on the values and reality of the Soviet system. Even better, the Afghans weren't satisfied to shame Soviets, an endeavor of dubious prospect; they wanted to kill them. And they were doing it, although at terrible cost. While I was there a reasonable estimate of the casualties on each side during almost three years of *Mujahideen* rebellion might have been 300,000 Afghan dead, almost all civilians, and perhaps 6,000 Soviet citizens killed, almost all soldiers.

The Afghans fought on, brave men; many did intend to fight until the blood of the last child. "Why are you, who have everything, afraid of the Russians? We have nothing and we are not afraid of them," said Dr. Mohmand at his hospital for the wounded. "Why won't you give us weapons? Answer that to me?"

"The answer is we do," said a high U.S. official in the country at the time. "But they want heavier weapons, stuff they probably couldn't handle. They have enough to keep this going. That's what we want: to keep this going as long as possible to make the Soviets look as bad as possible to the rest of the world."

The Soviets, in turn, seemed to think the price was worth paying. They were getting what they wanted—control over the land of Afghanistan. I couldn't be sure of all their reasons, but they certainly included control of Afghanistan's natural resources and a military buffer zone, avoidance of the embarrassment of the overthrow of a client Communist government, the quashing of the flow of Islamic fervor into their own Asian republics, and an eventual path (through Baluchistan) to the warm water ports of the Arabian Sea and the water routes of the world's oil supplies.

The Soviets were patiently gaining control over one of the most uncontrollable countries on earth by depopulating it. No one ever really conquered the fierce tribal people of Afghanistan—the British and the Russians had tried for all of the nineteenth century, but the mountain snipers had always driven them out—and the Soviet strategy this time seemed to be to conquer the country if not the nation. The nation, or at least the difficult people, was being eliminated in one way or another. There were fifteen million Afghans when the Soviets invaded. By the summer of 1983, a half million were dead, almost three million were in Pakistan and hundreds of thousands were in Iran.

Among the missing were the most troublesome—the tribal warriors in the camps of Pakistan and the small educated elite of Kabul who were scattering to richer places. There had been, when the Soviets came, about twelve hundred physicians in Afghanistan, said Dr. Mahmond, who had studied five years at Texas A&M and was jailed for ten months by the Communists in Kabul. He told me that there were only two hundred left, almost all of them recent medical school graduates. He said that proudly, as proof of the unpopularity of the Soviet rule. But I drew a different meaning from his figures.

"How many Afghan doctors are there in Peshawar?" I asked.

"Between fifty and a hundred," he said.

So, nine hundred physicians, three-quarters of his country's doctors, were gone. They were in Europe or the United States, aching perhaps for their land and people but making new lives for themselves in places where their skills made them welcome. The same was true in other professions and among merchants. The upper classes and the upper middle classes had been driven out or fled. Those pitifully small elites were gradually being replaced by cadres of physicians, teachers, engineers and administrators being trained by the thousands in Moscow. There was going to be a new Afghanistan.

And for the refugees, the Afghans driven from their lands: life was better. I was told that many times—by Pakistani and Afghan doctors, by foreign and U.N. relief officials, even by refugees—before I began considering that it might be true. "You must not look at this as if you were in America, by your standards, so neat, so clean," said Dr. Firdaus Khan (economics, not medicine, was his field of study), the Jamatt-i-Islami (the rigid and fundamentalist "Party of Islam") organizer who ran the party's Afghan Surgical Hospital. "Pakistanis are too soft to understand these people. We are not as strong as they are in the sense that we are more sophisticated. We have been softened by the amenities of life. They are hard."

If the people of Pakistan were too soft to grasp Afghan tribal life, it was infinitely more difficult for an American to understand that the refugees might be better off than they had been across the mountains. They were being given something—for the first time in their lives, for the first time in their history. Food. Medicine. Education. Wages.

Each refugee, each day, was supposed to be provided, by the World Food Program and the United Nations High Commission for Refugees, with this food: 500 grams of wheat, a little over a pound; 30 grams of edible oil; 30 grams of powdered milk; 20 grams of sugar and 3 grams of tea. That would add up to 2,250 calories per day, which was also the average Pakistani intake and just below the 2,500 calories a day considered the minimum daily requirement by most Western health agencies. Each refugee was also, on paper, receiving 25 liters (roughly quarts) of "potable" water each day; that, however, was impossible in a country whose own water supply, by its own government's most optimistic estimates, was less than 25 percent potable.

The government of Pakistan, the UNHCR and twenty-eight voluntary agencies—the Red Cross and Red Crescent among them—had set up more than two hundred medical units of various sizes and sophistication to serve the camps. Most of them were little more than dispensaries—and they really dispensed. "The Afghans and the Pakistanis, too, are drug-crazy, especially for anything in syrups," said Dr. Hennessey, who was on a one-year leave from his position as an anesthesiologist at Columbia Presbyterian Medical Center in New York. He was in the camps for a year, directing ten physicians, nurses and technicians working in the tents set up by the International Rescue Committee. One of the days we talked, he was working in a field near Hangu, fifty miles from Peshawar, vigorously scrubbing scabs from the scalp of a girl about five years old. Then he put the soapy blob of cotton he was using into the hand of the girl's sister, about ten years

old, and made her do it. "Now, every day . . . ," he began saying
to the older girl, then turned and said, "I need someone who
can speak to this child. . . .

"They're amazingly healthy people," Hennessey told me. "There
was a high incidence of tuberculosis among them in the beginning, but there isn't anything wrong with two-thirds of the people
who line up here every morning. They come to schmooze or
because they think the medicines are part of their rights here.
They want what they see other people getting. They can get
really obnoxious about it. Each day you have to decide whether
you're going to give them what they want—syrups and injections;
they don't believe in pills, especially white pills—or whether
you're really going to get down to what should be done."

"What's that?" I said.

"Teaching them the connection between filth and disease. Basic
sanitation and personal cleanliness. It's going to take a long time."

What could they think of Jack Hennessey—the Afghans who
walked miles over dry, scrubby hills to this tall, red-faced, gray-
haired man, all in white, dispensing miracles? The first doctor
most of the people crowded around the tent ever saw was from
one of the most important hospitals in the world, and all he
wanted to do was to tell them they should be washing their hands.
But they saw him, and they must have known that something
was never going to be the same for them, even inside their own
bodies.

Other things were happening at the same time inside the heads
of the refugees—and of their children. What did the women and
their daughters, sitting silently in the sun, think of the two doctors
with Hennessey, women physicians from Pakistan? Muslim women
were dispensing the same miracles. And there were schools and
teachers in the camps. The literacy rate among rural Afghans was
said to be something like 4 percent—7 percent for men and 2
percent for women. The numbers were undoubtedly made up to
complete the records of international organizations, but they made
the point: the people who came across the mountains could not
read or write. By the time I was there, the UNHCR had set up
more than 400 primary schools, using about 2,000 Afghan and
Pakistani teachers, and had enrolled 55,000 boys and 12,000 girls.
The literacy rate among boys was said to have reached 30 percent,

but there was great resistance among the refugees to educating their daughters. There were also large numbers of *madrasets*, religious schools run by Afghan political parties and other organizations, some of them financed by Arab countries, particularly Saudi Arabia, which sporadically but erratically pumped large amounts of money into the Jamatt-i-Islami in Pakistan and the most fundamentalist of the Afghan political parties loosely linked to *Mujahideen* inside Afghanistan.

Another statistic going the rounds, this one supplied by the International Labor Organization, was that just about 70 percent of the men registered in the camps had some sort of paid work in the North-West Frontier Province. Again, the number might be off, but it was an indication not only that were hundreds of thousands of refugees assimilated into the local economy—almost all transportation and construction work in the region was being done by Afghans—but that many of the refugees had become wage-earning parts of a cash economy for the first time in their lives.

It was also impossible to calculate exactly how much all that cost and precisely who was paying for what. One of the reasons was that no one knew how many refugees there were. The official figure, issued by the government of Pakistan, was just under three million. Most of the foreigners I talked with guessed that that number was an exaggeration of 20 or 30 percent. The rationale for overcounting was that the bigger the numbers, the more money the government got from the outside. The official cost figure for refugee relief, again supplied by the government of Pakistan, which retained administrative control of refugee programs, was $441 million. On paper, that was broken down to 150 rupees per refugee per month, about $12 each per month, plus a 20 percent override to cover Pakistan's internal transportation costs to move around food, material and people.

But that 150 rupees figure was clearly a phony. It was made up of 70 rupees per month for food—$5.38 per month for each person—30 rupees for all other direct and indirect services and a 50-rupee cash grant to each refugee each month. I did not meet a refugee who had received 50 rupees from the government, and I did not meet anyone else who had met a refugee who had received the 50 rupees or had ever heard of anyone who had witnessed such a transaction. It's possible that a few *malik*s were getting some cash—$3.85 per head, and they could argue about how many females were behind the walls—but if they were they probably weren't distributing it to the people under their control. When I asked Pakistani refugee officials—nine thousand Pakistanis were employed in refugee programs—about the obvious lack of payments, they began talking about "administrative problems." There were certainly plenty of those around the camps, but the real reason was pride. The Pakistanis, from Zia-ul-Haq down, were too proud to admit that for all practical purposes all the refugee money was foreign money, so all their records showed the government of Pakistan paying almost half the cost of relief—$139 million in cash allowances and $72 million in inland transportation costs.

There was real tension about the money and about power over the refugees. Just by refusing to pass the paperwork necessary for any foreigner to function in Pakistan, Commissioner Abdullah of N.W.F.P. pressured the international relief organizations to hire, reluctantly, Pakistani administrative and medical personnel. "I wouldn't call it pride. The Pakistanis are just xenophobic," said a Red Cross official with contempt. "They think foreigners are troublemakers. We're a constant reminder to them that Muslim brotherhood is still a dream. We are efficient, they're not. We make it obvious that they could never do this themselves."

"Anyway," a U.N. official added, "only a third of the money that comes into Pakistan for this actually gets to the refugees. The rest of it goes into someone's pocket along the way."

That was another statistic no one was ever going to be able to calculate. Corruption was pervasive in the refugee program. It did not involve the 50-rupee payments—those rupees never existed—it was basically a skimming operation. Army officers and officials were taking a cut of everything along the way. Food, clothing and drugs intended for refugees were in every bazaar, often being sold from the original WFP or UNHCR boxes. There was fatigued bitterness about that among foreign relief officials. But the Pakistanis were determined not to do things "the Western way." And the Westerners hadn't figured out a Pakistani way: a lot of them weren't sure there was a Pakistani way. Humanitarian work bred a certain cynicism. The United States government—

providing 40 percent of WFP funding and 35 percent of UNHCR funding—was probably accounting for half of what was called "The Afghan Money." That money included the secret U.S. and Saudi Arabian funds for arms and ammunition for the *Mujahideen*. But it was a given in Islamabad that American generosity was directly related to Soviet discomfort. The Pakistanis made much of their hospitality—*melmestia* in Pushtu—toward Muslim brethren, but they were more hostile than hospitable to other Muslim refugees inside and just outside their country. There were at least 2,000 Iranians in Pakistan, refugees from the Khomeini regime, shunned as leftists and Shia troublemakers in a conservative Sunni society. Then there were the Biharis, perhaps 250,000 of them, the wretched refuse of the 1971 war that transformed East Pakistan into Bangladesh. They were the East Pakistanis, many of them civil servants, who sided with West Pakistan. Some of them made it to the new Pakistan, where they, too, were shunned. Many more were trapped in Bangladesh, where they waited, miserably and vainly, for Muslim brotherhood from their old friends in Islamabad.

There were contradictions and hypocrisy in Pakistan's actions, and there was griping all day every day about the way the refugee programs were run, but the Pakistanis and the foreigners working together, and not particularly liking it or each other, were, on balance, a pretty impressive bunch: they supervised Major Mulk's "miracle."

A fragile miracle. The Afghan refugee situation was not exactly under control when I was there; it was just in balance.

"Regulate?" Commissioner Abdullah answered my question with his own. "No one can regulate these people. We can't. The Russians can't. They have family on both sides of the border, and they come and go as they please." Indeed. The Afghans did not seem to have thought of their migration in terms of whether they were "welcome" or not. They had always considered the Northwest of Pakistan, the home of their ethnic cousins and Muslim brothers, an extension of their own lands, separated only by the mountains and a line an Englishman named Durand drew on a map 150 years or so ago and and called a boundary. They were living as they had lived for centuries before this Durand ever heard their language. They did not accept Moghul law, British law, Afghan law or Pakistani law. Much of the frontier province, a band 200 miles long and 30 to 60 miles wide, was not under Pakistani or any other national law; it was governed, officially, by tribal law. In the Khyber agency, the land between Peshawar and the Khyber Pass, the border, only the main road was under the legal control of the central government. If someone shot you off the road—and it happened—that was not a matter for the government, any government. The case would be handled by a *jirga*, a tribal council. In at least one case, refugees dealt with adultery charges in the old way: a man and a woman were stoned to death. In July, when the heat on the plains built up to well over 100 degrees (Fahrenheit) day after day, thousands of refugees just disappeared into the mountains someplace. They came and went as they pleased. When it was cool again, they would become refugees again.

The Pathans have always been among the most independent people on earth. They lived by old codes including *melmestia* (hospitality to strangers), *nan awati* (asylum to fugitives or refugees) and *badal* (an eye for an eye). They have always done whatever they wanted to do, and if anyone didn't like it, the Pathan response, particularly in the tribal areas, began with harsh, threatening screaming—and quickly escalated to killing and blood feuds for generations.

The world relief agencies supplied the refugees with soybean oil (from the United States government) for cooking. The Afghans threw it out or sold it. They would use only *ghee*, butter from buffalo milk. The UNHCR gave them kerosene for their fires. They used only wood until they had stripped the barren land of every bit of loose firewood, then began uprooting bushes and killing trees by hacking up from their lower branches until not enough tree was left to survive. And if their Pakistani cousins needed that wood—well, the Afghans had guns.

"They are wild men who will end up destroying our country," said a Pakistani sociologist, a woman, with a passionate hatred of the refugees which I heard many times from educated men and women. "The government wants these people as an excuse to maintain the state of emergency and to get the money and sympathy from the international community. But they are terrorizing our own people. After all the years it took us to persuade the

Pathans in the Northwest to give up their guns—in exchange for roads and the things a modern government could provide—and now they are invaded by these barbarians. The Afghans are living better than the masses. Are Pakistanis being treated by American doctors? They are going to destroy us because one day they will revive the Pukhtunistan issue."

There might be unhappy endings to the great Afghan migration and the generous spirit of the masses of Pakistan. What would happen, as Major Mulk said that night in Chitral, if the refugees lost hope and began to believe that they could not go back to Afghanistan? What would happen if the men of the North-West Province, Pakistani men, were no longer needed or wanted in the oil fields of Arabia and came home, hundreds and hundreds of thousands of them, for their jobs and their lands and their women?

"Pukhtunistan!" was one of the fears. The cry for an independent Pathan nation—*Pathan, pushtu* and *pukhtu* were all Westernized versions of the same sounds in the language of the frontier—had been heard in this land over the years, particularly in the 1950s. "Baluchistan!" was another separatist dream, and until the early 1970s, there was civil war in the hills of that even poorer province south of N.W.F.P.

"Pakistan!" had been only a separatist cry less than forty years ago. The Land of the Pure didn't exist before the 1930s when Muslim intellectuals, led politically by Muhammad Ali Jinnah, the *Quaid-i-Azam*, "Father of the Nation," began agitating for a separate state for the Muslims of Hindu-dominated India. It was an artificial country—from 1947 to 1971 its eastern and western parts separated by one thousand miles of India—created along another set of lines drawn by another set of Englishmen. Half of it, East Pakistan, disappeared in 1971, and there was always a real chance (and real fear) that all of it could disappear—perhaps with the Punjab and the Sind aligning in some way with India, and autonomous states of Pukhtunistan and Beluchistan coming into being, then, sooner or later, falling under some kind of Soviet control exercised through the new Soviet-trained cadres in Kabul.

The centrifugal forces on Pakistan have been many and great for a long time—four provinces in uneasy alliance, twenty-two regional languages, powerful neighbors, suspicious or hostile, in

India and the Soviet Union, and, perhaps, a fierce new population owing allegiance to nothing modern, including the flag of the country.

The one thing that united Pakistan was the religion—the original *raison d'être*. The bonds of Islam, which had not been strong enough to hold together East Pakistan and West Pakistan, were still the only bonding. It was inevitable that the rulers of the nation, whether civilian or military, would always resort to appeals to "Islamic socialism," as Zulfiqar Ali Bhutto had done, or to "Islamization," as Muhammad Zia-ul-Haq was doing while I was there.

There would be an Islamic Republic of Pakistan or there would be no republic.

6

LAND
OF THE PURE

Islam's Holy Month of Fasting, Ramazan, ended in Pakistan with the sighting of the beginning of a new moon on the evening of July 11. There were cheers in the streets of Islamabad and the lighting of dazzling displays of colored bulbs draped on public buildings and the embassies of other Muslim countries. Great necklaces of red and green lights hung in strand upon strand, drawing crowds all through the night. Eid-ul-Fitr, a joyous holiday of feasting, gifts and family visiting, had begun.

Down the road in Rawalpindi, the President, Zia-ul-Haq, issued an Eid proclamation in the way an American President would offer a little inspiration as he lit the White House's Christmas tree.

"Let us beseech him in our Eid prayers to grant to Muslims throughout the world the will and the wisdom to promote and strengthen bonds of brotherhood and respond to hostile challenges as a single, united people. . . . It is fitting that a period of self-denial be followed by the reward of rejoicing. But it is no less binding that the sense of enjoyment be tempered with the feeling of solicitude for the indigent . . . enable the less fortunate members of the community to make arrangements to celebrate this auspicious day. . . .

"We bow our heads in gratitude to the Almighty Allah that we have been able to take important steps toward the establishment of a truly Islamic order in our country. . . . Let us above all in our prayers today invoke Allah's blessing to infuse in us the spirit of unity and solidarity as an Islamic nation and banish from our midst regional, parochial, sectarian and similar other divisive tendencies."

I had never heard of Eid, but I had certainly heard all that before. In fact, to me, it sounded pretty much like Nelson Rockefeller's old BOMFOG speech—the standard Brotherhood of Man, Fatherhood of God stuff he used to run for President (of the United States) a couple of times. It was what any politician says when you wake him up in the middle of the night—sacrifice, compassion, unity except that the symbols were a little different from the ones I was used to hearing.

"This shouldn't be all that exotic to an American," said Hamid Alvi, a Pakistani who worked in the offices of the United States Information Service in Islamabad. "Pakistan is working out all the problems of national identity and rapid modernization that the United States worked out a 150 or 175 years ago. But you were lucky enough to be able to do it *in absentia* from the world. There was no one around then. But Pakistan is being pressured on every side, on every border. Our real problem and the real gaps in our society are that you can't tell where each man stands on the scale of modernity. The trick is always how to embrace and advocate modernism without making it a rejection of the old values."

"What are the old values?" I asked, expecting a list beginning with "family. . . ."

But Alvi needed only one word:

"Islam."

I thought then, not for the first or last time, that what Pakistanis, sincerely and cynically, were calling "Islamization"—and were arguing over—was really, in the end, going to be a cover for the modernization of a very backward society. Pakistan was going through the agony of becoming new by talking about the old. They had to talk in the context of the only thing all Pakistanis knew—Islam. Newspapers were packed with rambling and redundant essays on "Islam and Science" and "Islam and Democracy"—all of them quoting the Holy Quran, almost all of them arguing for more and more technology and scientific education and for elections! elections! elections! A symbol of the process could have been a truck I saw near Peshawar. Pakistani trucks were rolling, smoking galleries of folk art, brightly decorated like circus wagons with paintings of landscapes, animals and religious symbols. This one listed a litany of Islamic saints and heroes— Ali, Fatima, Hasan, Husain—symbolically flying on a painting of an F-16.

The American jet, the material confirmation of Pakistani's status as a "frontline state," had quickly become the ultimate symbol of modernism in the country. But it had to coexist with old symbols and ritual. On the same day I saw that truck, July 2, in the morning, hundreds of people assembled in Kohat to follow Maulana Muhammad Naeem and Colonel (retired) Sultan Ali Shah Kateeh to pray for rain—after weeks of drought—by confessing their crimes and sins. At 1:30 P.M., it began to pour in Kohat.

The pull between the new and the old has been a part of the national identity crisis that has been Pakistan's curse since its hasty founding on August 14, 1947. On that day, the British, well aware that the Indian subcontinent would explode in the religious violence between its dominant Hindus and minority of Muslims, carelessly divided their Indian empire into India and Pakistan. The creation of the Islamic Republic—or of a stubborn Muslim intransigence that made a united India seem even more impossible than the divided one—was principally the doing of Muhammad Ali Jinnah, the leader of the All-India Muslim League, whose impeccably tailored three-piece suits and cool, secular Anglophilia were as much a symbol of what he was doing as the great Hindu Mohandas Gandhi's simple dress was a symbol of his devotion to the old ways. Even today, almost forty years after Partition, the Majlis-e-Shura (Federal Council) and city and village governing bodies in Pakistan seemed to be endlessly debating whether to replace the ubiquitous paintings and photographs of the *Quaid-i-Azam*, Jinnah, in suit and tie—including the portraits on currency—with pictures of him in traditional dress. The problem was that Jinnah rarely wore Indian or Pakistani dress. Also, he had visited East Pakistan (now Bangladesh) only once in his life, and although he had been born in Karachi, he lived most of his life in Bombay.

Even so, Jinnah, with family in Karachi, was one of the few leaders of the new Islamic Republic who could claim some connection, other than religious heritage, to the new country formed in 1947 when the British drew new lines on their old maps of India. The strains between modernism and traditionalism were not, in fact, the original new-versus-old issue in Pakistan. First, the new country had to absorb the tensions between new and old residents. The original Muslim inhabitants of the Sind and the Western Punjab were overwhelmed by Muslim migrants from other parts of India, including Jinnah and a twenty-three-year-old soldier from the East Punjab, Lt. Muhammad Zia-ul-Haq. That migration was one of the bloodiest in the history of the world as Muslims fought their way west through killing mobs of Hindus and Sikhs, and other Hindus and Sikhs fought their way out of Karachi and Lahore as their families were butchered by murderous Muslims. Millions of people were killed on both sides, all in the name of God whether He be called Allah or Ram. I met men and women who could point to gutters in Lahore and say they had seen them overflowing with blood that August when Pakistan was born.

It was that pending slaughter, driven by the dark energy of ages of hostility and by forces even more mysterious and frightening to Westerners, which convinced the British to run—leaving the people of the subcontinent free and independent to pick up the bodies and the political pieces.

Pakistanis still identified each other by whether or not each was a *mohajir*, a "migrant" of 1947, or a descendant of the migrants. It was one of too many nonreligious divisions for the good of the country. Next they identified each other by region, with Punjabis set against Sindhis or Baluchs or Pathans, and by the two dozen languages spoken across the thousand miles, including Urdu, the official national language, which came from central India with the migrants, and English, the language of Pakistani elites. Then they looked at each other on Alvi's scale of modernity, which was often a test of whether a man or woman identified with Western or Eastern traditions. Beyond that, those drawn to the Eastern world were often torn over whether Pakistan should identify with India or whether, as Muslims, they should identify with the Arabic countries across the Arabian Sea. (Some, usually Shia Muslims, wanted to identify with Iran and the Ayatollah Khomeini.)

There was something a little sad, at least to a foreign infidel, about the Muslim reach toward Arabia, the historic center of Islam and a modern petrodollar benefactor of Pakistan through foreign aid and the oil-field jobs. The Saudi Arabian presence is something like the American presence: neither ever lets the Pakistanis forget they're there and they're rich. My neighborhood in Islamabad was coming under the shadow of the new national mosque, Shah Faisal Masjid, a huge structure donated by the late King Faisal of Saudi Arabia, under construction just down the street. It was going to be the largest mosque in the world, they said, with a capacity of fifty thousand worshipers in the hall and courtyards covering more than forty-four acres. The minarets rose 350 feet and, local brochures emphasized: "There is an entrance for VIPs on the west side of the prayer hall."

This immense tribute to a foreign king was replacing the Badshahi Mosque in Lahore as "the largest in the world." (That's what they say in Pakistan; the title is also claimed in other Muslim countries.) That symmetric and beautiful red brick colossus, part of one of the most impressive public squares in the world, was built in 1673 by Aurangzeb, one of the great Moghul rulers, and is a national and historic treasure—but with towers 176 feet high on a six-and-a-half acre courtyard Pakistan's jewel was not as big as the foreigner's gift. The Pakistanis had forgotten or ignored the charge of the poet Muhammad Iqbal, who first proposed the idea of a separate Muslim state on the subcontinent in a 1930 speech in which he said it would provide "for Islam, an opportunity to rid itself of the stamp that Arabian imperialism was forced to give it."

Islam was a conqueror's religion, brought to India by Arab invaders in the eighth century—and, even after Partition, there were more Muslims in India than in Pakistan. Its message of equality before God was understandably attractive to lower castes within the rigidly hierarchical world of Hinduism. Untouchables became Muslims—a fact that has more than a little to do with

Indian attitudes toward Islam. (Many of the Hindus who stayed in Pakistan were Untouchables, and they and their children were still doing the dirtiest work of the society, cleaning streets and toilets. But many of them changed religions, becoming Christians; they made up the entire congregation of churches like Saint Michael's, the Roman Catholic church on the Mall in Peshawar.)

Pakistani attitudes toward Indians seemed more complicated— tortured, really—mixes of fascination and fear. After three losing wars, over Kashmir and East Pakistan, the Pakistanis seemed finally to have accepted the fact of India's domination of the subcontinent. There were fewer illusions of political, economic or military parity. Pakistan must play Canada, an antagonistic Canada, to its more powerful neighbor. Pakistan had many problems, and one of them was maintaining the myth that its people were fundamentally different from Indians, but the similarities between Indians and Pakistanis often overwhelmed the differences—at least in the eyes of foreigners—and the confusions of that unwanted similarity made the quest for national identity even more difficult, deepening the pervasive national inferiority-complex of Pakistan.

They wanted to be liked. "Do you *like* it here?"—Pakistanis asked that question of us again and again. They pleaded to be understood but did not yet understand themselves. They still had not decided who they wanted to be.

Pakistanis had not yet defined themselves. That was one of many similarities I thought I found between them and us, between Pakistanis and Americans. Who were we but a nation thrown together from the wretched of Europe? There were more than a few of the untouchables of the Old World among the people who made the United States of America. People didn't come to the New World because they were successful and honored in their own countries. With fewer natural resources—"meager resources"—older and more complicated problems and handicaps, and in a more dangerous and difficult time, Pakistanis were trying to do in decades what had taken Americans more than a century.

When Anwar Kamal, the lawyer in Lahore, had talked about the heavens on earth he had seen in Europe and America and how he wanted to be part of building a modern country with his own people, I envied him. Most of that had been done for me;

it's something I had read about—the challenge, adventure and triumph of other Americans.

I heard similar dedication again and again from Pakistanis. "Progress" was talked about as a god. But not God.

There is only one God and His name is Allah.

Modernization and Islam were spoken of together, comfortably sometimes, uncomfortably sometimes. But they were not dealt with as mutually exclusive. How could they be in the Islamic Republic? Islam was the environment. The ideas of Islam were the only way to reach all the people joined together now as Pakistan—the shared values, assumptions and knowledge of the nation. There was nothing else to begin with.

But what is Islam? Who defines the faith? First, the believers did not see it as "a religion"—as somehow separate from the secular—in the way that most Western Christians and Jews do their faith. "We can't separate God from Caesar," Abdullah, the zealous refugee commissioner, had said. "You do that."

"Islam is not *merely* a set of beliefs and a way of worship," stated a position paper prepared by the government of Zia-ul-Haq to explain its Islamization program to outsiders. "It is a complete way of life. It provides guidance in all walks of life—individual, social, material, moral, economic, legal and cultural. It is worldly and other-worldly."

Almost everyone I talked with in Pakistan, even the most Westernized (and personally secularized) of the country's elite, the men and women who went to embassy and consulate parties for the French wine, agreed with that and restated it in their own words. But that was where agreement ended. There were many Islams—sometimes, it seemed, as many as there were Muslims. When the Zia government, with the help of his Saudi Arabian advisers, interpreted the Holy Quran as supporting *zakat*, an alms tax on bank deposits, hundreds of thousands of people took angrily to the streets: Shia Muslims, the minority in Pakistan, who read the Holy Book differently.

The great division in Islam, but still one among many, is between Sunnis and Shias. Pakistan was a Sunni nation—85 percent of the population—and Iran, for instance, was a Shia nation. Saying that to a Muslim explained almost everything about the differences between the countries—and explained why Pakistan would never become a theocratic state on the model constructed by the Grand Ayatollah Khomeini in Iran.

There were no ayatollahs in Pakistan—only local *maulanas*. There was no hierarchy among Sunnis; in that way the two sects could be loosely compared with Roman Catholicism (Shia) and Protestantism (Sunni) in the days when Western nations were more inclined to fight religious wars. The Sunnis and the Shias divided over succession to the Prophet, Muhammad, after he died in 632 A.D. and ascended into Heaven on a winged horse from the spot where the Dome of the Rock now stands in Jerusalem. A fitting site, because Islam considers itself the last of man's three great monotheistic religions, after Judaism and Christianity. The stories revealed to Muhammad over twenty years and recorded by scribes as the Holy Quran were of the Flood and Moses and Abraham—fiercer in tone but similar to tales of the Bible—but Muslims believe that Jesus of Nazareth was the next to last in the line of prophets that ended with Muhammad.

After the Prophet's death, Islam (the word means "absolute submission" or "surrender" in Arabic) was ruled by a series of Caliphs ("successors") selected by the family and men around Muhammad. At the death of the fourth Caliph, Ali, the Prophet's son-in-law, a dispute broke out among factions, and two lines of succession were established. The Sunni line, to oversimplify, eventually petered out, ending ambivalently in the twentieth century with the fall of the Ottoman Empire in Turkey. The Shia line ended, after a fashion, in 873 A.D., when the Twelfth Imam ("leader") died or disappeared mysteriously. The "Hidden Imam" became an omnipresent factor in Shiism—"We are waiting for you, Twelfth Imam" was a revolutionary slogan in Iran—and the Ayatollah Khomeini (or Imam Khomeini; the title applies to all Shia leaders) wears, for many, the mantle of the Hidden Imam. Those connections gave Khomeini a temporal power over many people that it would be virtually impossible for any Sunni leader to accumulate. In talking about Pakistan's Shias, the hundreds of thousands of them who demonstrated against Zia's *zakat* proposals, I asked someone what it would take to trigger such a demonstration by many of the Sunni population.

"I don't know," he answered. "You couldn't get a hundred Sunnis to agree on anything, much less a hundred thousand."

I have obviously oversimplified all of this enough to outrage
any thinking Muslim. But it would be impossible for me to do
justice to these disputes. Millions of men have been arguing—
and going to war—over these differences for centuries. I have
also ignored the hundreds of smaller sects that have broken off
from these two over those centuries, including the Ahmadis, a
sect that followed a nineteenth-century prophet and was declared
"kafir," non-Muslim, by Prime Minister Bhutto, and the Ismaelis
of the North West, the followers of the Aga Khan. The closest I
could come to describing the passion and angels-on-the-head-of-
a-pin nature of those debates—and, too, the intellectual vitality
of Islam—was by comparing them with the arguments of American Constitutional lawyers working for very high hourly fees.

Apart from sects, the Islam of India, and then Pakistan, developed in ways unique to the subcontinent. After the invasions
of Arab and then Turkish Muslim armies into the territories that
would become Pakistan, new invasions through the Khyber Pass
by Genghis Khan and Tamerlane in the thirteenth and fourteenth
centuries reached Delhi, weakening Hindu rule in all of India.
Muslim princes gradually took control of more and more of the
subcontinent until the great reign of the Moghuls was established
in the sixteenth century. In two hundred years, those Muslim
rulers built the spare and disciplined monuments that came to
symbolize India to the world—the Taj Mahal at Agra, the Red
Fort at Delhi, the Badshahi Mosque at Lahore. Hindus, in larger
and larger numbers, converted to Islam during those years, drawn
from their musical religion of many gods to the faith of the one
God by their own ambition—Islam was the religion of opportunity
while the Moghuls ruled—and by the oppression of the Hindu
caste system. It was, by and large, Untouchables, the lowest of
the five *castes*, who embraced *Allah*. That fact had a great deal
to do not only with enduring Indian attitudes toward Pakistan,
but with the kind of Islam practiced in the Land of the Pure.

In India, higher *caste* Hindus, particularly the highest, *Brahmins*, would not touch food in the presence of Muslims; they
were still treated as Untouchables even as they ruled. When the
British came, gradually expanding their rule as the Muslim ma-
harajahs divided and were conquered, the Hindus not only began
to reassert their numerical superiority—there were 300 million

Hindus and 100 million Muslims in India at Partition—but they enthusiastically seized the opportunities of British education and modernization. The Hindus became the businessmen and bureaucrats of British India; the Muslims, uncertain about confronting new knowledge, remained landlords, soldiers and peasants.

But whatever the tensions between the religions—village slaughters periodically followed such provocations as the playing of music by Hindus while Muslims prayed, or the killing of a sacred cow by Muslims—the new religion of one God never totally abandoned the culture and ritual of Hinduism. The Muslims of India, then of Pakistan, worshiped at the tombs and shrines of *pirs*, local saints and demigods, in the most un-Quranic ways, and sang and danced and threw flowers at weddings in most Hindu ways. One of the enduring traditions of Lahore, which Muslim purists had been trying to stamp out almost forever, was the giving of garlands of rupee notes as wedding gifts—a Hindu custom. The city's bazaars are still filled with merchants patiently folding and weaving the money into elaborate paper jewelry. I was reminded more than once in Pakistan of North African Jews who sometimes seemed more North African than Jewish. Perish the thought in the Islamic Republic, but Pakistani Muslims sometimes seemed more Indian than Muslim.

Then there came a day when the military government ruling the country of those Muslims decided they were not Islamic enough. Gen. Muhammad Zia-ul-Haq decreed "Islamization." The official definition of that process was stated this way: "Islamization in Pakistan is a positive effort to build up a system of human relations—on the individual and collective level—on the principles of justice and morality as enunciated by Islam. It is an attempt by the people for whom religion is a living faith to remodel their private and public lives."

"Who the hell is Zia-ul-Haq to Islamize us?" said a prominent writer. "I was Islamized a long time ago."

I heard that question a couple of times a day. The short answer was that he was the man in charge of the army—and the army ran the government. He gave a longer answer of sorts in a press conference on August 14, 1983, the thirty-sixth anniversary of the country's independence, at the Rawalpindi Presidency. It was, I thought, one of the most extraordinary performances I had ever seen by a political leader. Humble in personal manner, intelligent, articulate, committed, the self-appointed President of Pakistan suddenly seemed a bit mad to me, drunk on his own power and destiny. I did realize, however, that not all of his sense of power was delusionary.

"My only ambition in life," he said that day, "is to complete the process of Islamization so that there will be no turning back. . . . The Islamization process is a lifetime job. It is not only the changing of certain laws from the Anglo-Saxon character to Islamic character. Islamization is complete whenever we can have the social environment turned into an Islamic character. You have to bring some of the fundamental elements of the educational system into line with Islamic values. Also, the general society itself. You have to put their aims and objectives straight on the path of righteousness. And that's what I call Islamization."

It also might have been called "hubris." The Army Chief of Staff who had taken over the country—for ninety days, he said at first—also thought he could take over the mission of the gods. Whatever tragedy lay ahead for him—and for his nation—Zia-ul-Haq did not seem totally in touch with either general society or righteousness that August 14. It was not only the question of who he thought he was. It was also that leadership is often best achieved by example, and not only the example of personal piety. The people he expected to lead on the path to righteousness noticed that a few other paths were being traveled from army headquarters to Rawalpindi. "The man in the street—the illiterate masses—knows Islamization is a hoax," said a young writer who took his own Islamization seriously. "It's just a way to keep the military in power. The people know the difference between the way the Prophet lived—the clothes He wore, the house He lived in—and the way our leaders are living."

The word *hoax*, which was widely used, in safe privacy, by Zia's opponents, was too strong, even if many generals and colonels were obviously feasting on the spoils of power—including the money the United States was delivering in the name of its own governmental religion, anticommunism. There were, I was sure, some admirable aspirations behind the official quest for a modern Islamic identity. But "Islamization" fashioned on the austere and repressive monarchical religion of Saudi Arabia was choking Pakistanis—who were coming to despise the Saudis anyway as stories of life under the Islamic mastery of the desert princes were brought back home by oil-field laborers.

Really changing the social environment and the behavior of millions of people would require more than arresting young couples for publicly embracing, or laying eighty lashes on the back of some pour soul caught drinking a can of beer or the home brew made out in villages. But more substantial attempts at Islamic reform quickly ran into the realities of modern life—modernization was changing the way Pakistanis lived more than Islamization ever could—and as much resistance as could be prudently mounted in a police state. Better and presumably righteous minds in Islamabad had not been able to figure out a way to construct a banking system faithful to their interpretation of the Quranic ban on "the curse of interest"—to use a favorite phrase of Zia's. The women of the country were in open and dangerous (to the new regime) revolt over attempts to institutionalize the new laws of evidence based on conservative interpretations of the Holy Quran—the work of the *maulanas* who wanted to mandate the supremacy of male over female words in court. So, the Islamization of Zia was often reduced to silliness, like his announcement to the nation that he would ask the *Shariat* Courts—created to review all civil and criminal verdicts and sentences to determine whether they were "Islamic"—to decide whether book piracy was Islamic. Pakistan had never been signatory to any international copyright agreements. Local publishers just stole any foreign books of local interest—if they were passed by military censors—and reprinted them without paying fees or royalties to authors or foreign publishers. So a court of *maulanas* was delegated to determine whether the Prophet would approve of that.

But there was more to Islam than things like that, and there could be more to Islamization than the hastily conceived and self-serving games being played with the lives of the faithful of Pakistan. It seemed obvious to me that Islam was rich and complex enough intellectually and idealistic enough not only to provide the material for Brotherhood of Man, Fatherhood of God speeches, but to create the environment for technological modernization and for modern political systems providing the rule of law, social justice and economic opportunity for most of the people, most of the time.

Despite the angry and vengeful message of many Quranic verses, Islam was, after all, the faith of the *tonga wallahs*—men as good, in the eyes of Allah, as Zia-ul-Haq. There was a determined egalitarianism projected in the pages of the Holy Quran, and the religion grew on the subcontinent as the alternative to caste systems. Despite the VIP entrances at mosques, the faithful were taught that all men—women, as they had been at the beginnings of the United States, were a different matter—that all men were equal if they performed, with belief, the five duties of a Muslim: (1) to say, with full acceptance, *"La ilah illulah, Muhammadur rasul-Allah,"* the Arabic for "There is no god but God, and Muhammad is His messenger"; (2) to pray five times daily, facing toward Mecca, and say Friday noon prayers in a mosque; (3) to give alms generously; (4) to keep the fast of Ramazan; (5) to make *hajj*, the pilgrimage to Mecca, once in a lifetime, if it is financially possible.

"Wherein the principles of democracy, freedom, equality, tolerance and social justice as enunciated by Islam, shall be fully observed, . . ." begins the Constitution of the Islamic Republic of Pakistan, written in 1973. "Now, therefore, we the people of Pakistan . . . faithful to the declaration made by the founder of Pakistan, Quaid-i-Azam, Muhammad Ali Jinnah, that Pakistan would be a democratic state based on Islamic principles of social justice . . . Do hereby . . ."

That Constitution was suspended by Zia-ul-Haq, but as I found out, and more importantly, as he did, too, it was still a document of great weight to the people of the country, even the illiterate masses. "There seems to be a consensus emerging in the Majlis-e-Shura"—Zia's rump parliament—"during the debate on the future system of government that the 1973 Constitution was a sacred document that should not be touched under any circumstances," reported *The Muslim* on page one of its July 26, 1983, edition, during the period leading up to the Chief Martial Law Administrator's promised announcement on Independence Day, August 14, of a framework for *Nizam-i-Mustafa*, a "System of the Prophet."

The formal commitment to equality was not questioned in

RICHARD REEVES · 103

Pakistan. Mufti Muhammad Hussain Naeemi—*Mufti* is a title for
interpreters of religious law—one of the country's more prominent Muslim teachers, offered this definition of the responsibilities of an Islamic government: "There are five responsibilities:
providing jobs, education, medical facilities, residential accom-
modations and security of life and property."

That commitment has been all too rarely honored in Islamic
countries, and it shouldn't be confused with a religious commitment to democracy or to what we call freedom. The Islam I heard
being debated was egalitarian, but it was not necessarily democratic—and the debaters generally rejected Western concepts of
individual freedom. "Islam is a system of duties and obligations,"
said Commissioner Abdullah in Peshawar, "not a collection of
rights like your religions."

"If the head of an Islamic government is qualified according
to Islam, he is solely authorized to make all the decisions, after
consulting knowledgeable people," the Mufti Naeemi continued.
"Islam doesn't bother about how a head of state comes to power.
If a true Muslim with full knowledge of the Quran and the *Sun-
nah a Muttaqi*"—the Sunni book of contemporary descriptions
of the life of the Prophet—"becomes the head of state, Islam
permits him to remain in power."

The Mufti, I suspected, was going to discover that he parted
company there with the faithful. So did the General. It was
Elections!—the un-Islamic idea of majority rule and democracy—
that mobilized the illiterate masses that August. Demonstrations,
then riots, began after Independence Day when it became apparent that General Zia had no real intention of holding elections
he couldn't control.

Civil disorder had been the traditional method of overthrowing
Pakistani dictators. If riots were as close as the masses could get
to democratization, there would be riots. Islamization could not
stand up to that more modern, more powerful idea. Zia's ideas
and prayers would be drowned by other voices of Islam, sooner
or later.

"Why General Zia's Regime Cannot Last Long" was the cover
headline of the June 1983 issue of *Arabia*, an important Islamic
journal. The article inside stated that the government of Pakistan
was riddled with corruption and would never allow elections.

When the issue, predictably, was banned in Pakistan, the publishers of the magazine—Muhammad Salabuddin and Muhammad Al Wazir—responded with a letter, in their next issue, which could have been written by Thomas Jefferson if he knew the Quran.

"We, the editors and publishers, share the firm belief that contributors to this magazine are entirely free to express whatever views they may hold. . . .

"In so doing, it must be clear that we are not practicing a secular belief in democracy and civil liberties but upholding the precepts of Islam, as stipulated in the Holy Quran. . . .

"What are the limits, according to Islam, within which one can express his views? No limits or restrictions whatever. On the contrary, it is the highest duty of each and every Muslim, male or female, to voice his or her views very strongly when it comes to public life or the nation's affairs:

" 'Let there arise of you a band of people inviting to all that is good, enjoying what is right and forbidding what is wrong. They are the ones to attain felicity.' (104 Al-i-Imram) The Quran.

"The major achievement which the General, as a true Muslim leader, can offer to his Muslim nation in general and his country in particular, is to lead the Pakistani nation to democracy."

I had asked a Pakistani publisher, of an Urdu-language daily newspaper, whether there could really be such a thing as Islamic democracy.

"If it's really democracy," he answered, "who cares what they call it?"

"Can you preserve the old ways as modernization comes?" I asked an important Pakistani intellectual, who had just been telling me how important it was for his people to find their own way rather than simply imitating the West.

"Preserve the way people live here?" he said with a look I took to be perplexed. "Why would anyone want to do that?"

Islam had tried to resist modernization once—for centuries. The price had been enormous, and Pakistan was one of the Muslim countries still paying it. In the Middle Ages, the Dark Ages of Western civilization, science, mathematics and medicine had all flourished in the Arab world and Persia. It was our ancestors, not Muslims, who painted themselves blue and danced around rock piles to combat drought and plague.

But over time, the efforts of xenophobic Muslim leaders determined to resist the "sinful" advances of Western philosophy and science—earlier and greater versions of the Gujranwala *maulana* who cast out anyone who believed men had walked on the moon—drove entire nations back to their origins, back in time to the sullen bliss of the ignorant. But what they didn't know was hurting them. In India, the descendants of the Muslim rulers of the seventeenth century gradually lost their feudal domination of the subcontinent's Hindu population. As the nineteenth century was ending, with the British in control of the subcontinent, earlier roles were reversed as the Hindus grabbed at the opportunities offered by education and the English language while the *maulanas* cursed white men and the darkness. Between 1858 and 1878, of the 3,155 graduates of Calcutta University, only 57 were Muslims. During the 1880s, fewer than one of every twenty-five Indian students in British colleges were Muslims. Some of that was a product of British discrimination against Muslims because of their principal role in the Mutiny of 1857—an Indian army uprising against British rule—but much of it was also by choice. Muslims buried their heads in the sands of time.

One hundred years later, in 1983, Pakistan, the home of the 95 million descendants of the men who built the Taj Mahal and discovered much of early modern medicine, had nineteen universities and thirteen physics professors. There were, according to one study, 45,136 scientists and engineers working on research and development in all the Islamic countries combined, compared with 34,800 in Israel alone—or 400,000 in Japan, or 1.5 million in the Soviet Union.

But, there was no debate, not anymore, about whether the Islamic Republic should accept and learn the technological ways of the West.

"We must be like the Mormons I have seen in your country," said Fazl-ur-Rehman, the *maulana* from Lahore. "They are a religious people like us, who have known persecution as we have. They push their people into technology and the advanced fields. Television and universities are part of their church. They are not only up to date. They are ahead."

The debate now was only over how to become part of that world of "advanced fields," and Islam, the vessel of the old ways, was also being used, finally, as the agent of change. The Science and Technology section of the government's Sixth Plan began by quoting the Quran: "In the change of the winds . . . are signs for a people that are wise"—and then got down to the business at hand: "Quantum jump in Science and Technology allocations—from Rs. 1,838 million in the Fifth Plan to Rs. 5,855 million—to accelerate progress towards early attainment of self-reliance in Science and Technology." "Islam and Science" was practically a standing headline in newspapers. One analysis in a government-owned journal estimated that Islamic science was at least ten years behind the science and technology of the People's Republic of China. Those entreaties for more technical education also began with appropriate verses from the Holy Quran, including this one: "And He has subjected to you what is in the heavens and what is in the earth, all together, from Him. Surely in that are signs for a people who reflect."

On reflection, the Islam I found in Pakistan was a more positive force, or field of force, than I had expected—and it was less important than I had expected. It was not Islam that oppressed Pakistanis and enslaved the illiterate masses of the country. They were victims not of their faith but of the forces that have always oppressed men and women; the Pakistanis were victims of force and greed. The worst thing I could say about Islam was that it made the oppression more bearable. Dreams of the next world, a paradise of gardens for the pure, made men—and women—more tolerant of the injustices of this one.

Islam was used for many things. The Jamatt-i-Islami, the country's disciplined fundamentalist party, a sort of Moral Majority with guns, used to accuse Pakistan's founder, Muhammad Ali Jinnah, of cynically using Islam for his own ends. They were absolutely right. Everyone manipulated the symbols of Islam in Pakistan—and the words of the *Quaid-i-Azam*—as American power brokers manipulated arguments and people through the words of Jefferson or Abraham Lincoln.

As Zia-ul-Haq tried to restructure Pakistan to fit his own images by using the term "Islamization," Zulfiqar Ali Bhutto did before him with the term "Islamic socialism." That is the way of the words and worlds spiritual and political. But materialism and self-interest—wanting first what is necessary to survive and then wanting what other people have—are the way of the world, too. Pakistanis had not voted for Bhutto because he was a Muslim. Everyone was a Muslim in the Land of the Pure. In the villages and the slums of the cities they voted for *"Roti, Kapra aur Makon,"* for Food. . . .

Abdul Hafia Kardar, a Lahore businessman who was once captain of the National Cricket Team, told me about the first day he campaigned, in 1971, as a candidate for the Punjab State Assembly on the Pakistan People's Party ticket headed by Bhutto.

"I went outside the city, where the farms began then," he said. "I saw a lady sitting—her husband was farming—and I asked her whether I could talk to her. She just stared at me, coldly, and finally said, 'Why?'

" 'Who owns the land where your husband is farming?' I said. She told me a name and pointed to a mosque far away and said this man owned everything up to the mosque.

" 'I'm running with Mr. Bhutto,' I said, 'and if Mr. Bhutto wins, you're going to own the land where you're sitting.'

" 'Sit down, brother,' she said. 'Tell me about that.' "

"Bhutto created the perfect slogan for Pakistan," said one of his worst enemies, Hussain Maududi, the publisher of the journal of the Jamatt-i-Islami and a son of the militant party's founder and the foremost Pakistani religious thinker, Maulana Abu'l A'la Maududi. "Islam means everything to the masses, but the needs of their bodies have to come first. They went to Bhutto in a landslide and they would do it again. Their needs are too great. To eat, to educate their children instead of sending them out to work. The difference between the rich and poor is just so great here that the masses can't be mobilized around Islam until much more work is done. There is so much work to be done before there can be real Islamization."

7

WHO RUNS PAKISTAN?

Who runs Pakistan?

The first time I asked that question was in Washington in April of 1983, at a briefing set up by the State Department. The short answer I got that day was "The Military. The Civil Service. The old oligarchy, the landowners. And the underground economy, the smugglers and black market people."

I had expected the answer to be: "Islam." I thought I might hear about the structure of a theocratic state, perhaps with councils of elders or God-fearing edicts issued hourly from temples. "No," I was told. "Islam is just there, everywhere. Nothing challenges Islam openly, but everyone tries to use it to their own advantage." Islam, then, was the *environment*; I began thinking much more conventionally of a state with the usual contenders for power and influence but less of a sizable middle class or the kind of influential business-finance class in more (capitalistically) developed societies. That model served me well: the Pakistan I found was a country of illiterate masses exploited and feared by a powerful, rich and ruthless few; there weren't many people in between the extremes.

The briefing was a good one, the first of many informed and frank briefings, interviews and conversations I had with official

Americans. It was comforting—at first—to know that we knew what was going on in a far part of the world. Later, I became more and more troubled by the fact that we knew exactly what we were doing out there. Before I went to Pakistan, I generally believed in a sort of American innocence abroad, that, for instance, we were taken by surprise by the depths of feelings and turns of events during the Islamic Revolution in Iran. After a while in Washington and South Asia, I didn't believe that anymore. We, officially, seemed competent and consistent. The official Americans I met knew which side they were on in Pakistan and were doing what they could to keep that side in power. Muhammad Zia-ul-Haq was on our side and we were on his.

But maintaining anyone in power in Pakistan has never been an easy thing. "The country has three strikes against it already," said Louis Dupree, the American scholar, as we talked away an afternoon with forbidden beers in his Peshawar hotel room. "One: There are too many definitions of Islam to really unite everyone. Two: The country is run day to day by an imperial bureaucracy. They're set up to raise revenue and maintain order, and that's all they do. Three: There won't be time to break down the regionalism. There are just too many ethnic groups, too many languages."

What he might have been saying was that there never should have been a Pakistan. Perhaps it was never anything more than a relic of British colonialism and a tribute to Mr. Jinnah's willful vanity. The British had been tired and broke; they had been defeated by winning World War II. They had just wanted to get out of India before the killing began, so they drew some lines on a map, said this was India, that was Pakistan, and then they ran. They left behind an infrastructure of roads and railroads, and civil and military bureaucracies that could outlast the concrete and steel. On August 11, 1983, thirty-six years after the British left, I watched the President of Pakistan coming to the docks in Karachi to bid Godspeed to thousands of pilgrims leaving on government-arranged *hajj* to Mecca. "This is the greatest moment in their lives as Muslims," Zia told me with feeling as we stood among the white-clad believers. I listened, respectfully, I hope, but I was still in bemused shock from watching him led to the pilgrims on this most solemn Islamic occasion by the Karachi Police Band dressed in Tartan plaids. Bagpipes wailed the Presbyterian hymn "Amazing Grace."

British rule was the last great wave of modernization which Pakistan absorbed. The British imposed administrative practices—heavily dependent on carbon paper and on paperweights to hold everything down when big overhead fans were on—which did not seem to have changed since Rudyard Kipling's father was the curator of the Lahore Museum. The 1983 Islamabad-Rawalpindi telephone directory carried a message: there were 203 (white) pages listing all the individuals and businesses and institutions with telephones in a metropolitan area of more than a million persons, and there were 109 (pink) pages of government numbers. Somewhere behind those telephones—and the bend-over windows of the bureaucracy—sat the latest generation of civil servants of high education and low pay (often the children of the last generation) who had been administering, manipulating, avoiding and fearing the illiterate masses since the fateful day that the first Englishman showed the first Indian the proper elbow and wrist motion for banging paper with a rubber stamp. Whether you wanted to build a steel rolling mill near Gandani Beach or go to college or bury your recently deceased uncle, you needed the right papers. And a lot of them. And it cost. And it explained, at least to me, why a lot of people would rather be nomads in the desert or tribesmen in the mountains than face the men with pincushions to hold the pins used to hold the papers together— just the way the British did it in 1870.

"The Civil Service," as it was usually referred to, or "The Bureaucracy," seemed to lie on the country like a dead hand. My favorite story about the pincushion men was the explanation of why the flag of Pakistan shows a fading moon. The founder of the country, Muhammad Ali Jinnah, had approved a green and white flag with a sliver of moon almost encircling a star. The moon was placed to the left, rising, as it does on the flag of Turkey. His idea was passed along to government draftsmen, who did the final design. They handed that design, the first flag, to the *Quaid-i-Azam* moments before he was to unveil it publicly. When he did, the moon had been moved, it was down and to the right— fading.

The men who screwed up the flag and much more were part of the most conservative kind of institution, focused on a limited agenda: to conserve its own position and control of the society. If there was a larger and more complicated purpose to the sum of the service's individual actions and decisions, then I missed it. It was the institutionalization of *sifarish*—an Urdu word that means "special approach" or "special recommendation."

"In Pakistan, to buy a ticket in the face of a rush, to buy a bag of cement or fertilizer or a tin of *ghee* when those items are in short supply, to buy a residential plot in a government scheme to get a job, etc., one needs more than cash or merit," said one of the country's leading economists, the former Finance Minister, Dr. Mubashir Hasan. "One needs *sifarish*."

In the ideal bureaucratic world, no one would get anywhere or anything without *sifarish*. And Pakistan was close to being a bureaucrat's ideal. The civil service (at its higher levels, the VIPs and VVIPs) controlled the recommendations, the permissions, the passes, the letters, the telephone calls that made things happen in Pakistan—the things that the civil service wanted to happen. In its most refined form, the special recommendation was family. Nepotism was the nervous system of Pakistan. It was sometimes difficult for foreigners to trace the lines running out from the complex webs of extended families, but they were always there, just under the surface of theoretically open selection systems involving familiar things like comparative examinations and waiting lists.

The first level below the surface was preferential quotas—for the children of civil servants and military officers—for the seats in universities or on the country's only air-conditioned train (from Rawalpindi to Lahore to Karachi). Beneath that, the society was simply corrupt—sometimes only by sticky Western standards, sometimes by any standard. Not only was *bakshish*—bribes and tips—necessary to move papers and permissions through the underpaid (officially) bureaucracy, but test scores were affected by traditional practices such as allowing rich students (VIPs) to bring servants into examination rooms. The servants then shuffled out to get refreshments and to recite the questions to smart brothers or hired tutors. Then they came back in with tea, cookies and the answers. Even after that, the scores and rankings and the other niceties of meritocracy were subject to adjustment. The adjustments, I was told many times, were arranged after the *sifarish* call, or the *bakshish* payment, or because of threats, particularly from Jamatt-i-Islami members and other fundamentalist students who stockpiled guns and ammunition in university hostels.

Whatever we might think of it, the mix of nineteenth-century administrative practices, *sifarish* and *bakshish*, which had been India's and then Pakistan's way to modernize the last time around, was still working for them. The wheels grind slowly, but somehow they keep moving. "There is no such thing as what you call honesty and of the kind of honesty I would like to see here," said Maulana Rehman, the Lahore preacher who also acted as a chaplain at the city jail. "The jailkeepers are paid 700 rupees a month [less than $60]. That is nothing in Lahore. They have to abuse their power or trade favors for bribes. They have to."

There was always something to trade—if nothing else, some restriction. Large areas of Pakistan, for instance, were off limits to foreigners. Gadani Beach was one because of a Pakistan naval base near the shipbreaking beaches. The Khyber region was another; military security was the official reason, but, actually, the government was afraid that foreigners might get caught in the sporadic crossfire of feuding smugglers and narcotics traffickers.

But there always seemed to be a way to go where you wanted to go or get what you needed.

I spent a lot of time sitting in the bare offices of Assistant District Commissioners, being served cup after cup of sweet and milky stewed tea wondering, even though the conversations were in English, what was going on as forms were passed back and forth. In one office, my companion, a Pakistani businessman, seemed unreasonably confident that he could get me into a restricted area, even though the ADC seemed intent on making small talk about the weather—hot!—for twenty minutes. Finally a car with an armed guard pulled up outside and we were off through the checkpoints.

"I thought we weren't going to make it," I said.

"No problem," said my friend. "Did you see that telephone on his desk? I gave that to him last week. In his position, it could take six months to get one out here."

Another man I knew, one of the country's leading financiers, had once studied the private books—there were double books everywhere—of the company of a friend, a major industry. "Forty-seven out of each one hundred rupees in the business went for illegal transactions," he said. "Bribes to bring imports into the country. Smuggling. Bribes to avoid charges and taxes. Paying off to get things done or not done. There is no such thing as straight business in this country."

All that commerce, crooked and straight, has traditionally been controlled by the civil service, from inspectors and policemen to provincial governors and federal ministers. The great challenge to that power came during the early 1970s when Zulfiqar Ali Bhutto became Prime Minister and a new power grouping began to emerge—politicians. Leaders of Bhutto's Pakistan People's Party and its opponents—particularly the regional parties in control of the North-West Frontier Province and Baluchistan—began exercising power that had been the exclusive prerogative of the civil service elites. It was no accident, then, that the civil service quietly encouraged the army's takeover of the government, General Zia's *coup d'état*, on July 5, 1977. The Supreme Court ruled that the coup was legal because of something called "the doctrine of necessity," and then, on October 16, 1979, also upheld the legality of the banning of all political parties and activities. In between, Zia, who had promised elections within ninety days of the coup, announced to the nation that an overpowering voice had come to him in a dream and convinced him that Western-style democracies were "un-Islamic."

The coalition of the civilian and military bureaucracies had been time-tested in Pakistan. For one thing, the upper ranks of both services were dominated by Punjabis. The Punjab contained 60 percent of the country's population, and more of its wealth and power: the relationship of the Punjab to the rest of Pakistan could be compared to the first-among-unequals relationship of the Russian Republic to the other republics of the Soviet Union. Lahore, to Punjabis, *was* Pakistan. Karachi, with a population of at least five million, was considered an "island city" off somewhere in the wastelands of Sind, and Peshawar and Quetta, the capitals of the Frontier Province and Baluchistan, were thought of, when they were, as outposts.

In one way or another, Punjabis in fancy offices and fancier uniforms had usually controlled the affairs of the country under various constitutions (four) and martial law orders (three). But as Zia-ul-Haq's regime carried on from one promise of elections to another—the letters CMLA came to mean not only Chief Martial Law Administrator, but, jokingly, "Cancel My Last Announcement"—the military gradually moved from junior partner to senior partner in the alliance for order that was formed in 1977 when the country was being ravaged by demonstrations over charges (and evidence) that Bhutto had rigged the elections of March of that year.

After March 24, 1981, the nation was governed under—that word is appropriate—Provisional Constitutional Order, 1981. Generals moved in then as provincial governors and federal ministers. The Majlis-e-Shura, the Federal Council appointed by the President as a mock legislature, was established to advise but not consent. But that was for show, and for squeamish American officials; the core of Zia's rule was in Article 15, officially described in these words:

"The Proclamation of July 5, 1977; all Presidential Orders; Orders of the CMLA, including Orders amending the Constitution made by the President or the CMLA; Martial Law Regulations; Martial Law Orders; and all laws made on or after July 5, 1977, are hereby declared, notwithstanding any judgment of any Court, to have been validly made by the competent authority and shall not be called into question in any court on any ground whatsoever."

The rule of law was eliminated in Pakistan. The military stood alone and above. In case anyone misunderstood that, martial law courts were established with absolute jurisdiction over any matter—no spectators, no attorneys, no appeals. Any Pakistani's life and property could be in the hands of an army captain seated behind a bare table with paperweights preventing the charges from flying away in the wash of an overhead fan.

The unofficial powers, the rich families, of the society pretty much stayed out of the way of all that. The people with great economic power in Pakistan were generally not interested in national political power. Their interests were local, in the land around them. The wealth of the country was in the land, particularly the agricultural lands of the Punjab and Sind, which was owned in vast parcels and managed feudally. Tens of thousands of tenant farmers and their families made up the province of one man or one rich family—a *wadera*, "landlord." In 1964 a bright young economist in the Federal Planning Department—it was Mahbubul Haq, the same man who went to the United States for twelve years and came back to become a federal minister— did a study of the distribution of wealth in the country and concluded that two-thirds of the available industrial capital in Pakistan was controlled by just twenty families.

That had not changed or it had only begun to change over the next twenty years; and the illegal commerce of the country, from *bakshish* to the smuggling of tires and narcotics, seemed to a very large extent, to be financed by and profiting the same old oligarchy. The gap between rich and poor in Pakistan, I was told in my first State Department briefing back in Washington, might be the widest in the world. Some members of those families, or lesser landowners, might become interested in or be delegated to handling political affairs—particularly as local leaders and legislators—because they could not afford to have new power centers and politicians attracting and agitating their own illiterate masses. In 1977, 13 families held 100 of the 143 seats in the Baluchistan Provincial Assembly. But such participation was essentially defensive, and what the great families really wanted was a minimal government that defended Pakistan's borders and maintained order at home. The military was fine, for them, at the center, as long as they, the families, owned and operated government in their own great fiefdoms.

In a way, those people lived and were still living in a place separate from Pakistan and, as much as their peasants, in another, earlier time. They could, as long as there was not genuine land reform, buy their way out of inconveniences like Islamization. Pakistan, the land of arrows pointing to VIP entrances and lounges, has always been so rigidly structured along lines drawn by Hindus and then Englishmen that there were even classes of prison. The highest was house arrest, reserved for the prominent, including the surviving members of Bhutto's family. The second was "Class A"—a cell like an apartment with air-conditioning and personal servants. Then came "Class B"—usually one room with a fan and the right to hire common prisoners as servants and cooks. "Class C" was for the illiterate masses, built and maintained by the descendants of the Muslim mutineers of 1857 who kept their British prisoners in the Black Hole of Calcutta.

But *class* was a word I was warned about by an American in Lahore, another impressive representative of my government. "You cannot analyze Pakistan in terms of horizontal groupings," he said. "There are no 'classes.' No 'workers' or 'managers' as we know them in most of the world. The society is made up of vertical groupings." I found myself drawing a fasces, a bundle of rods— but without the axe in the middle of the bundle that the Romans and, later, Italian Fascists used as a symbol of authority. Islam, particularly Sunni Islam, did not provide that kind of authority. "That's why political parties don't work very well. They're not much more than regional vertical groupings, most of them anyway. People don't know how to organize themselves the way Americans organize political parties. The classic way for a peasant to deal with a problem is to go up the vertical ladder to his landlord. Tribals do the same thing; they go up to their clan chief, who goes to a member of the tribe who is a Minister or someone else high in the government."

So, in my bundle of rods, a peasant in the Sind and a tribesman in Khyber might be at the same level of society—and of modernization—but their view of power was different, each looking straight up the rod to a feudal lord or tribal chieftain. The ship-breakers at Gadani Beach were recruited through and loyal to Pathan chieftains. The army was organized the same way (it was a thick rod) from the lowest private to General Zia, with all its own facilities including transportation, hospitals, schools for the children of officers and enlisted men. The fundamentalist Islamic Party, the Jamatt-i-Islami, was a smaller rod, tightly organized with its own institutions meeting all the needs, spiritual, material and social, of its membership from candidate member students to its single leader. The peasant, and tribesman, the army private, the poor student coming to the city from a village, might seem to have a great deal in common to me—or to Thomas Jefferson or Karl Marx—but in Pakistan they almost certainly would have no relationship or even contact with each other.

The many arms of modernization, though, were hacking away

relentlessly at that bundle of rods. The most dramatic examples of that were the explosive growth of the slums of Pakistan's cities and the hold of Bhutto's PPP on the imagination of the masses four years after the early morning he was taken from a "Class C" cell in the Rawalpindi central jail and hanged by the neck until he was dead.

The Canadian agricultural technician I had met on Bastille Day was a part of the restructuring—one modern arm hacking away. He was right to have the uneasy feeling that somehow he was doing more than just teaching men more-productive farming methods. Modern farming was creating the muddy slums of Karachi and Lahore—mud houses in muddy fields, boys playing cricket in the mud—and the people there had been made redundant by mechanization and had come from the countryside to the cities, or their outskirts, to see whether there was a place for them in a more modern world. There had been a day when such things did not happen—centuries of days—when fealty to the landlord was exchanged for cradle-to-grave subsistence. Those days were ending, even in Pakistan. Some farms were now being plowed by tractors rather than water buffalos, or were turned into orchards, which require less labor. The machines were cheaper than animals, including humans.

Zulfiqar Ali Bhutto had been another great agent of modernization—and unrest. His rhetoric—*"Roti, Kapra aur Makon"*—had mobilized the masses. He created a kind of modern politics in Pakistan. The Pakistan People's party, more rhetoric than program when Bhutto was alive, became more legend than program after his execution, but it also became, after the secession of East Pakistan, the first truly national political organization in a country whose politics had been, at best, the disconnected politics of five, then of four regions.

Why he did what he did—what made Ali run?—was a question guaranteed to produce a night of argument anywhere in Pakistan. The *Quaid-i-Awami*—"Leader of the People," a title he encouraged the controlled press to print as often as possible—was one of the great landlords of the Sind, and there were those who thought he represented landholding interests by giving the masses the impression of land reform without too much of the land. He was a graduate of Oxford and the University of California at

Berkeley who preached social democracy and democratic socialism and practiced repression, including the creation of a personal
secret police force. Worse, I was told many times, than anything
Zia had done.

Bhutto, too, had come to power as Chief Martial Law Administrator—after an election, but also after a sequence of events
that mocked majority rule. In 1971, after thirteen years of martial
law, President and Chief Martial Law Administrator Yahya Khan
allowed elections. The Pakistan People's party won 82 of the 138
National Assembly seats in West Pakistan, but, in East Pakistan,
the Awami League, seeking greater autonomy for the province,
won 160 of 162 Assembly seats. It was a totally unexpected result—East Pakistan, ethnically Bengali, had been governed from
Islamabad, as virtually a colony of West Pakistan—and from the
moment the votes were counted there was never any intention
in the capital or in Lahore or Karachi to honor the choice of the
majority. The army was sent to East Pakistan and was conducting
a brutal campaign of terror against Awami League leaders and
anyone else who got in its way, when the Indian army intervened
in the civil war and captured 93,000 Pakistani soldiers and officers
without too much trouble. East Pakistan was gone. West Pakistan
was in panicked turmoil—afraid India would invade—and the
decimated, humiliated army under Yahya Khan turned to Bhutto,
a civilian, as Chief Martial Law Administrator.

He ruled—and that is the word because he regularly imposed
"emergency" laws—until demonstrators brought him down after
the government announced that the PPP received 68 percent of
the vote in the 1977 elections, and evidence of systematic vote
fraud began coming out. Demonstrations and riots, again, proved
to be the effective substitute for democracy in Pakistan. What
happened was a massive national vote of no-confidence. The economy was near collapse after widespread nationalization that turned
industry over to the civil service, so expert in preventing things
from being done or made. Believing Muslims were led into the
streets by *maulanas* outraged at Bhutto's high Western living and
thinking style.

But Pakistan would never be the same. The masses had been
brought into the processes of power for the first time, or they
had been used by a brilliant demagogue. It did not matter which.

What mattered was that they did not forget what it was like. In 1973, at a PPP conference in Karachi, a group of peasants from Sind confronted Bhutto about the promises he had made, and broken. "Many of the points you have made are true. We have proceeded slowly," he answered, and his voice began to rise. "But let me ask you one question. Who gave you the courage to stand up and confront the prime minister of this country as you have done? *Who gave you a voice?*"

Zulfiqar Ali Bhutto. He also gave women positions of power and, more importantly, access to education. Even as he gave the civil service more to do by nationalizing private companies, he reduced its power by putting career administrators under the supervision of political appointees. He tried to bring the army under control by skipping over the highest ranks to appoint his own man as chief of staff, Gen. Muhammad Zia-ul-Haq.

Zia was the front man for "Operation Fairplay," the public code name for the coup of July 5, 1977. But the other generals behind him and around him gradually disappeared, into ambassadorships to Western countries and other comfortable and profitable sinecures. Soon enough, he was in charge, and he presided over the hanging of Bhutto on charges of complicity in the murder of the father of a political opponent. It was a very daring and brilliant stroke: Bhutto, it seemed, had been among the first to underrate Zia. The General was risking his own life, because he raised the stakes of future transfers of power. He must have known that he might be the next one, that he might be killed when the wheel turned. But by eliminating the force at the very center of Pakistan's politics, he created the "political vacuum" which he then began citing as the justification of continuing martial law. The argument against executing Bhutto was that it would make a martyr of him—and it did—but that martyrdom was the force that held together the PPP, and as long as it seemed as if the People's party would win a national election, other parties were ambivalent about pushing for elections.

They seemed a pathetic bunch to me, the leaders of the officially "defunct" political parties, none of which had any internal democracy. They were practically fiefdoms, too. Those feudal and feuding democrats allowed one clever and ruthless general to institutionalize the conflict of 1977, then they functioned as if their enemy and the enemy of democracy were not a military dictator but a dead prime minister. The intent and effect of the Chief Martial Law Administrator's seven years of election announcements and canceled last announcements were to play the parties off against each other. He manipulated the pettiest fears and ambitions of petty men in the hope of eventually finding some arrangement in which the parties would publicly legitimize military rule rather than just privately tolerating it. Whatever role they might play in Pakistan's future, the politicians of the country spent seven years producing little more than the stuff of newspaper stories like this one in *Dawn* on July 11, 1983:

"LAHORE—Defunct Pakistan Muslim League has confirmed that the political alliance between the league and *Jamiat Ulema e Pakistan* (defunct) does not hold anymore."

Many things were not going to hold anymore in the Pakistan I saw. The changes, and the agony and chaos that will come with them, had already begun all over the country. The decisions were not going to be made by defunct political leaders, but by the illiterate masses, who were only beginning to learn that there were such things as decisions to be made about machinery and votes and cash.

When Mahbubul Haq, the Planning Minister, began putting together the Sixth Plan, the document of Pakistan's modernization, he listed as the priorities for the development of the country's 45,000 villages: "1. Education; 2. Health centers. . . ."

But in the villages themselves, Haq discovered, when he did some traveling around, the priorities were quite different: 1. Roads; 2. Electricity; 3. Clean water; 4. Education; 5. Health centers. . . .

"We were talking about the software of modernization," said Haq. "They realized they could have power in the process, and what they wanted was the hardware. Roads, to them, meant liberation, the opening of options. They could eliminate the middle man in getting from farm to market.

"Roads meant needing a truck and being able to buy a Suzuki," he said. "People are materialistic."

8

DONKEYS
AND SUZUKIS

On the way to Pakistan, I passed through Dubai, one of the tiny, rich, oil-producing states that make up the United Arab Emirates. It happened to be the day that the government of Pakistan released the "Pakistan Customs Tariff and Import Trade Guide, 1983–84." That was important news in the Emirates, where hundreds of thousands of Pakistanis worked as laborers, drivers, clerks, technicians and physicians.

The day's *Khaleej Times*, in addition to the usual advertisements for meat from "lush, fertile farms in Pakistan . . . a taste of home," and housing projects sponsored by the government of Pakistan's Overseas Workers Cooperative in Lahore, published in detail the new duties and sales taxes announced in Islamabad on "items usually taken home by Pakistanis."

The list, with items listed by frequency of purchase and transportation to Pakistan, was led by air conditioners. The new duty was 200 percent of the purchase price, plus 30 percent sales tax, up from 100 percent duty and 25 percent sales tax the year before. The average increase was somewhat lower than that for the rest of the list, which included, in order, refrigerators, color televisions, sewing machines, washing machines and video cassette recorders.

"Overseas Pakistanis"—there were approximately two million

of them—were bringing in or sending between $2.5 billion and $4 billion each year to Pakistan. (The statistic was imprecise—on the low side—because many Pakistanis were abroad illegally, or were deliberately understating their income to evade taxes.) Whatever the precise figures, those remittances represented at least 10 percent of Pakistan's gross national product and almost 50 percent of the country's foreign exchange earnings. Pakistan's exports, for instance, totalled less than $1 billion in 1981–82.

That money earned abroad was spent this way, according to government studies: 63 percent on consumer goods and 23 percent on real estate. Not much was saved or invested. That spending on things like air conditioners, I was told several times by concerned men in air-conditioned offices, was the best example of the rampant materialism of the masses.

If I argued that other people—Americans or Russians, for example—would probably do the same thing, especially if they lived in a place as hot as Pakistan that manufactured few air conditioners, I was told: "Ah, but, you see, these people live in villages that don't yet have electricity."

Usually, though, the same people had just told me that village electrification was one of the most successful of government programs—that 9,000 villages had been wired in the last five years and 22,000 more were already scheduled in the next five. One man's foresight, it seemed, was another's materialism. Or, common sense in a country with per capita income of just over $300 per year. Most Pakistani men were going to work overseas only once in their lifetime, and that was the time to get what they were going to need at home in a country that had developed depressingly little heavy or consumer industries. One of the differences that developed between Pakistan and India during the years after Partition was that successive Indian governments encouraged and protected domestic industries, while the Pakistanis continued to depend on imports.

From what I saw, the people of Pakistan were about as hardworking and resourceful as anyone anywhere. I kept hearing how lazy Pakistanis were—from foreigners. Then I would see the people of the country crowding airports, traveling to far lands for four or five lonely years to provide for their families; in dry fields, straining behind a rough plow pulled by a buffalo; risking their lives at Gadani Beach; carrying pots of water or loads of bricks on their heads past my window for ten hours of a brutal summer day. And as far as the televisions and video cassette recorders were concerned, if a man owned one in an electrified village, he had a theater and could begin charging his entertainment-starved neighbors to watch banned movies: almost everything was banned in Pakistan. "A TV and a VCR together cost maybe 25,000 rupees," said a municipal officer who was leading police raids in Islamabad to confiscate cassettes of forbidden films. "But with the right cassettes, a man can earn 6,000 rupees a month." What money was being saved was usually for property or to buy a Suzuki minitruck. Owning a Suzuki meant a man was in the transportation business and moving up to a new economic class. The masses may have been illiterate, but, as far as I could tell, they were not stupid.

It was not only uneducated villagers who left home for opportunity. Muhbubul Haq was only one of hundreds of thousands of examples of the best and the brightest of Pakistan going overseas to make their mark and their contribution; the only thing unusual about him was that he came back after twelve years in Washington. There was, in fact, a sad little United Nations program in Pakistan called TOKTEN—Technical Know-How Through Expatriate Nationals and, while I was there, five expatriates working in the United States and Europe consented to return to Pakistan for from three to eight weeks to consult with local agencies and companies.

The brain drain began early, because most Pakistanis seeking advanced education have to leave the country. They were expert at taking advantage of the generosity and loopholes of Western systems. The largest bookstore in Karachi, Sasi's, featured stacks of Barron's guides to American colleges and medical schools, along with how-to manuals for taking Scholastic Aptitude Tests and English-language examinations. In the first two days I was in Pakistan, I met engineering students at the University of California (Berkeley) and the State University of New York (Albany) who had registered as in-state students by using the addresses of relatives or friends of friends. "Red Flag, Green Card" was the title one American diplomat said he should give his memoirs. He said he wanted to dedicate the book to Pakistani students who stopped demonstrating against the United States only long enough to apply for the green tickets issued to aliens allowed to study or work legally in the United States. "In November of 1979," he said, "after they burned down our embassy—there were false rumors that America was in some way involved with a hostage-taking situation in Mecca—some of the same students who did it were back complaining that their visa applications weren't being processed. And they weren't, because the little bastards had destroyed all the records and machinery."

People were Pakistan's most important product. The nation was barely able to feed itself, had very little industry, not much oil and gas so far and had just managed to produce enough cotton and rice and carpets to export token amounts. But in a bit of national bravado, the government and the press had taken to referring to the country as an exporting nation, as in this commentary by a professor named Farhatullah Babar in *The Muslim*: "Countries like Pakistan which have been exporters of raw materials, lately in the form of manpower . . ."

But even Babar, after proposing the formation of OMEC—the Organization of Manpower Exporting Countries—had to mention a dark side to this unusual definition of trade balance: "Pakistan may face the grave possibility of hundreds of thousands of Pakistanis bundled home with high expectations, luxurious life-styles, spoilt habits and no opportunity for gainful employment in the country."

"The prosperity you see here is artificial, ephemeral," said the man who assigned Babar's analysis, Suroosh Irfani, an editor at *The Muslim*. "There have been a few lucky years of good weather and good harvests. But there will be bad weather again and the overseas workers will be evicted; then there will be chaos here. If we are impoverished and confused, we will be moved by any political slogan."

"Prosperity" was obviously in the eyes of the beholder. I was told about it, proudly, everywhere, but it took time and effort to see things as they were to others. There was no starvation, and people, even the refugees in the Northwest, had shelter— the same shelter every night. That was no small achievement, and Pakistanis were quick to compare their modest success with the problems of their bigger rival. "If you want to see real poverty now, you have to go to India." Several Pakistanis I met in different parts of the country used those exact words.

Life in Pakistan, the weather and the oil countries willing, did get better after the economic chaos of Bhutto's last two years, when, no matter who made up the statistics, the gross national product was declining as the population continued to grow and grow—at close to 3 percent a year. The area that became Pakistan in 1971 (West Pakistan in 1947) had increased its population from, roughly, 30 million at Independence to about 90 million thirty-five years later. With some modernization in the country, the average life expectancy had increased from thirty-two years to fifty-five years.

Increased life expectancy was one of the measures of modernization. But it could be an agonizing curse in old societies built up from millions of strong families. To prepare for old age, parents usually wanted to be sure they had three surviving children, preferably males; children have always been the social security of the subcontinent. In the old days, only three out of ten babies would survive into maturity, so people had ten. By the 1970s, with rudimentary sanitation and some modern medicine, most children were surviving to become adults. But people continued to have children at the same rate, and the average family size was up to almost seven people. The population kept growing. More food, more work, more country were needed, perhaps more than Pakistan could produce.

Food production, still increasing with the agricultural modernization of the late 1970s, was beginning to be affected by drainage problems in the irrigation of the Punjab, the "breadbasket" of both Pakistan and India. Lahore, the center of the Punjab, was 800 feet above sea level and 800 miles from the sea, so natural drainage had always been slow. Water doesn't move very fast when it drops only one foot per mile. Salt from the sea had been slowly seeping into that sluggish water, and into the fields of the Punjab, turning thousands of miles of fields into barren salt plains.

There was also real tension—fear—among Pakistani elites about the possibilities of social and political combustion if declining production curves ever intersected rising demand curves of masses who were becoming more sophisticated about the ways of work

and of the world. Jobs overseas were creating a revolution of
rising expectations, paying wages undreamed of in Pakistan—
$300 a month for a driver compared with $38 at home—and the
money was going directly to the people actually doing the work.
The remittances were foreign aid to the masses. In a rigid world
of "trickle-down" economics, for the first time real money was
actually trickling somewhere near the bottom of society. People
in Pakistan had cash to spend, and human experience argued
that they would never willingly go back to the subsistence economy of their elders. Rampant materialism developed a momentum of its own.

There were people betting on a very materialistic future in
Pakistan, investing in it. Japanese people. I mentioned Suzuki's
minitruck a few times, because they were impossible to avoid in
Pakistan. You could only hope they avoided you as they careened
through bazaar alleys and around mountain curves. I mentioned
them the way a traveler in northern India one hundred years ago
might have mentioned donkeys. The donkeys were still there—
capable of carrying a couple of hundred pounds—but more and
more of them were being replaced by the little pickups and vans,
most of them purchased with money earned abroad, used for a
couple of thousand pounds of cargo or passengers. More passengers than seemed possible—just like the tiny old circus car full
of clowns—men and boys jumping recklessly on and off (to push
the thing up hopelessly steep grades) during the runs between
mountain villages.

"That Suzuki is Japan's gift to the developing world," said
David Brantley, the commercial attaché in the U.S. Consulate
in Karachi. "They cost $4,500 here, which is cheap. They don't
use any gas, and most important of all, they're easy to repair."
That last was important in a country of great wastelands. Larger
trucks carried three-man crews; one of the men was the mechanic,
whose job was to keep the thing running with or without the
right spare parts.

Brantley wasn't speaking with much joy. Before he took the
trade job two years before, the U.S. government considered
abolishing the position, figuring there was not enough money
around to bring in American companies and salesmen.

"Pakistan isn't a big enough market for us yet," said another

American official. "General Motors, Ford and Chrysler all came in here in the mid-sixties, but they pulled out when they realized how long it would take to make their investment worthwhile."

When it does become worthwhile, it will be Japanese. That could be very soon, even though by 1982 the United States and Japan had about equal market shares in trade with Pakistan. Each country did almost one billion dollars a year worth of export business, but the American share was heavily weighted toward military equipment. In Pakistan, after all, the total number of car sales for the fiscal year 1975–76 was 5,278 units—discouraging numbers for an American company. But the estimated unit sales by 1995, according to the United Nations Industrial Development Organization, will be 100,000 a year. That number was encouraging enough to Suzuki, which began assembling cars and trucks in Pakistan in 1983, building facilities capable of producing 25,000 a year. Suzuki, Toyota, Sanyo, Sharp—the Japanese brand names were everywhere, usually on cars or televisions or air conditioners assembled in Pakistan from parts made in Japan. The Japanese style was, with liberal credit, to build factories in the host country as part of joint ventures under which the entire operation would be turned over to locals when they could meet Japanese quality-control standards. That would take a very, very long time in Pakistan; a lot of rupees will have become yen before Pakistanis are capable of handling the fit-and-finish of the components of a modern technological society.

"I feel as if I am visiting a Pakistani plant," President Zia said when he went to Japan in July of 1983 and made Suzuki his second stop, after the Premier. "This miniature mechanical revolution which you have brought to Pakistan is not only welcome but appreciated by us."

Toyota was Zia's third stop (it may have a bigger future in Pakistan than he does). The future, barring a Communist government, which seemed very unlikely to me, belongs to Japan out there. The Japanese, speaking local languages, were literally "out there" selling themselves and their products in plants and offices where businessmen had never seen an American. It was as if America's commercial energy or interest ran out after the Coca-Cola and Pepsi-Cola signs went up. Chauvinist that I am, and ignoring the argument that Pakistan might be better off developing its own industries without either the Japanese or us, I was thrilled (and surprised) when I saw newspaper advertisements, in Urdu, one day in July announcing that IBM was introducing "the first ever Urdu electric correcting typewriter."

As far as I could tell, IBM and frustrated commercial attachés were the only American "civilians"—military trade with Pakistan was big business—who had read and understood a 1982 United Nations report that concluded: "Pakistan has an intelligent populace, an attractive labor rate, a growing economy and a retarded industrial base that promises rapid expansion to the investor."

"The workers going overseas are accelerating the rate of modernization in Pakistan," one foreign diplomat told me. (Bureaucrats of all countries insist on the protection of vague identifications.) "There may be confusion about how to do it, but the commitment is almost total. More importantly, there is total recognition of the inevitability of the desires of the population."

People had been off the farm, and they wanted the things they had seen. That materialism displeased some of the devout and many of the ignorant. Others, like Mubashir Hasan, who had been the country's Finance Minister during the Bhutto years, were concerned because they feared that international bankers— organized as the International Monetary Fund and the World Bank—were invading Pakistan's sovereignty by imposing conditions before lending the capital for modernization. A colonial modernization, in Dr. Hasan's view.

"They impose a rigid framework on an economy, a framework that suits the purposes of the United States and the rest of the West," he told me, after a series of speeches he had made on the subject had been generally ignored by his successors in power. "We no longer have the power to determine tax policy or import policy or to subsidize the price of electricity or fertilizer or *ghee*. Independence becomes a myth. Loans with these conditions bring a continuous deterioration in our ability to produce, making us open our doors to foreign products. We have seven hundred miles of limestone deposits, we have gypsum and natural gas—ideal conditions for cement, but we are importing it."

I had no doubt he was right about that. We had conflicting nationalistic concerns. Mine was that Americans should profit from economic colonialism rather than the Japanese. But I also thought he was almost certainly going to be frustrated, that his country was already on a roller coaster of modernization. If the trade doors of Pakistan were open enough to bring in badly needed technological assistance, they were also open too wide to force development of local production. The bright lights of the world were showing. People wanted to go through those doors. The push and pull between the traditional, which was often the sensible, and the dazzle of the new was discomforting to watch for me. For those committed to the old or skeptical about the new, it must have been excruciating. On July 3, the District Language Committee in Rawalpindi met and decided that, to promote the "national language," Urdu, all entries in the city's Independence Day display contest on August 14, 1983, would have to be in Urdu. No English!

But that day's *Pakistan Times* carried a full-page advertisement for a company called Pemref, offering an impressive array of jobs, good-paying jobs, as secretaries, at 3,750 rupees per month, and as accountants, technicians, clerks, warehousemen and laborers—in Saudi Arabia. The last line of the advertisement was: "Proficiency in Written and Spoken English Language is an Essential Requisite of these Jobs."

You couldn't deal with the rest of the world in Urdu, or in Punjabi, or in Pushtu. Pakistanis were scrambling to learn English, the language of opportunity. The language of materialism.

9

THE SECOND
ENGLISH EMPIRE

For at least twenty-five centuries, invaders and missionaries from Europe and China, from Persia and Russia, came through the land that became Pakistan, creating civilizations that rose and fell. Near one town, Taxila, off the road from Rawalpindi to Peshawar, there were ruins left, successively, by Bactrian Greeks, Scythians, Pathians and Kushans. The Taxila Archeological Museum, repository of one of the great collections of Gandharan Buddhist art, was surrounded by the excavations of three cities believed to date back to six hundred years before the birth of Christ. A sign in front of the museum warned:

BEWARE

False Sculptures and Coins
Are Sold in Plenty Around Here

The language of that sign was brought there by the latest of the invaders, the British. A veneer of the English language was laid over Pakistan; it became the way the country's elites communicated with each other and with the outside world of modern missionaries and potential invaders.

There are twenty-four officially recognized languages spoken

130

across the one thousand miles of Pakistan. *Spoken* is the word because many of them do not have standard alphabets. There is a debate, for instance, about whether Baloch, the language of Baluchistan, should be written out in the Roman or Arabic alphabets. Other languages in Pakistan used the Persian or Sanskrit alphabets. The nation is a Babel. That confusion of tongues, and a confusion of attitudes about the language of both colonialism and modernity, English, has provided the background music for Pakistan's long march into a modern future. Perhaps the best example of how the country communicates is the operational language policy of the army: Manuals and orders intended for officers are written in English; manuals and orders for noncommissioned officers and enlisted men are written in Urdu, the official "national language"; face-to-face orders and conversation between the noncommissioned officers and enlisted men are usually in regional languages—principally Punjabi, Pushtu, Sindhi and Baloch.

No language united Pakistan when the country was created in 1947, and choosing one of the indigenous languages as the national language would almost certainly have led to civil war. In fact, the early disturbances in East Pakistan, which eventually led to war and the formation of Bangladesh, were over attempts to suppress the local language, Bengali, in favor of Urdu. In 1972 there were language riots in Sind Province over claims that Sindhi was being denigrated to promote Urdu.

Urdu was selected as the national language by Muhammad Ali Jinnah, who did not speak it, precisely because almost no one in Pakistan spoke it. The idea was not to favor one region over another. Urdu, the name derived from the Turkish word *ordu* or "army," which was also the root of the English word *horde*, was a mongrel language spoken in north central India, where it was called Hindustani or Hindi. (Written Urdu and Hindustani appear different from each other because the Pakistanis use the Arabic alphabet while the Indians use Sanskrit.) The Hindustani (or Hindi) connection, however, was never mentioned officially in Pakistan, where the language was defined as a combination of Turkish, Persian and Arabic which evolved as a working language for successive conquerors of northern India through the eighteenth century.

The only native speakers of Urdu in Pakistan at the beginning were the *mohajir*, the migrant Muslims from other parts of India who came north and west at Partition. Not a particularly popular group, the *mohajir*, whose children, like Muhammad Zia-ul-Haq, took much of the property and many of the bureaucratic posts held by Hindus who fled to India that bloody summer of 1947. They were, in many ways, new colonizers who just happened to share the same religion, and their imported language was not embraced with particular enthusiasm. Thirty-six years later, Urdu was the first language of less than 10 percent of Pakistanis, compared with the two-thirds of the nation native to Punjabi. A little more than 10 percent of Pakistanis each spoke Pushtu or Sindhi as their first language. Those four languages, which were similar enough so that many speakers of one understood a great deal of one or more of the others, along with Baloch, spoken by less than 5 percent of the population, were the country's major regional languages. But not the only ones. On the roads north from Peshawar, language changed gradually from Pushtu to Khowar, a Turkish-Sanskrit language without an alphabet spoken in Chitral, to Kalashwar, also unwritten, the language of the Kalash Kafirs. We talked with Kalash through three cheerful interpreters. We were in the valley of Bumburet at the same time as an Afghan shepherd from across the mountains who spoke Pushtu and some Kalashwar, our driver, a Chitrali, who spoke Khowar and some Kalashwar, and an American missionary who had taught English in Kabul and spoke Pushtu. The husband of the Kalash couple we spent time with spoke a little Pushtu and a little Khowar in addition to Kalashwar. It was a wonderful, laughing afternoon, but it took about five minutes of multilingualism to figure out that the Kalash's wife did not know how old she was—in years—because her people do not use calendars.

"How old are your houses?" my wife asked.

The question passed from language to language. So did the answer, which finally came back as "Many thousands of years."

"That can't be right," said the missionary translator. "Maybe the question got changed to 'How long have your people been here?' Maybe the Afghan changed the answer into numbers because they all know we love specific numbers. They probably just said the houses were here when their grandfathers were and that is as far back as they can know."

The changing of the question and answers was at least as old as the houses. There was only so much we were going to learn in Bumburet speaking English.

English was spoken by between 2 and 3 percent of Pakistanis, usually but not always as a second language. "English is really the official language of the country, just as it was under the British—except on paper," said Anjum Riyazul Haque, secretary of the Study Group on the Teaching of Languages, one of the official bodies attempting to formulate a comprehensive and *realistic* language policy for Pakistan. Although English was haphazardly suppressed after August of 1947 as the language of the country's colonial masters, it was only in August of 1982 that orders came from on high—Army Headquarters—that all official government correspondence and transactions should be recorded in Urdu as well as in English. It would certainly be many more Augusts before those orders were actually followed—if they ever would be. It had proved to be no easy matter to create and promote a "national" language in a nation in which education was the exception rather than the rule. More orders were given than followed in Pakistan. One of the newer orders, part of the drive toward Islamization, was that Arabic, the language of Islam, be taught as a mandatory language from the sixth grade through the eighth grade. But there was no such teaching, because there were no teachers of Arabic in the country. (The Arabic of the Holy Quran, which believers heard at mosques, was an elegant but archaic version of the language. It was eighth-century Arabic. The obvious, but religiously still unthinkable, way to promote a national language in Pakistan, it seemed to me, would have been to print and teach the Holy Book in Urdu.)

The language policy orders were given and supposed to be enforced by the people who spoke English in Pakistan, many of them educated abroad or in the private Christian academies that were another British legacy. That elite, as far as I could tell, was more than comfortable retaining for themselves, only, the skill that set them apart as a nobility inside and outside the country— command of the modern language of science, technology, trade, diplomacy, pop culture and materialism. "Our books are all in English," said a medical student in Peshawar. "The government keeps promising scientific books in Urdu, but no one really believes they are efficient enough to do the translations. Even if they were, the books would be obsolete by the time they were printed. What really happens is terrible. The government insists on teaching in Urdu at the lower schools, and the students from poor families get here and can't understand the teaching in English. The professors scream and scream at them, but that doesn't help. If you don't understand enough English, you're not going to be a doctor."

Learning English, then, became a national obsession among the ambitious of the society after the government banned its use as a medium of instruction—an order that was enforced only in public schools. Families, I was told, were going without a meal each day to get together enough money to keep a child, usually the oldest boy, in private (and totally illegal under "national language" laws) "English medium" schools all over the country. "The mushroom growth of English medium schools should be checked, or they will be a source of trouble for the public, . . ." according to *The Pakistan Times*. Small chance. The English medium schools were, in fact, a source of hope—English was seen as the language of opportunity—and the same bureaucrats and police officials charged with closing down the private schools were instead enrolling their own children. That was happening even though many of the new English medium schools seemed to be frauds run by bilingual illiterates. "A-1 English Speaking Medium School" was a sign I saw outside a building in Karachi.

"Those who can afford it would still by and large like to send their children to English-medium schools," concluded the 1982 report of the Language Study Group. "English is the main repository of modern knowledge and one-third of all the books printed in the world each year are in the English language. . . . [It] is essential for international intercourse. There is no escape for any country in the world from learning English well and thoroughly and it would be very unwise, in fact almost suicidal, for Pakistan to destroy by neglect all the advantages we already possess in respect to past knowledge of English."

But they saw themselves damned if they didn't and damned if they did. The same report, a tortured document that recognized the many uses of an elite language and officially conceded that the men and women preparing the report might not know enough about people who did not know enough English: "The ruling elite was trained to do their official work in English. This produced a class of people unrelated to the mainstream of the masses and interested in perpetuating themselves as an elite group."

True—and the Pakistan civil service were the foot soldiers of that group—but modernization was dictating the expansion of that linguistic elite. The history of the English and English in Pakistan was of no concern to the world. The world was interested only in whether enough Pakistanis could speak enough English to get things done. The Associated Press Pakistan transmitted news of the country and the world to all of the 135 newspapers in the country—six of them published in English, one hundred and twenty-nine in other languages. But all the machines in APP offices worked in only one language, English. The news clattered into APP headquarters in Islamabad on English-language teletypes from Washington, Paris, Moscow and Riyadh and was sent back out in English to Quetta, Multan and Hyderabad. The rich, flowing script of the Arabic alphabet did not adapt easily to eco nomical mechanical demands of devices like typewriters, tele types and linotypes. One of the most extraordinary sights I saw in Pakistan was the city room of *Nawa-1-Wagt*—Persian for *The Voice of the Times*—the second largest Urdu-language newspaper in Pakistan. Reporters wrote out their stories in pencil, and their copy was run over to long tables where dozens of men sat or squatted in rows—men in woven caps and lamb's wool hats, in brocaded robes and polyester pants, in boots and barefoot—cal ligraphers with brushes swiftly writing out the stories in Arabic script on one-column-wide sheets of transparent paper. Those beautiful columns of painted words were then pasted upon pages, while other calligraphers, a little better paid, did the headlines. Then the whole page was photographed to make printing plates.

It was often easier just to give in and use English officially.

When Prem Tinsulanonda, the prime minister of Thailand, visited Pakistan in August, he was greeted by signs he understood, because they were in English: "Long Live Pakistan-Thailand Solidarity." He came from another country where all high school students were required to learn English.

It was not only Pakistan and Thailand that depended on English. Seventy-seven percent of the secondary school students in the world were studying English in 1981, according to the United Nations. The language of Great Britain and the United States had become the *lingua franca* of the world, spread now by technology and popular entertainment, often to the official dismay of countries from Pakistan to Tanzania to France which had made or were making some attempts to slow the spread of English. But those attempts—except for a while, in places as brutally governed as Vietnam and Iran—usually just meant that more English was being spoken less well. "One of the lessons Pakistans learned during the years it was friendly with Russia, when students were being sent to Moscow," said Simon Cole, the director of the British Council in Islamabad, "was that the teaching at Lummumba University, the international university in Moscow, was in English. Whatever the official policies, people got the message about what that meant for the future."

More than 700 million people around the world, by some estimates, spoke English by 1983, with perhaps 400 million of them speaking it as a second language. The growth of the language was one of the phenomena of the second half of the twentieth century, paralleling the growth in American influence in the politics and business of the world. Before World War II, fewer than 200 million people spoke English as their first language, and another 20 million or so spoke it as an additional language. Forty years later, English was the mother tongue of twelve countries and *an* official language of twenty-six more, including Pakistan. Even though the percentage of the world's people speaking the language might decline—because the world's population growth would be dominated by poor rural people speaking only local languages—English was already more widespread and dominant as the *lingua franca* of the educated world than Latin had been during Roman times or Italian during the sixteenth and seventeenth centuries, or French in the eighteenth and nineteenth centuries.*

What began as the language of the people of a small island off Europe and then of the colonies those people established—in North America, later in India—developed a momentum of its own around the world. Each person who learned English as a second language had a selfish interest in other people's learning it—particularly if he or she was selling something. A German selling pharmaceuticals in Pakistan or Costa Rica, or a Russian selling ideas in Algeria or Greece, would probably be doing it in English.

This growth of the new international language, not because of government policies but because of millions and millions of individual needs and ambitions, created political and educational conflicts and contradictions all over the world after World War II. Pakistan was one among many countries that were ambivalent about English. Israel, ironically, was one of the new countries grappling with the same linguistic problems as Pakistan during the same years. There was irony in that because no one in Pakistan would allow himself to see any link, even one of shared conflict, with Israel. The Islamic Republic, and all its citizens I met, identified totally with Arab hostility to the Jewish state. On July 4, 1980, as part of an issue commemorating American independence, the *Khyber Mail* printed quotes attributed to George Washington calling Jews "the white ants of society." I heard a lot of that in Pakistan.

---

* English, in 1982, was the mother tongue of the United States, the United Kingdom, Ireland, Australia, New Zealand, Barbados, Jamaica, Trinidad, Canada, Guyana, Grenada and the Bahamas. It was a co-official language in Botswana, Cameroon, Fiji, Gambia, Ghana, India, Lesotho, Liberia, Malawi, Malta, Mauritius, Nambia, Nauru, Nigeria, Pakistan, the Phillipines, Sierra Leone, Singapore, South Africa, Swaziland, Tanzania, Tonga, Uganda, Western Samoa, Zambia and Zimbabwe. In addition, English had some official status in seven other countries: Burma, Ethiopia, Israel, Kenya, Malaysia, Sri Lanka and Sudan. Beyond that, it was the language of international contact with many of the world's most important countries including the Arabic countries, China, Japan, and the Soviet Union.

But that hostility did not change the fact that Pakistan and Israel were new, religiously identified countries that chose to designate a national language few people spoke—Urdu and Hebrew—as a means of uniting ethnically and culturally diverse peoples. And despite government pronouncements in both countries, educated or ambitious people chose to learn English as the way to get ahead or get out: the language was the key to foreign employment or to emigration. Then, with a certain ambivalence and not particularly effectively, each government attempted to eliminate English medium schools but made English a compulsory foreign language in public schools.

English by the 1970s was mandatory in most countries of the world. More than 100 million students were studying the language at any time. It was not that English was superior as a language. I had that illusion when I first noticed my native tongue's growing tyranny over serious international discourse. I thought that, somehow, English was more direct and perhaps a more democratic language without distinctive high and low vocabularies and grammars. But in Islamabad, as well as Paris, I've been assured that you can say most of what you need to say quite well and often more beautifully in Urdu, or in French. The power of English was its role as the language of modernity. It simply had more words and newer words; there are 550,000 words in some English dictionaries, compared with 50,000 or so in Urdu or Hebrew dictionaries. Even in France, the words describing whatever was the latest—from computers to rhythms—tended to be English or English adaptations. Actually *American* might be a more accurate word than *English*. Americans created new words in the twentieth century to name the new things that were being created by American scientists, engineers and hustlers of various sorts.

So, not only did more and more people have to learn our language if, for instance, they wanted to keep up with medical or electronic journals, but their own language had to adapt to these new things around them, usually by just adopting an English (American) word or adapting it for local ears. "Urdu or the regional languages are perfectly serviceable languages for everyday living," said David Queen, an officer in the United States Information Service in Islamabad whose job was promoting the teaching and learning of English. "But when you watch someone repair a typewriter here, you hear a lot of English. The parts don't have names in Urdu, or in a lot of other languages. People just use the English."

Sounding out the words "typewriter ribbon" was not speaking or understanding English, but for many people in many places, language experiences like that were the beginning of determined personal modernization. Many realized that the language of the Yanks—that's what it really was after World War II—was the language of opportunity, of upper mobility, of access to technology. English was the code of modernity itself. It was the code of computers, and that technology became another reason to learn English. It was not that computers operated only in English—they could easily be programmed to transmit their mathematical logic in any language—but the literature of the field was in English, and to play with the newest machines and programs you had to know the language of the people who made the stuff. You had to know English to keep up—to stay on top of almost any modern field. More than 80 percent of the technical papers published each year in the world were published first in English, then translated into the other four languages of science—German, French, Russian and Japanese. It will take a very long time for that information to be translated into Urdu—if it ever is—and it would never be accessible in Punjabi or Pushtu.

The original literature in any field had enormous reach. One of the reasons English spread over the globe was the expansion of mass higher education. The idea itself—of educating masses beyond the reading, writing and arithmetic they needed to get by—was essentially American. So the literature and the curricula of large university systems were produced first in English and used or adapted everywhere, including Pakistan. Even though less than one-half of one percent of the population of the country entered universities, those educated few would almost certainly run the country no matter what happened over the next few decades. And they would speak English.

In much of the world, too, popular entertainment—from Walt Disney and Elvis Presley to *Star Wars* and the video games in Peshawar—created a thirst for English, among people if not their governments. That sinful craving, under "Islamization," was being curbed in Pakistan. In *Shame*, his bitter novel of Pakistan, Salman Rushdie imagined the entire nation beginning to bang their television sets at the same time after a pious military dictator took over: people were convinced the things were broken when they couldn't get anything but *maulanas* chanting the Holy Quran. Zia-ul-Haq was determined to protect his people against the enticements of modern entertainment whether they wanted to be protected or not.

The resistance to English, in Zia's mind, must have been part of his struggle against what he saw as the flotsam and jetsam of modernization—mass culture, liberated women, independent young people, cultural and social revolution. A tough fight, complicated for him by his stated commitment to modernism and his personal command of its language, English, which he learned from Englishmen at Saint Stephen's College in Delhi in the late 1930s and early 1940s.

One of the English teachers at Saint Stephen's in those days was a young Cambridge graduate named Michael Close. He came to Delhi in 1937 and moved to Peshawar in 1947, after commanding Pathan troops during World War II. And there he was, in a small apartment at Edwardes College—still teaching English.

"Yes. Oh, my, yes. We do teach in English here at Edwardes. It may be illegal, but I think they made an exception in the rules. The children of the elite of the province go here, you know. Always have," he said. He seemed to be the last Englishman in Peshawar. Someone told me there were only 140 foreigners in the city, which had 300,000 or 400,000 people. The apartment was decorated with color photographs of scenes of English countryside, great homes and churches, all clipped from magazines. A handsome young Pathan served us tea and crumpets—"My adopted son," Close said fondly. Then we walked about the campus, fading at the corners but still a pleasant collection of courtyards bordered by red stone buildings in an Islamic Gothic style—English buildings softened by the symmetry and curves mastered by local builders. He was, he said, actually the last Englishman there, at Edwardes, which was a private high school for boys. He was also an adviser to the Provincial Police, who were setting up an English medium high school for the sons of officers; that's what they wanted for their own children.

"English was the official language when I came. Still is, really. But it was totally unambiguous then. There was a high standard when I taught at Saint Stephen's, and I taught, at least I imagined I taught, at a Cambridge level. Then I got this liking for Pathans. Rather lost my heart to them. I came up here and the standards were lower, but I didn't mind. Since then, there has been, I'm afraid, a steady qualitative erosion accompanied, of course, by a quantitative explosion.

"The government," he said, "seems to encourage and discourage English at the same time. Quite confusing. But it doesn't matter. Nearly every rational person recognizes the necessity of English for advanced study in every subject but the Oriental ones. Parents want it for their children. They don't have the books in Urdu, you know."

They had the books in English, though, and ironically, that was one of the reasons the language was deteriorating as it spread in Pakistan. "H. G. Wells English," one young British teacher called it in Islamabad. "And that's the best of it," he said. "What we try to do out here is prevent them from doing too much damage to the language." Educated Pakistanis sometimes speak as if they were reading aloud; many conversations I had in Pakistani homes were punctuated with references to or lines from *Vanity Fair* or *Wuthering Heights*—and the national concept of teaching the language had a great deal to do with reading Thomas Hardy.

"I love the literature, of course," said Mrs. Riyazul Haque of the language Study Group. "I taught English literature for ten years, and more and more, I began to realize that students no longer understood what they were reading." So, she decided to go to the University of Hawaii to study the teaching of the language itself.

Her work, the group's work in trying to integrate English into modern Pakistan or, perhaps, integrate Pakistan into the modern world, was part of her country's painful attempts to digest its own history—to get beyond the humiliation of colonialism and get on with the often-humiliating processes of accepting Western models of modernism. "The colonial compromise" was a phrase used by the head of the British Council, Simon Cole, whose job, like that of his American counterpart, David Queen of the United States Information Service, was to promote English in Pakistan.

"Rejecting English as the colonial language is the first phase," said Cole, who had worked in other former British colonies. "Very natural. You saw it in Burma, where Ne Win tried to eliminate the language completely.

"The second phase comes hard—the realization that English is vital for development and for communication with the rest of the world.

"Then comes the compromise, the third phase. The new governments realize that they have been throwing away one of their greatest advantages, a history of speaking English. They begin to train people functionally—doctors, scientists, diplomats, tourist people who must have good English."

That process, in fact, was most dramatic in Ne Win's Burma, which was also once part of British India. As an absolute dictator determined to guide the development of his country without foreign influence, he not only banned the use of English but cut off almost all contacts with the outside world. That all ended after his own daughter applied for admission to a British medical school and was rejected because she could not pass the English-language examination. Soon, English instruction was mandatory for all high school students in Burma.

Pakistan, Cole thought, was coming to the end of the second phase. "There is still great confusion here," he said. "The government is promoting Arabic, while Saudi Arabians are learning English as fast as they can. But, then, as you know, the Pakistanis are learning English as fast as they can, too, in all those private schools. Unfortunately, they're not learning it very well—all these people reciting Wordsworth and Shelley by rote.

"The fact is that anybody who is anybody in Pakistan speaks English, which means we, the British and the Americans, will always have influence far out of proportion to our resources in trade and commerce—here and most of the world.

"English is a force of its own now. In Pakistan, the demand for English far outstrips the ability to deliver, and the demand will keep growing."

10

BEHIND
THE VEIL

Modernization was making many demands on Pakistan, and it would make many more. But the greatest of them would not concern language; the use of English, Urdu and the regional languages showed strain lines in the country but did not cause them. The great trauma coming to Pakistan would be over the liberation of women. "Half-liberated and half-shackled" had been the Lincolnesque phrase at the end of the introductory paragraph of the Sixth Plan's chapter "Women's Development: Equality of Opportunity."

"In all societies, women's development is a pre-requisite for overall national development; indeed, no society can ever develop half-liberated and half-shackled."

In a plan (and a country) where statistics were generally used to put a brighter face on things, the next couple of paragraphs indicated that, whichever sets of figures were believed about national literacy, the ratio between male and female literacy was about three to one; the highest figure, certainly exaggerated, estimated the number of rural women who could read and write at one in seventeen. Then, discussing health in a country that was poor but where daily nutritional levels apparently averaged out close to world minimum adequacy standards, the chapter mentioned that of the Pakistani women who received some sort

143

of medical care during childbirth, which set them above many
others, 90 percent were suffering from anemia.

On Independence Day, August 14, the principal national ceremony was at the Presidency in Rawalpindi, and two thousand
people were invited to watch President Zia-ul-Haq hoist the flag
of Pakistan in the morning. "A cross section of citizens . . . ,"
reported *The Pakistan Times* the next morning. It did look like
most of the high-level gatherings I had seen. There were, by my
count, three women there—and one of them was my wife. It was
only when I read that phrase, the next day, though, that I thought
about what I had seen. I was quite surprised at how quickly I
took things for granted—water buffalos on the street, but no
women. Pakistan, for miles or hours or days, was a society without
women. None. Offices seemed somehow strange, until I realized,
time after time, that every single person inside them was male.

"I know what it's like in Peshawar," said a nineteen-year-old
medical student, a woman. "I do not keep *perdah*"—the veil—
"in the bazaar, and when the men stare, I stare back and call,
'What is the matter with you? Have you never seen a woman?
Have you no mothers or sisters?' " But, she added, at home near
Kohat, she did keep *perdah* in the streets. "I must," she said.
"To do otherwise would cause great embarrassment to my family." So, when the Sixth Plan used the phrase "Equality of Opportunity," it innocently distorted Pakistan to the sensibilities of
any Westerner. The reality was outside American twentieth-cen-
tury experience. One survey published recently as part of a book
on the status of women in Pakistani cities—*Metropolitan Women*
by Sabeeha Hafeez, director of research of the Federal Women's
Division—reported that experience and somewhat dated data
showed that the proportion of women in the paid working force
was highest in Karachi, a city of perhaps five million people.
Listing the number of women in selected positions several years
after Independence, Dr. Hafeez wrote: "49 secretaries, 48 typ-
ists, 28 receptionists and 162 stenographers are cited to be present in Karachi."

"The metropolitan woman, then, is a model of change for the
rest of women . . . ," she concluded. "Unlike other cities a woman
in a big city like Karachi is less restricted in her physical movements. . . . Perhaps as more and more women become mobile,

ease in the acceptance of women outside home will also increase. Compared to the metropolitan woman, the woman in the medium-sized cities of Pakistan are slow to emerge from seclusion. The mobility of the few educated ones in those towns is mostly from home to workplaces, which in most cases are segregated educational institutions. Otherwise a male escort or a *burqa*— the tentlike garment with the veiled slit for seeing out—"guards their movements. The village women, however, are somewhat physically mobile in that they work in the field outside their homes."

The village women, in fact, worked like animals, beasts of burden weaker and less surefooted than donkeys. Pulling veils to cover their faces from strangers, they were in the fields chopping into the rough earth to plant alongside their husbands and brothers. But they were not Dr. Hafeez's subject. She was only writing about more "advanced" Pakistani women, the bolder ones whom Islamization would force back into the traditional ways. The Zia regime not only began resegregating the country's schools—by sex—but, in March of 1982, ordered that women's events be dropped from the Pakistan National Games. That was also when Zia decided that the women's national teams would be withdrawn from international competitions. The idea was to end the display of female bodies to spectators at sporting events at home and abroad.

"Do not take Islamization seriously. It is lip service," said a woman with a position in the government, one of the very few. I asked her whether it was true that women in the diplomatic service—they had been actively recruited during the Bhutto years—were no longer being assigned to overseas posts unless they had husbands who were diplomats assigned to the same place. Yes, she said, but that affected only a few women.

Later—we were seated next to each other at a government dinner—the woman turned to me and said, "Islamization *is* mostly talk. But not always, not where women are concerned. That is what the men here care about."

And that was what I had been told by Altaf Yawar, the foreign editor of Associated Press Pakistan: "Pakistani men are afraid that the place of women in an agricultural society can't be maintained in an industrialized society."

"We are not going to force our women into the streets," Zia-ul-Haq had told me. We were talking just after he had given his *Nizam-i-Mustafa* speech on August 12, 1983, speaking for more than an hour and a half to the Majlis-e-Shura about his plans for the eventual shift of federal power to a civilian government based on the "System of the Prophet."

As part of that speech, he had defended the military *coup d'état* of 1977, and an important part of that defense was chivalry. "The country reached a point of civil war," he began. "The country's economy, too, was shattered. Life was disturbed. Democracy was shattered in the name of democracy. The Honour and sanctity of mothers, daughters and sisters became unsafe. . . ."

Then, in words that were guaranteed to cause trouble, either deliberately provocative (unlikely) or an indication of personal belief, he said: "Drafts of the laws of evidence . . . are under consideration of the government and they will be promulgated very soon, *Inshallah.*"

The Laws of Evidence, which had provoked demonstrations by female attorneys and other educated women, particularly in Lahore, were the focus of a festering domestic debate—among elites—about the role of women in Pakistan and under Islam. Based on a fundamentalist interpretation of a verse of the Holy Quran, those were the new laws that would make the legal testimony of one man worth the testimony of two women. One person's word against a half-person's word. That was based on one Quranic verse—or an interpretation of the verse favored in some Arabic countries—regarding financial transactions and the repayment of loans. Put it in writing, said the Quran, and get witnesses:

"Oh ye who believe: When you deal with each other in transactions involving future obligations in a fixed period of time, reduce them to writing; let a scribe write them down faithfully as between the parties. . . . If the party liable is mentally deficient, or weak or unable to dictate, let his guardian dictate faithfully and get two witnesses out of your own men, and if there are not two men, then a man and two women, such as ye choose, for witnesses, so that if one of them errs, the other can remind her." (Holy Quran, II, 282)

There were also words to be found in the Quran for those who believed that men should have double the financial rights and powers of women. "God thus directs you as regards [the inheritance of] your children, to the male a portion equal to that of two females." (Holy Quran IV, 11) Leaving aside the questions and problems of dealing in a modern world with thirteen-hundred-year-old Quranic directives that are unambiguous, the interpretation of God's word in all religions and systems was done by humans, usually male humans.

A man could make the faith be anything he wanted it to be, and men in Pakistan wanted to keep women in their place. Zia-ul-Haq was one Pakistani who made that a central tenant of his own public belief. In August of 1983, laying out "the manifesto of this government," the third priority he listed, after "advancement of Islamization" and "improve economic conditions," was: "To improve law and order conditions, to protect the life and property of the people and preserve the sanctity of *chador* and *chardiwari*"—to keep women behind the veil and behind four walls.

That has been a dark place for many people for a long time. While I was in the country, a blind fifteen-year-old pregnant village girl named Safia charged a man named Maqsood with *zenna bil jabr*—"rape"—but she could not prove it because she could not produce four male witnesses to the penetration. So, it was she who was convicted, of false accusation and *zenna bil raza*—"sexual intercourse"—and sentenced to fifteen lashes and three years in prison. I wanted to reject judgments of fanaticism, but the evil hidden by *chador, chardiwari* was too obvious to ignore. I had to believe the many, many stories I heard of the ordinary abuse of women. Beatings. Rape. Lust. Incest. One of the common curses in most of the languages of Pakistan was *behan chod*: "sister fucker."

The news of any day in Pakistan was heavy with crimes of great violence—two kinds predominated, sudden and almost inexplicable, and plotted revenge—and much of it seemed a brutal testament to repressed sexuality and an assertion of men's convictions that they had the right to control the lives of their women. *The Muslim* of July 10 reported from Gujrat on the trial of three brothers named Biba whose sister Sakina had dared to marry "her own choice," Muhammad Sharif. The brothers attacked the wedding house and killed the groom's brother, with hatchets, when he got in their way while they were carrying their sister out. They then hanged her and threw her body in a canal.

A few days later, the same newspaper reported from Rahimyar Khan: "One Abdul Ghafoor of a nearby village allegedly axed to death his young wife as he suspected her modesty. . . ."

Islam could be used to provide a rationale for many definitions of modesty and protection and sanctity, but a great deal of what went on in Pakistan seemed to me to have more to do with men and women than with their Maker. Men asserted their dominance in the traditional way of many societies, by brute force. Many of them were determined to maintain that power for as long as possible. The "protected" ladies of Pakistan—to use Zia-ul-Haq's word—were walking gracefully under loads of wood or produce or water on their heads, in the great heat of the plains, past men sharing the smoke of a bubbling *hookah* under a tree or beside a building. Shade, like food, went to men first. Even in poverty, a man was king over one or two or four wives.

The traditional polygamy of many Islamic societies—men were allowed four wives because that was the number the Prophet, Muhammad, had had in his time—was restricted, officially, but not banned by Pakistan's 1961 Family Laws. That legislation required the signature of earlier wives and a reason—sterility or physical infirmity were acceptable—before a husband could take additional wives.

The Family Laws also ended, officially, the traditional power of husbands to divorce their wives by simply pronouncing the word—"Divorce!"—three times in front of a witness. A ninety-day waiting period was mandated, and women were given the right to seek divorces. But almost none did. Except among the rich and Westernized, divorced women lived truly cursed and impoverished lives, scorned by the men and women of their village.

Laws, after all, had to be enforced to mean anything, and many in Pakistan existed only on paper, including restrictions on such ancient rituals as dowries and arranged child-marriages. In the case of the Family Laws, even that existence was being challenged when I was there by religious leaders who demanded that those laws be eliminated as part of the process of Islamization.

Village *maulanas* were also a significant factor in stalling another drive of modernization—birth control. The official goal of the government's Population Welfare Plan of 1981, complete with detailed statistics, was to, within four years, "increase the level of [birth control] practice from an estimated 12.7 percent to 25 percent . . . to decrease the crude birth rate from 41–42 per 1,000 population to 37.5 percent, and to reduce the annual average growth rate of the population from 2.9 percent to 2.7 percent."

All on paper. In the real life of Pakistan and despite United Nations and foreign aid totaling almost $100 million for birth control programs, success eventually may be linked to female literacy. Wherever the money actually went, the government never began the kind of effort that would be necessary to reach illiterate women "protected" by the walls of *chador, chardiwari.*

Enforced sexual segregation before marriage and male dominance forever after were the highest and thickest of the Islamic walls against modernization of the country. The treatment of women was considered central to the political and economic thinking of Pakistan by Mubashir Hasan, the former Finance Minister, who had written extensively not only on his own field, economics, but on the culture of his country. A subculture of homosexuality, particularly among upper-class men—"the female," he said, "came to be considered not worthy of a man's love"—and the antimodernist instincts among poorer men, he thought, were both inevitable curses of the rigid roles created for men and women. "I believe that one of the important reasons why our society refuses voluntary acceptance of a capitalist or socialist pattern of socioeconomic development is that the male dreads the prospect of emancipation of the female. He is terribly apprehensive that if he loses his right to rule over women, the world will come to an end."

Well, the world that the men of Pakistan had built was coming to a painful end. Dr. Hasan and his antagonist in planning and interpreting the economics of Pakistan, Mahbubul Haq, disagree on many things—they are something like the John Kenneth Galbraith and Milton Friedman of their country—but they agreed, as we talked separately, that modernization was inevitably breaking down Pakistan's male-female caste system. "We have to take

advantage of the talent and energy of our women to become a
modern nation," Haq said, "and families need two incomes, a
man and a woman's, as the society becomes more mobile and
more materialistic. Economics! —not Islamization. Iran, with all
of the rhetoric, has more women working than ever before, even
when the Shah was in power. I have heard figures as high as 40
percent of the workforce. Women are directing traffic in Teh-
eran—because the men are away at war and the work has to be
done. Societies respond to economic necessity. We will need our
women, and they are knocking on the door."

It was Dr. Haq who selected the verse from the Holy Quran
at the beginning of the Sixth Plan's section on Women's Development: "To men is allotted what they earn. And to women what
they earn."

What men were earning in foreign countries—the remittance
economy of millions of Pakistani families—was also redefining the
roles of men and women. The preferred Pakistani way to handle
the affairs and daily decision-making of families when the man
had gone overseas or to another part of the country for work, was
to pass the authority to a brother. But there were only so many
brothers around—and there seemed to be a lot of strong women
who would take orders from their husbands but not from their
brothers-in-law or their sisters-in-law's husbands—so, wives, even
if they were not working for cash, suddenly assumed the responsibilities, power and privilege that had been men's since the
first male demonstrated that he was physically stronger than the
first female. But those women were also taking their share of the
pain of that modernization. It was hardly a country of psychia-
trists, but Pakistani journals had begun to write of "Dubai Syn-
drome" in telling the stories of depressed, confused women having trouble coping at home while their husbands worked far away.

The tradition of women taking over for men has always been
strong in Pakistan—a society of family above all, even female
family—and it has produced the great irony of the country's repressed political life. The most dramatic leaders of the opposition
to martial law and Gen. Muhammad Zia-ul-Haq were two women,
the surviving wife and daughter of Zulfiqar Ali Bhutto.

Begum Nusrat Bhutto— *Begum* means wife—who had been
living in Europe and receiving treatment for cancer, and Benazir

Bhutto, the daughter under house arrest in Karachi while I was there, carried on the family name and business, demanding and receiving the power to speak for the Pakistan People's Party, even when such political speech was officially banned. "Defunct," of course, under martial law; but the PPP would probably win a national election, if one were held, and Benazir Bhutto, a thirty-year-old graduate of Radcliffe and Oxford, conceivably could become the prime minister of Pakistan.*

That was not going to happen if Zia-ul-Haq could prevent it. But there were many things that Zia and many other Pakistani men, ruling in the present, living in the past, were gradually losing the power to prevent in the future.

On August 2, 1983, the results of the annual Secondary School Certificate Test, the test that determined university entry, were announced in Karachi. A total of 56, 915 students had taken "The Matric"—one of the few gateways to success in Pakistan not tied directly to family name—in two divisions, Science (the higher one) and General. The top three finishers in each division were young women.

Saira Jamil of Habib Girls School, the daughter of a junior executive in the Pakistan National Bank, scored highest at 88.70 in the science division. The highest male score was 87.41, made by Muhammad Asif Khan Mateen of Saint Lawrence's Boys High School. The next day's *Dawn* reported that Miss Jamil was happy "sharing domestic responsibilities with her mother." The second-place finisher, Shabana Anwar of Government Delhi School, who scored 88.47, said the newspaper, "is fond of sewing and shares kitchen work with her mother." Number three, Shabana Saeed of Saint Jude's High School, who scored 87.88, the newspaper said, "studies but without neglecting kitchen work."

I had no doubt the generals could keep Benazir Bhutto under house arrest or in exile for a very long time. It would be interesting to see how long they could keep Saira Jamil, Shabana Anwar and Shabana Saeed in the kitchen.

* In January of 1984, Benazir Bhutto was released from house arrest to go to London for medical treatment of ear problems.

11

TO THE
KHYBER PASS

In his August speech defining his plans for the "System of the Prophet," the Islamic system, the Chief Martial Law Administrator, Muhammad Zia-ul-Haq, proudly took credit for enforcing laws against the "heinous crime . . . of alcohol drinking." And it was enforced; the penalty for a Muslim caught drinking was eighty lashes.

But it was actually Prime Minister Zulfiqar Ali Bhutto who had banned drinking. On April 4, 1977, with his personal life-style, including drinking, under mounting attacks in the mosques, Bhutto had instituted his own Islamic system. He banned liquor, wine and beer. He changed the Sabbath from Sunday, the Western world's day of rest, to the Friday mentioned in the Holy Quran (Pakistanis worked six days a week, but between the Friday Sabbath and time zone differences, their country was really in working communication with the West for only about three and a half days a week).

Bhutto's Islamic reforms, which never really fooled anyone about his personal piety, remained in effect after he was placed under house arrest three months later by General Zia. Then on February 9, 1979, Zia, playing to the same persistent fundamentalist constituency, announced a "Prohibition Order," extending the alcohol laws to include narcotics. He banned the production, distribution and use of opium, of which some 880 tons a year were being grown and processed, and of cannabis (hashish and marijuana), which was growing, cultivated and wild, all over the country. The Holy Quran was cited but with new interpretation; the definition of the word *intoxicants,* which Muslims traditionally took to mean the products of the grape and hops, was broadened to include the products of the weed and the poppy.

"Satan's plan is to excite enmity and hatred between you with intoxicants and gambling, and hinder you from remembrance of God, and from prayer," said the Quran. "Will ye not then abstain?" (Holy Quran, V, 90–91)

That effected more Pakistanis than the ban on whiskey, wine and beer. Although home brews of various kinds helped pass the long nights in many villages—I was depressed by the oppressive darkness in the unelectrified villages—the illiterate masses didn't drink all that much. But hashish and opium were widely used and always had been. The roads of Pakistan have always been among the most dangerous on earth, and one of the principal reasons was that the country moved by truck and the truck drivers worked around the clock, staying awake with hashish and trusting their lives (and, sometimes, mine) to God. *Inshallah,* the man behind the brightly decorated overloaded truck or bus careening toward you on roads that are, by Western standards, only one lane wide was awake and abstaining. But if Zia's interpretation of the Holy Book was widely ignored at home—I saw poppies growing and hashish being sold in the bazaars—it became part of a worldwide chain of events that made Pakistan the most important heroin-distributing country in the world.

By the middle of 1983, narcotics control officials in the United States and Europe were reporting that between 85 and 90 percent of the heroin reaching the East Coast of the United States and the countries of Western Europe was coming from Pakistan. In the previous eighteen months more than eight thousand pounds of heroin were reported seized in Pakistan (compared with eighteen pounds in 1980), the equivalent of more than six months' supply for the American market with a wholesale value of more than $800 million. But at least three times as much was believed to be getting by customs stations at the airport and docks at Karachi.

This, according to American drug officials working in Pakistan, was what happened in the four hectic, profitable years between 1979 and 1983:

Pakistan, the home of peoples who had been growing poppies and making opium, legally and illegally, for at least five hundred years, had stores of more than eight hundred tons of opium at the time of Zia's order. The stuff, in large, sticky blocks, was stored in the Khyber region, around the town of Landi Kotal in the Khyber Pass, three miles from the Afghanistan border. That opium had been cooked from the scrapings of the poppies cultivated on both sides of the border for centuries. The top of each of the chest-high plants is a fist-sized bulb—it looks something like a green tomato—and when it is ripe and the bulb is lanced, a brown gum oozes out, opium gum. The opium in Landi Kotal had traditionally been used at home—the government of Pakistan estimated that there were 86,000 opium addicts in the country and hundreds of thousands more controlled users—and for export, legal and illegal, to Iran, Afghanistan and Turkey, where much of it would be made into heroin.

In the year of Zia's order, 1979, the United States was having some success in persuading authorities in Turkey and in the "Golden Triangle" countries of Southeast Asia, Thailand, Burma, and Laos, particularly Thailand, to take measures to curtail heroin production in that part of the world. Then, later in the year, the government of Shah Reza Pahlavi was overthrown in Iran and the Soviets invaded Afghanistan. In the turmoil, it became more and more difficult to find a safe haven for the heroin business.

Pakistan, with its huge supplies of stored opium, was the obvious place. The Khyber District was still principally under tribal control; federal laws, like the laws of the British Raj, had no standing off the main road through the Khyber Pass.

"What does that mean?" I had asked when I finally received permission and an armed guard to travel in Khyber, which was officially closed to foreigners.

"That means," I was told, in the office of the District Commissioner, "that you are under the protection of the government of the Pakistan if you stay on the road. If you get off, you're in tribal territory. They can shoot you, and they've been known to do that. There's a drug war going on up there. The tribes, particularly the Afridis and the Shinwaris, blame you Americans for the crackdown on their narcotics business. Kidnaping you two and your children might be their idea of a way to get the soldiers off their backs. Have a good time."

Heroin production probably would have come to Khyber anyway, but the American officials told me the catalyst was the children of tribal leaders who were being sent away to universities in the United States and England. "The kids started coming home and telling the elders about heroin," one American drug official said. "They told them they were crazy to have all this sticky, smelly stuff around when it could be made into a powder that was worth much, much more and was much easier to smuggle through Kennedy or Heathrow airports."

Ten pounds of the raw opium gum, which would be worth about $250, could be distilled down to one pound of very good Western-grade heroin—water-soluable for injection—which, I was told, was selling in Landi Kotal for a little more than $2,000. That pound, if someone could get it past Kennedy Airport security, would be worth close to $100,000 in New York City.

The conversion itself was a pretty basic process, requiring nothing much more complicated than big pots and pans and some tubing; that kind of setup was what narcotics agents called a heroin "factory." There were dozens of factories in Khyber, fanning out from Landi Kotal, which has been known for as long as anyone can remember as the "Smugglers Village." The bazaar was the last stop on the Khyber Road before Afghanistan, and goods imported by that landlocked country had traditionally been delivered to the port of Karachi and transported north one thousand miles through the Khyber Pass in sealed trucks. Only, somehow, trucks seemed to get unsealed in Landi Kotal. Its bazaar, called the "Underground Bazaar"—not because of illegalities but because the shops and stalls were below the level of the built-up main road—was the place Pakistanis went to buy televisions or air conditioners or shoes or aspirin for a fraction of the prices these same high-duty items cost where they were available in other parts of Pakistan. That bazaar was also the place to go for the 60 percent of the country's tires that had been smuggled in without duty. When opportunity struck in the world narcotics market, Pakistani crooks were ready, willing and experienced enough to seize the moment, and the tribesmen of Khyber, who didn't consider themselves outlaws because they didn't recognize any law but tribal *jirgas*, were more than willing to run the factories to cook the poison of the West.

The factories were set up in little valleys or caves hidden in the mountains, or inside the fortresses in which the Afridis and Shinwaris live along the Khyber Road. They were the most extraordinary contemporary homes I had ever seen. I had been told that the Khyber Pass, despite its history as a gateway of invasion, was actually kind of boring to visit, that it was a relatively wide pass with a good asphalt road winding through a thirty-mile-long cut in the Hindu Kush at 3,500 feet.

The road was wide, wider than two lanes, but I wasn't bored. Not by the geography and certainly not by the history. Or, for that matter, by Gul Rachman, the guard provided us by the Tribal Militia, who would pat his old Lee-Enfield .303, the British rifle that was the favorite of Khyber, whenever we tried to walk somewhere he thought we should not.

The military history of the world was written along the Khyber Road. The armies of Alexander and Mongol hordes had come this way, usually only once, because going, uninvited, through Pathan lands was running a gauntlet of hell. In 1897 the British, whose abandoned picket forts, machine gun nests, bunker hospitals and regimental plaques still decorate the sides of the road, sent forty thousand men just to subdue one tribe, the Afridis. "People were expected to keep quiet, not to shoot one another, and, above all, not to shoot at travellers along the road," wrote one of the British, Winston Churchill. "It was too much to ask. . . ."

Little had changed since then. *Badal*—an eye for an eye—was still the code of the hills, and no one had persuaded the tribesmen that there was much difference between a British soldier and a Pakistani soldier. They lived in forts, these people. I have driven half a day in the Sahara to see an abandoned medieval *casbah*, one of the fort-villages first built on desert oases sometime in the Middle Ages. In Khyber, there were tract developments of fort-villages, and they were not abandoned. There were people living in them, probably watching the foreigners through rifle slits.

The forts, sometimes only one hundred feet or so apart, were the same reddish clay color as the barren, hilly landscape inside the Khyber Pass; the construction was of rock and burned brick and mud. Walls, perhaps thirty feet high and hundreds of feet around, surrounded the buildings and yards of one or more extended families. One hundred people or more might be living inside, prepared for siege—perhaps from the people in the fort next door. There were huge gates, made of wood and corrugated metal, into the compounds, and there were few windows, usually none. Some of the forts flew family flags from the watchtowers. More had television antennas up there.

Landi Kotal overlooks the barren land that is the border between Pakistan and Afghanistan. It is a classic border town, with Bedford and Suzuki trucks rolling in and out and the Under ground Bazaar built around and under a bend, almost a right angle, in the Khyber Road. The hotel was at the corner, three stories high, with a balcony overhanging the road. A cow was walking across the balcony. Stepping down from the road with our guard, we were in the alleys of the bazaar. The stripped carcasses of sheep hung in butcher shops next to glass counters filled with Lanvin perfume; mud-walled cafés with food being cooked on the ground in large pans of sizzling ghee were next to stacks of Sharp televisions from Japan. Men with guns on their backs sat patiently, being shaved by barbers squatting in the streets. Shouting schoolboys, in neat uniforms and berets with red felt crescents sewed on them, ran around a corner, headed for a stall of Coca-Colas floating among blocks of ice in a washtub. Hashish was for sale on the ground, two stalls down. Life went on in the Khyber Pass.

The trail that began in the pass—many smugglers did not use the road but walked with their camels and donkeys a few hundred feet from the asphalt, behind the federal inspectors whose job and authority began and ended on the blacktop—could end anywhere near the docks and airports of the West. Pakistani heroin traffickers were still not very well organized outside their own country. They were just greedy amateurs—at least that was what

American officials believed. The trail ended for some of them, respected businessmen, with arrests in hotels in Karachi or West Germany or England. At Heathrow Airport on July 15, 1982, British customs inspectors arrested two of Pakistan's world-class squash players, former world champion Mohibullah Khan and Hidzyatullah, carrying just about one million dollars' worth of heroin in the false bottoms of their suitcases.

"This took us by storm. We did not know what heroin was when this began. It was still called *charas* like opium," said Mairaj Husain, the chairman of the Pakistan Narcotics Control Board at a press conference in August. It was basically a slide show, presenting imaginative statistics and graphs to back up federal requests for more narcotics control money from the United States and the United Nations. It was true that heroin was new as the illicit cargo, but Pakistanis knew a great deal about narcotics, and even more about smuggling before some of them found the mainstream of world drug currents. Two Americans and a German were arrested in Karachi in 1974 for attempting to smuggle eleven liters of hashish oil under the seats of an automobile being shipped to Los Angeles. That was fairly routine, but the Pakistani police also found detailed plans for hashish oil factories to be set up in Southern California—one of the few transfers of technology from this part of the world to hi-tech America.

Drug use was always extensive in what became Pakistan, long before the region was part of British India. Cannabis was growing wild all over the country and I saw poppies growing—and bound up to collect their seeds—in roadside fields and even in the flower beds around the government hydroelectric station in Garum Chasma, near Chitral. The favorite sport of our children was to take photographs of each other among the eight-foot-high marijuana plants that covered the lot next to our house in Islamabad.

Pakistanis also had a reputation for indiscriminately using any pharmaceutical drug they could get their hands on—a deserved reputation I was told by foreign doctors working in the Afghan refugee camps—and the country has been something of a dumping ground for the obsolete or potentially dangerous products of American, European and Japanese pharmaceutical houses since the 1950s. Among the drugs I saw being sold by "compounders"— local pharmacists—were some that had been linked to blindness, brain damage and anemia in the West. But, of course, names like Entero-Vioform, Novalgin and Chloramphenical had no meaning to the men buying them at the compounders clustered along the road in places like Hangu. The customers described symptoms, often the symptoms of their women behind four walls, and the compounders reached for handfuls of small boxes marked in strange languages.

Heroin, too, had been sold openly along with the hashish in Landi Kotal until November of 1982. One day that month the Attorney General of the United States, William French Smith, was being taken through the bazaar by officials of the Pakistan Narcotics Control Board who wanted to show the Americans how effective they had been in convincing the tribes to get out of the heroin business—and one of Smith's assistants spotted heroin on display. It was after that incident that the Khyber District was closed to foreigners.

Four months later, in March of 1983, narcotics control was listed as the number two priority in the State Department's briefing on the purposes of U.S. aid to Pakistan in closed session before the House Foreign Affairs Committee—right behind "the stability and security of . . . a frontline state resisting Soviet expansionism." State Department and Defense Department briefers told the congressmen: "Our program of economic assistance also supports the Pakistan government's efforts to suppress poppy production . . ."—a timely statement, backed up by proposed narcotics control aid of between $20 million and $50 million over three years, because members of Congress from urban states had begun to question making Pakistan the second largest recipient of United States foreign aid when it was also the largest supplier of heroin to the U.S. One of the members, Senator Daniel Patrick Moynihan of New York, had even managed to get himself photographed in a field of poppies north of Peshawar.

"Our commitment to the elimination of production, processing, trafficking and consumption of narcotics is total and unqualified," Mairaj Husain said at his August press conference for a dozen Western reporters. It was one of those vaguely uncomfortable affairs where East and West tried to meet each other halfway. The press conference was hardly an indigenous Pakistani entertainment, and Husain seemed nervous, smiling and chatting too much as a seven-page press release containing the latest set of government statistics was passed out to the reporters seated around a table, along with cookies and bottles of Seven-Up. Then Husain read the seven pages aloud, word for word and number for number, while the reporters pretended to take notes. During questioning after the reading, he was more polite than informative. A British correspondent persisted in asking why, if as the government reported, eight thousand pounds of heroin were seized in eighteen months, there had not been more than occasional reports of seizures in the newspapers? "We need international efforts, help from the consumer countries," Husain began, elaborating on the day's theme, and concluding, "If the Russians with all their might cannot control poppy production in Afghanistan, how can we do anything with our meager resources?"

At any rate, the official figures announced that day were that the number in acres of poppies growing in Pakistan had been reduced from 81,000 in 1979 to 6,300 in 1983. The amount of heroin reported seized in 1982 was 5,264 pounds, and in the first five months of 1983, 2,750 pounds. That compared with 175 pounds seized in the United States during 1982.

"We accept their statistics, and we accept their assurances that whatever corruption is involved in the narcotics trade has not reached high levels of local law enforcement or government," said an official of the United States Drug Enforcement Administration assigned to work with Pakistani officials to train policemen and customs inspectors. The training had been successful enough that our teenage sons could not move through airports in the country without having themselves and their backpacks handled and sifted for ten, sometimes fifteen minutes and watching helplessly while inspectors did things like slowly squeeze out the contents of a tube of toothpaste onto the floor. "We have to believe them. It is their country, and we're not here to question their honesty," the American agent said. "If we think they are corrupt, we try to remember that what we call corruption is not what they call corruption. The perks of power are greater over here than in Washington. Maybe those perks include a piece of the heroin business, but we are not in a position to say that."

"It's going to get a lot worse out here before it gets better.

There are fortunes to be made, being made," another agent added. "We can put pressure on the Pakistanis, and they respond because of the big $3.2 billion, the economic and military aid they're getting from us. But whatever they say, it's not a top law-enforcement priority with them. Not yet. No country really cares when they think drugs are just an American problem. Why should they? If we want to kill ourselves, that's our problem, not theirs. What we are trying to do is convince them that it is a Pakistani problem."

And it was becoming one.

By the middle of 1983, the government had opened twenty heroin addiction treatment centers around the country. Addicts coming into the Quetta Treatment Centre said that there were more than twenty-five *saqi khanas*—"heroin dens"—open all day and all night in the city's bazaars and estimated that about one thousand men visited them daily. The heroin sold and used in those dens and others around the country, especially in the slums of Karachi, was amazingly cheap (and strong) by Western standards. The price of a gram of heroin in the streets, I was told, varied between 20 and 60 rupees—$1.50 to $4.50. The price for the same weight in the United States might be $100. But the purity of the heroin in the U.S. would be about 5 percent; in Pakistan it could be as high as 70 percent.

The number of heroin addicts in Pakistan, by then, was estimated, by the Americans, to be fifty thousand. But no one really knew. Many of the new addicts were not new at all; they were opium addicts who switched to heroin because it was cheaper and more plentiful as the suppliers in the Khyber region switched their basic product. Most of those addicts were not of great concern to the government or anyone else. They were the dregs of a very poor society, concentrated in slums like Lyari in Karachi. In that district of a half-million people, according to Dr. Yasmin Ahmad of the Karachi Civil Hospital, at least 70 percent of the male population was addicted to one or more drugs—usually hashish or opium but, more and more, heroin.

Addicts in Lyari, though, never caused much official (or elite) concern in Pakistan, no more than addicts in Harlem did in the United States before drug addiction spread to upper-class and middle-class American families in the 1960s. The concern in Pakistan began only toward the end of 1982 when it became apparent that the best and the brightest of young Pakistan, particularly in Lahore, were using heroin, by sprinkling the powder into ordinary cigarettes, or cooking it on small squares of tin foil and using straws to inhale the fumes.

It should not have been a surprising thing in a society of stunning boredom, a puritan society becoming more puritan under military rulers who were banning movies, books, music and anything else that might offend a devout middle-aged Muslim in uniform. The reaction to that new addiction reflected the mindset of those rulers. A report of the Pakistan Narcotics Control Board in March of 1983 said:

"The most disturbing experience at the [Karachi] Civil Hospital in the summer of 1982 was to find a medical student suffering from heroin addiction. Here was a man of science who should know more about the destructive qualities of heroin than, say, the rickshaw driver Shafi, yet he was still lured into the heroin trap. He picked up the habit not from the drivers and mechanics of Lyari, but from his colleagues. Heroin, the deadliest of drugs, is making inroads in the youth culture worldwide, just as pop music and hashish did in an earlier era."

12

BREAD
BUT
NO CIRCUSES

The military puritanism of Pakistan was the kind that had trouble seeing a difference between heroin and "pop music"—and it was the dangers of pop music that Chief Martial Law Administrator Muhammad Zia-ul-Haq had specifically told me he wanted to protect his people against. He was doing a good job; his people were being protected against many things that might make them relax or laugh.

A scene on Eid-ul-Fitr, the day after the end of Ramazan, the Holy Month of fasting, stuck in my mind the entire time I was in Pakistan. We were driving in the morning to Lake Rawal, the large, placid artificial lake between Islamabad and Rawalpindi, and we were overtaken by a large truck painted like a carousel with brightly colored animals and birds, calligraphic religious symbols and, incongruously, snowy Alpine scenes—another exhibit of the rolling folk art of Pakistan—and the truck was filled with teenagers, mostly girls who seemed to be thirteen or fourteen years old. They gaily waved and cheered as they passed on. There were more than twenty of them, packed onto the flatbed of the open truck. They pulled up just ahead of us at the lake and began leaping off, *shalwar kameezes* flying as they ran laughing toward the water for a picnic. Laughing. I rarely saw joy like that in Pakistan.

163

There was no entertainment in the country, or very little of it. I saw a hundred men gather one Friday before prayers in Abbottabad, north of Rawalpindi, to watch a trained bear. The big, dusty animal danced or lumbered about while his owner played a flute. Then it wrestled with the owner's young son, the boy and the bear rolling around in the dust. The men mainly just stared; there was not much smiling.

Just watching had to do as entertainment. Men sat by the roads in the mountains watching the trucks and buses go by, with people rocking and bumping and holding on for life itself on the roofs and sides and any little place they could squeeze in a hand or foot. The bright paintings and elaborate patterns of hammered tin and small mirrors on those vehicles seemed to advertise a people who knew how to celebrate life, but there was not the waving and yelling back and forth you might expect between the roadside and the road. I had the uncomfortable feeling that the spectators were waiting for something else to happen. An accident, perhaps—as the crowd at a circus is thrilled by the possibility of death from the trapezes.

The trapeze analogy seemed appropriate. The trucks and buses sped wildly on roads cut, not all that deeply, into the sides of the mountains, with spectacular views—and drops—off to the side. The driving was skillful and brave in Pakistan. We hired drivers, always, not only because they were cheap, but because I did not believe I could survive behind the wheel the way cars raced toward each other before swerving on narrow, broken roads. Foreigners closed their eyes and explained it to each other by mentioning hashish or *Inshallah*, the fatalism of men who believed their life was in God's hands—or, perhaps, they had a certain lack of respect for the power and danger of machines. Whatever the reasons, psychological or physical, the men and their machines regularly self-destructed, quite spectacularly. I kept track of small items about the buses in the English-language papers for a couple of weeks in July. Leaving aside the routine run of crashes and runnings-over, there were these: On July 1, twelve persons were killed and eight injured when two buses collided between Lahore and Rawalpindi. On July 2, seven people were killed and nineteen injured when a bus from Rawalpindi to Malot missed a turn on a blind curve and dropped three hundred feet into a dry riverbed; on July 3, three people were killed and twenty-five injured when a bus from Sialkot to Pasrur crashed into a tree; on July 9, four persons were killed and twenty injured when a bus from Mianchuan to Chickawatni overturned; on July 21, thirty-eight persons were killed and sixteen injured when a bus from Dir to Peshawar plunged one thousand feet into a gorge.

Death and violence, accidental and purposeful, did seem to be just around many bends in Pakistan. And not just on the roads. Sudden violence. Some of it came during inevitable skirmishes along the borders of affluence and poverty. Some of it was the bloody work of bandits—dacoits—roaming the countryside generation after generation. But an extraordinary amount of it also came out of the normal comings and bumpings of ordinary people. There was enormous pent-up energy in Pakistan—positive and negative—and some of it was expressed in savagery. The English-language press used murder reports almost as fillers, and the Urdu and regional newspapers carried even more of the same kind of story.

Here was some of the daily report in the July 9 issue of *Dawn*, Karachi's English daily: "Dacoit Sadiq Taddani, Sind terror, opened fire in the Civil Hospital premises at the time of *sehri* in an attempt to kill an indoor patient. Two persons were seriously injured." . . . "Local police were alerted on Friday after an alleged notorious outlaw, Bashira, released from the jail recently, went on firing sprees in two areas of the city." . . . "A young man, father of an infant, was stabbed to death by two men of his hometown in the Zoological Gardens on Friday. They worked together in a plastics factory and had a quarrel." . . . "A four-man armed gang of *dacoits* was smashed by a special squad of the special interrogation cell of the Civil Lines Division in a Defense Housing Society cemetery on Thursday night. [The gang was led by] Nadir Khan, 25, who after committing eight robberies, went to perform *Haj*"—the pilgrimage to Mecca. "On his return, he went to the tribal areas, bought 2,000 rounds of ammunition and formed a gang. . . ."

Two days later, the daily report in *The Muslim* of a not particularly unusual day in the area of the city of Multan began with these two items:

"A violent mob of citizens of Mailsi protested against the mis-
behavior of the S.H.O. [police] towards a *pakoro* vendor by
surrounding the police station for six hours.

"Khushi-Muhammad Luqmon was frying *pakoro* after Asr prayers
at Dharampurk Chowk. S.H.O. Malik Muhammad Ramzan came
to him and scolded him for violating the sanctity of Ramazan
. . . he kicked a frypan burning the vendor with boiling oil. The
vendor is in critical condition at the local hospital."

"According to details available here, Abdul Rehman of Moza
Baggreen paid 2,000 rupees to a schoolmaster, Hussain Bakhsh,
to get his uncle, Ghulam Rasool, appointed. The schoolmaster
neither repaid the amount, nor did he get him appointed. When
Abdul Rehman demanded his money, the accused's mother abused
them, and the schoolmaster threw a brick at Abdul Aziz's head.

"In the meantime, the victim's relations . . . joined the argument. The accused's brother, Imam Bakhsh, opened fire, resulting in which Ghulam Rasool died on the spot and Abdul Aziz
succumbed to his injuries on the way to the hospital."

Some of that violence existed just because there was a great
deal of the Wild, Wild West in wild parts of the East—and that
was there long before there was anything called the American
West. But there also seemed to be rage surging just below the
passive surface of daily life everywhere in Pakistan. A young man
in Karachi, carrying sand on his donkey, somehow intruded on
a property line one day and in minutes two men were dead and
two more were dying. Incidents like that sometimes seemed
about to happen everywhere. There was no way to blow off steam.
If the puritanical military regime of Zia-ul-Haq has been competent at providing bread to the people, it also has allowed no
circuses. It seemed quite possible to me that the next big one
might be the crazed entertainment of riotous rebellion.

Pakistanis were starved for entertainment—and younger people for excitement of any kind. "Nothing to do, no place to go"—
the lament of children everywhere was heard again and again in
conversations with adults. One of the imperatives of military rule
was the elimination of politics as an entertainment form. The
repression came just when any people find politics most exciting
and engaging, in the beginning years of a democracy. Rallies,
speeches, marches, elections—those celebrations had really be-

gun in Pakistan less than forty years ago, but they were stopped and stopped again by the military. There was a passion beneath the nation's passivity, and I had the feeling it would burst out: there would be dancing or blood in the streets—or both at the same time.

Zia's personal devotion might take him to ecstasy—in the great local traditions of Sufism, or what startled Westerners first called Whirling Dervishes—but most of his countrymen did not seem to be getting much fun out of his clumsy attempts to replace new entertainments with old religion. "There is nothing to do here," said a taxi driver standing idly outside the Karachi Sheraton. "There is no fun here anymore. They took it for Islam."

Inside the hotel, bored Westerners, mostly communications and aviation technicians and consultants staying for a few days of repairs and planning, acted as if they were prisoners in their rooms. In the hotel, they could buy liquor or beer after filling out a form swearing they were not Muslims and having their passports photostated to prove they were not Pakistanis. And they could watch television, including a channel of censored films.

"We apologize for not being able to schedule a larger number of films as we have to remain confined to those movies which are approved by the government of Pakistan": that sign was posted in each room of the Karachi Sheraton.

The approved list when I was there listed five films, all American: *The Bad News Bears, The Birds, Thoroughly Modern Millie, The Front Page,* and *For Whom the Bell Tolls*—all cut by military censors. I was surprised one night to realize how short *For Whom the Bell Tolls* was without hugging and kissing. Anytime a man and a woman, even if they were father and daughter, came close to each other in the censored American and British movies and television series, the screen suddenly turned gray and snowy, and buzzy static replaced the sound track. It was hilarious, at first, then maddening. So was the mysterious process of the selection of what could be seen by travelers. Gary Cooper and Ingrid Bergman heroically—and, in the uncut version, romantically—fighting a civil war was not what I would approve if I were running a military dictatorship. Particularly when anything that moved electronically on a screen anywhere was being taped on the video cassette recorders Pakistanis were bringing back from overseas—and then being shown around the country in homes temporarily converted into neighborhood or village theaters. In his room around the corner at the Holiday Inn, William Stevens, a *New York Times* correspondent visiting from Delhi, was even more amused to see the film *Cromwell*. He found the puritanical English military ruler of the seventeenth century a plausible role model for General Zia—except that Zia had already ruled for a year more than Oliver Cromwell.

The television that Pakistanis saw at home (in electrified areas) was one government channel dominated by discussion programs featuring *maulanas* and other religious figures and live concerts of local music. The favorite shot seemed to be the fade, with pictures of the singer on stage fading into a picture of the audience and then back again. One Sunday night in Peshawar, we watched a *maulana* in Western dress, a well-known "evangelist," earnestly arguing for a more Islamic system of taxation than the Western systems used in Pakistan: "Your money is not yours. Your house is not yours. Your time is not yours. Your children are not yours. They are His. . . ."

One foreign dramatic show, almost always American, was shown each night—I often saw "Little House on the Prairie" subtitled in Urdu—along with a half-hour of semieducational programming featuring animals or landscape. I say "semieducational" because one of the regulars in that time slot was a syndicated American show called "You Asked for It!" with an impressionist named Rich Little. I saw people gathered at a set one night in Abbottabad watching Little imitate John Wayne.

There were also two half-hours of news each night—in Urdu and English—read by a man and a woman in traditional dress. Like Rich Little, the news programs were imitations—of the American originals. There was film, but every piece I saw was silent footage of President Zia smiling and shaking hands across his own country or Japan or wherever he happened to be. The broadcasts were literally the American form without content. The female anchor, with lowered veil, appeared in front of a still photograph of the appointed Federal Council one evening and said:

"Eighteen members spoke at the Ninth Session of the Majlis-

e-Shura today. They were Hajii Saifallah, Alla Rahmat Ullah As-
had, Begum Saliba Shakil. . . ."

What they said was never reported.

The next item, with a picture of the United Nations General
Assembly in the background was:

"The General Assembly of the United Nations will convene on
20 September in New York. The subjects to be discussed are:
disarmament, hunger, human rights. . . ."

Then would come the announcement of the orders of the day:

"The government announced today a program for the housing
and rehabilitation of deserving beggars."

Pakistan, it seemed, like the United States, had undeserving
and deserving poor. They could often be seen gathered around
giant movie theaters, featuring the limited product of Pakistan's
young film industry. "In all about 75 films were produced during
the year," reported the annual Pakistan Year Book of 1982–83:
"Most of them were not up to the mark while some of them were
simply moneymakers without any cinematic and artistic qualities.
This was all due to weak scripts."

No matter how weak the films, Pakistanis crowded for hours
to pay 10 rupees to see them, even if what they really wanted
were Indian movies, which were banned by the government. The
romantic melodramas from India, which traveled across the tense
Indo-Pak border more easily than people could, were the most
important product of the private theaters made possible by video
cassette recorders. It was not propaganda that made the Indian
films subversive; it was all that kissing. Public embracing between
sexes, live or on film, was against Section 294 PPC, Pakistan
Public Code. Men embraced cheek to cheek everywhere, but in
Ramalia on July 24, Khadim Hussain and his girlfriend, Sufia
Khatoon, were taken to jail for doing it, a violation of Section
294.

So, legally, Pakistanis saw only certain entertainment. The
regime's idea of entertainment was the documentary being prepared on the life of Muhammad Ali Jinnah. It was emphasized
about once a week that the Jinnah project was totally unrelated
to the worldwide success of the British film *Gandhi*, which de-
picted the *Quaid-i-Azam* as something of a sour old fellow. On

July 9, it was announced that the script of the film on the *Quaid* had been sent to the Cabinet for review before being submitted to General Zia for final approval. Dictators, it seemed, could indulge all human fantasies including the compulsion, in warm climates, toward screenwriting.

VCR theaters were big (illegal) business, and while I was there, police began a series of raids on stores and shops selling Indian films and, it was said, pornography. Four hundred and seventy-five cassettes were seized in Islamabad alone on one day, August 6. By that night, I assumed, they were either being copied for generals or were back on sale at a higher price to cover the handling costs of the police. That was when municipal officials announced that the average take for a home VCR theater was 6,000 rupees a month—not bad considering that the recorder itself cost 25,000 rupees.

The video game parlors were the other new entertainment in town. They had begun appearing in the spring of 1983—three in Islamabad and the "Star Trek" parlor out on the Khyber Road. The price was 2 rupees a game—16 cents.

"Video games attracted large crowds during last weekend," *The Muslim* reported on July 4. "There are some who noticed that during the Holy Month of Ramazan the elders are also turning to these games as the offices are closed much before the scheduled time. . . . Some wonder at the fact that in the very capital of a country where Martial Law is imposed for the last six years, and where all the high-ups of the law-enforcing authority sit and live, people are daring enough to indulge in an unlawful business."

The article went on to question whether the games were just an "amusing diversion" or another "trap" of the West.

Both.

Video games beat hanging out. And there was an awful lot of hanging out in the cities, at places like "*paan* shops," where flavored betel nuts were sold. Young men, in jeans and checkered shirts or in *shalwar kameezes* and sandals, lounged for hours at night, leaning against cars or lampposts. Talking. Occasionally pushing each other around for a moment. Nothing to do. "I don't know why they're not smart enough to allow more entertainment, more diversions," a Lahore businessman said of his military rulers. "The only thing that is saving them from riots is that the tough boys are all away working in the Gulf states. The young men who would carry the disturbances that would overthrow Zia just aren't in the country right now."

"Each time I'm here, there are fewer and fewer smiles," said an American who was in Pakistan for a few months, a man who had lived his life on the subcontinent and was working in India. "Pakistan used to be a happy, proud place. Now, I just can't wait to get back to India."

I did not have that kind of experience to check my own perceptions against. But I had been on both sides of the border between Pakistan and India in both Kashmir in the north and the Punjab in the south. The contrast was striking. Not only did I see women on the Indian side, but I saw women's faces, and there were smiles on those faces.

Smiles were rarer in Pakistan. I remembered them after a while—like one on my first full day in Peshawar. I was going through the International Red Cross Hospital for Afghan wounded with its director, Dr. Ian McPherson, a New Zealander. We were just coming around a corner when a young nurse ran into us, literally, with dark hair flying. "Excuse me! Excuse me!" she said, laughing merrily, and went on her way.

"Happy," I said, warmed by the encounter.

"She's Egyptian," McPherson said. I looked puzzled at that, and he added, "You're going to find that Pakistanis don't laugh very much."

And I did. I also heard a lot of foreigners blame that dourness on Islamization or on Islam itself. Well, the laughing nurse was a Muslim. When I crossed from Azad Kashmir, in Pakistan, to Kashmir in India—across the disputed northeastern border established after the countries' 1948 war—the people looked the same. They should have, because many of them were cousins of Pakistanis and practiced the same religion. But they smiled a lot more. The reason that there was less and less smiling in Pakistan, I came to think, had less to do with their God than with their rulers. It was not fun living in a police state.

THE
POLICE STATE

13

"Operation Fairplay" was the code name of the coup of July 5, 1977, in Pakistan. The country had been in chaos; most commerce and industry had been suspended in favor of demonstrations against Prime Minister Zulfiqar Ali Bhutto and the rigged national elections of the spring. "The sole aim of the Armed Forces is to organize free and fair elections, whereupon power will be transferred to the elected representatives of the people," announced Muhammad Zia-ul-Haq, the Chief of Staff of the army and the spokesman for the group of generals which had planned the takeover and the house arrest of the prime minister. General Zia pledged that the elections would be held within ninety days.

Very little was known about Zia-ul-Haq when he took power. He had been a Bhutto appointee and loyalist, and it was widely assumed, in the country and outside, that he was not much more than a front man acting, perhaps even reluctantly, for other military leaders. Even after six years in power, not much was known about him—at least not by the standards of Western democracies with free, inquiring presses and leaders driven to be liked and so fascinated with themselves that they assume their people can't get enough of the daily details of their lives and thoughts.

The best public information on the man who ran the ninth-largest country in the world was his three-page official biography. I also had some access to classified profiles prepared by the United States Department of State and American intelligence agencies. In terms of usable facts—"God, these things are short on information," said an American official reading the classified documents for me in Washington—the official Pakistani version was a little better.

"Fortified by deep religious conviction, animated by the spirit of Islam and sustained by an ideological 'elan vital,' General Mohammad Zia-ul-Haq, President and Chief Martial Law Administrator of Pakistan, is an enlightened and progressive soldier-statesman. . . ." That was the beginning of the Pakistani biography, and it did not lose its enthusiasm for the subject as it went on.

He was born in Jullundur, now part of the East Punjab of India, on August 12, 1924, the son of an army chaplain—a lower-middle-class *maulana* in uniform. He graduated from Saint Stephen's College in Delhi, one of the better English colleges in India, and was commissioned as a cavalry officer in 1945, serving in Burma, Malaya and Java at the end of World War II. "An upright officer, suave, austere and dignified," said the official biography.

The man I met did fit that description. We first spoke on August 8, on board the *hajj* ship, *Safina-e-Abid*—"The Ship of Those Who Make Their Prayers"—among 1,127 white-clad pilgrims about to leave the port of Karachi on the first leg of the journey to the Holy City of Mecca. Zia had come in a Mercedes-Benz limousine to the docks to bid the pilgrims farewell—*hajji* trips were sponsored and regulated by the government—and he walked out of his way to us when he saw my wife and me, the only foreigners at the ceremony.

"Are you going on the ship, too?" he said with a smile. We laughed at the small joke and introduced ourselves, then chatted about the devotion of the people around us. He made a point of reaching out to shake Cathy's hand—a Western gesture disdained, sometimes in disgust, by many Muslim men. He was charming and, I thought, extraordinarily relaxed for a man who must have just finished reading his morning paper. The lead story of that morning's *Dawn* was the overthrow of a military dictator because of his public and excessive religiosity, Gen. Efrain Rios Montt of Guatemala, a zealous evangelical Protestant.

After Partition, according to his biography, Lieutenant Zia, who was already married, attended Pakistan Army Staff College at Quetta and later served as an instructor at the college. In 1963 he attended the United States Command and General Staff College at Fort Leavenworth, Kansas. In the 1965 war between India and Pakistan, he was a lieutenant colonel, although it was not clear from official biographies whether or not he served in combat. The question of whether or not he led troops in combat in 1970 when he was in Jordan had long been debated—in whispers—in Pakistan. Whatever he was doing, he was in Jordan as an adviser to the Royal Army of King Hussein from 1969 to 1971, including the "Black September" of 1970, when Jordanian troops attacked the Palestine Liberation Organization, driving Yassir Arafat and his troops into Lebanon.

General Zia, who was by then a brigadier, returned to Pakistan—after the 1971 war with India over East Pakistan—and worked his way up the command ladder until he was plucked from its second rung and elevated to Chief of Staff by Bhutto in 1976. It was generally believed that Bhutto selected Zia because he found him dull, dedicated, loyal and controllable. For that misjudgment, the prime minister's body became one of many literally and figuratively littering the landscape. Many men paid the full price for underrating Muhammad Zia-ul-Haq.

Although his wife and children did not normally appear in public and were not named in his official biography, Zia had been married for more than thirty years and was, by all accounts, a devoted family man—especially, it was said, to a retarded teenaged daughter. He had four other children—two daughters, one married to an accountant in London, the other in medical school, and two sons, one a medical student and the other a Bank of America executive trainee in Bahrain. "He is a keen sportsman— plays tennis and golf," the official biography stated, ". . . a book lover and, of course, a man of the world.

"When he is out of uniform—sporting *shalwar* and *kameez*, and Peshawari *chappals* [the long shirt, baggy pants and sandals]—he drops the mask of officer and engages you in animating dialogue," that biography continued. "To make a point he would put his hands on his chest, gesticulate with both hands, fix his penetrating eyes on you and raise his voice to a lively pitch. You can enter into a contentious debate with him, at the Chief of Staff's house, criticize him for his acts of omission and commission, and he would react with his characteristic smile . . . he leaves you disarmed."

I quote all that because I found it, basically, to be true. The General was animated, forceful and charming on the half-dozen occasions I saw him. We did engage in a bit of uncontentious debate—about the role of women in a modern society—and I was disarmed by his manner if not his arguments. I thought he was an attractive man, personally. Not handsome. With his waxed mustache, slicked-back hair parted in the middle and deep-set, hooded eyes, Zia looked almost exactly like the villains who went "Hch! Heh! Heh! Now, my lovely . . . ," in old melodramas about mortgages being due. All he needed was a black cape and a high silk hat.

His personal manner was an enormous asset to General Zia. He projected humility, bowing slightly when he walked or stood— he was about five feet eight inches tall and portly—and wearing the *shalwar kameez*, a poor man's dress which Bhutto had popularized. "He's mastered the style of the double handshake and the triple embrace," said a newspaper reporter sarcastically, referring to the almost obsequious Pakistani formal greeting of gentle bows, hugs and handshakes in which the more powerful of the shakers holds the other man's right hand in both of his own. All of that, which took a bit of time, was usually accompanied by a long gaze from those "penetrating eyes."

"But, you know, he seems an honest bloke," said a Lahore businessman—a common but pertinent comment. Pakistanis were not used to honesty in soldiers or statesmen or soldier-statesmen. Zia's apparent religiosity was generally admired, and many people believed or hoped that personal honesty was part of that. The worst rumors about him were that he secretly owned land near Sacramento, California, where many Punjabis, particularly members of the Ararain tribe, from which Zia is descended, have settled as vegetable farmers.

Zia did not excite passion, which meant he was not personally hated, even by people who hated the regime. "Well, this is not tough martial law," said Maulana Fazl-ur-Rehman, who had been a leader in organizing anti-Bhutto demonstrations in Lahore in 1977. "I am against this martial law, but it is not the worst we have seen in this country. So, they're arresting political leaders; what regime wouldn't do that? The political people almost destroyed our country." That, like the little tributes to Zia's character, was a sort of comment I heard over and over again. That surprised me, but then I had never lived under dictatorship. "This is relatively benign," a political scientist in the same city told me. "Bhutto was more repressive. He created his own secret police and no one felt safe. He kept the courts in operation, but what he would do was arrest people and have them taken to the tribal territories where the laws wouldn't apply. Kidnaped them."

"There are no midnight knocks on the door," Zia boasted in one speech in August of 1983. That was not true, I discovered, but apparently there were not as many late-night raids as there had been when Bhutto, the democrat, controlled the police. Such things were relative. "Consider the fact that there was more democratic freedom available during the British rule than people have now," said a writer in a Karachi magazine, *Herald*, in about the frankest commentary I read inside Pakistan. "Not to be ignored is the fact that the Quaid-i-Azam [Muhammad Ali Jinnah, the founder of Pakistan] was never taken to jail."

Political arrests under Zia reached as many as three thousand in two weeks, according to Amnesty International, which, in 1982, asked the United Nations to investigate reports of "gross and reliably attested violations of human rights" in Pakistan. The international human rights group also asserted that it had received reports of rising numbers of executions—twenty in December 1982 alone—which were not being publicly announced. (That was a long time after the peak of Zia's often-stated concerns about terrorism. There had been more statements, it seemed, than incidents since 1981 and early 1982 when Al Zulfiqar, a terrorist group which included Zulfiqar Ali Bhutto's son, Murtaza, claimed credit for a PIA hijacking and an attempt to fire a small missile at a plane taking off from Islamabad with General Zia aboard.) "Amnesty International continued to receive detailed accounts of beatings and torture of prisoners detained in prisons and police stations," the organization reported at the end of 1982. "Among methods reported to Amnesty International were beatings with rubber hoses, clubs and sticks; being hung upside down by a rope; deprivation of sleep; burning and pulling of hairs; and electric shocks."

A police state is a police state. In the village of Chitral, north of Peshawar, foreigners were required to register at the police station as soon as they arrived. I was not sure why, but that procedure had been followed since British times. That didn't bother me, except for the time it took, and I was used to that in Pakistan. I sat for a while on the bench in front of the rough table in a small, square, bare room with nothing on the wall except a calendar. There seemed to be thousands of identical rooms in Pakistan. The table held the usual mix of rubber stamps, paperweights, pins and small stacks of mimeographed forms and reports.

"Special Report" was the title of the sheet on top of one stack. Someone had obviously been careless in leaving that on the registration desk. It was numbered 720 B and was a description of correspondence between politicians talking about elections and using the phrase, which was underlined, "Returning the country to its people." The report went on, quoting extensively from letters—and, I believed, telephone calls—before urging vigilance in surveillance of dangerous people. I was debating whether or not to turn to the next page, when a policeman came in and cheerfully asked about our children. He had seen them with us when we arrived at the Aerodrome.

The long arm of the lawless reached deep into the private lives of Pakistanis. In one case I knew of, a man who was a relative of someone on Zia's staff became involved in a fight involving both love and money with a middle-level federal bureaucrat. The bureaucrat, it seemed, liked to tell jokes about Zia, and someone, a friend who was a journalist, asked him to write some of them down. The paper with the jokes was taken to the Chief of Staff's house the next day, and whatever happened inside, the bureaucrat was dismissed immediately. He was told Zia had personally ordered it after reading the indiscreet comments of the night before.

"Supremacy belongs to the people," the Chief Martial Law

Administrator had said when scheduling elections, but his religious interpretation then and at other times more forcefully stressed the supremacy of God, and of His instrument in Pakistan, Muhammad Zia-ul-Haq. In his latest scheduling of elections, announced on August 12, 1983, Zia linked his plans and His plan:

"I want to make clear to my countrymen, companions, friends, admirers and all others that the measures I have announced today will *inshallah* be completed, under my supervision. . . .

"I have given the election program. But there are certain elements which want to sabotage it. They have already exposed themselves and people and the government are well aware of them. If the vested interests want to disrupt the election program or disturb law and order they will be dealt with with a heavy hand. I have said this so clearly that there remains no doubt about it.

"Remember the miscreant is not liked by Islam. . . . The Quran has clearly stated that the disruptionist and the miscreant should be given exemplary punishment. They disobey Allah and His Prophet when they try to create disruptions in the country. Such peoples are the enemies of Islam and the Islamic Republic of Pakistan."

But there was no law to disrupt in Pakistan. Zia-ul-Haq, ruling in the name of God, destroyed the rule of law in his country. People had no enforceable rights; each and every Pakistani was subject to the military courts. Courts of junior officers—courts without laws or lawyers, judgments without judges or appeals. The "heavy hand" was at its weightiest in 1979, according to the estimates of international organizations, when it directed two thousand political executions. Directives replaced laws, and they were changed to fit the crime as new crimes were defined or invented.

If necessary, a certain politeness was practiced in slapping or pushing people around. The military rulers, periodically sensitive to foreign criticism, particularly American criticism, used jail and executions only as a last resort. Professors did not have to be arrested for speaking out. They could simply be declared subject to the Conduct Rules for Civil Servants, which was what was done with the faculty of Punjab University in Lahore on July 9, 1983. From that date, it was a crime for them or members of their family to discuss politics. They could vote, if there was anything to vote on, but it would be illegal for them to reveal afterward how they had voted or, beforehand, how they planned to vote.

The day before, in Quetta, the governor of Baluchistan, Lt. Gen. Rahlmauddin Khan, announced that there would be Local Body Elections in the province—elections of town and village councils—but that members of political parties would be ineligible to run. Ten days later he issued a second directive ordering that the candidates who did run would be barred from holding public meetings.

"There is no compromise now in the politics of Pakistan," said a professor in Islamabad. "They say people like me are of 'The Left'—which means 'disorder' or, worse, 'communism' here. I am not Left. Most of the dissenters are not. I'm in the Western democratic tradition, but with this government there is no place for me because there can be no center. It becomes the army against everybody else; of course, everyone else doesn't have guns. It all comes down to that—the guns."

On the day the Punjab University faculty was silenced, the Executive Council of the Rawalpindi Union of Journalists passed a resolution expressing "deep concern over growing interference and harassment . . . of working journalists at the hands of various government and security agencies." It seemed that plainclothesmen of some sort, carloads of them, had taken to following reporters back to their offices or homes after government press conferences. Sometimes the reporters' cars would be forced off the road and they would be interrogated on what they planned to write—and pushed around a bit in the process.

It was hard for me to imagine what the bully boys could be so upset about. The tone for a lot of the Pakistani press was set by the government-owned *Pakistan Times*, which reported the Chief Martial Law Administrator's reception on the morning of the Eid-ul-Fitr holiday this way:

"An unprecedented number of people streamed into the Chief of Army Staff House to pay [Eid] respects to President Mohammad Zia-ul-Haq and offer their greetings to him on Tuesday. Surely, this speaks of the kind of popular image which the President enjoys in the eyes of the public. And the President, too, received them with open arms—a gesture which is untraceable in Pakistan history. While receiving them, the President's smiling face smacked of the humility which is peculiar to him. . . ."

The *Times*, which I had seen cited and heard talked of seriously outside Pakistan, was interesting reading inside the country because it seemed to have lost many connections with reality, domestic or foreign. But other newspapers, including the better independently owned journals, often got lost, too, after dancing and dodging day after day, sometimes quite bravely, through the alleys of government misinformation, censorship and financial coercion. On July 7, 1983, under a Washington dateline, *Dawn*, usually a pretty good paper, reported this:

"King Hussein of Jordan has expressed willingness to participate in the Middle East process with Israel, claimed a United States dignitary currently visiting Israel. . . .

"Hubert Humphrey, a renowned American politician and once Vice President of the United States, said King Hussein had asked him to convey to Israel . . ."

Each day after that, I looked for a correction and some acknowledgment that Hubert Humphrey had been dead for five years or, better yet, a follow-up analyzing the Holy Land's latest resurrection. But the incident was never mentioned again.

Despite blunders like that and a style both flowery and pompous—Pakistanis rarely used a short word when something polysyllabic was available—I developed real admiration for the more independent newspapermen of the country. They tried to communicate real news to the nation in code. There were understandings between editors and readers pointing the way to detours around government lying and censorship. "It's a tightrope walk every day," said the publisher of an important Urdu journal. "We try to stay fair to our readers but also stay in existence. Over time, they come to understand that if there's a demonstration or riot someplace in the provinces and we play it a little higher on the front page or give it a larger headline than the facts in the story would seem to warrant, that means that we know the situation is worse than the government is admitting."

During the early years of this Martial Law administration, there was strict official censorship. Officers with blue pencils were assigned to every newsroom in the country. But after 1982, the press was allowed, or ordered, to operate under "self-censor-ship"—a process that several journalists told me was more ef-fective than the clumsy interference of army captains and lieu-tenants who could often be fooled by clever reporters and editors.

"They figured out that they had the key to turn us on and off," one editor told me, making a motion with his hand as if he were locking a door. "Advertisements and paper. Sixty percent of the advertising in my paper and every other paper is from the gov-ernment; even the ads for the banks and PIA [Pakistan Inter-national Airlines] come to us through the PID, the Press Infor-mation Department. And we need an import license to buy newsprint. If they don't like what we're printing, we have no paper to print it on. They've showed what they could do. *Jang* is the largest newspaper, the richest in the country. But when *Jang* began reporting too much about demonstrations in Karachi, they brought it to its knees in just a couple of weeks. The owners had to beg for the ads and the paper; they were almost out of business. And they pulled the ads from *The Muslim*—it was giving too much attention to Shia demands last year—until they started to go along."

"What does 'go along' mean?" I asked.

"Usually it means ignoring or playing down civil disorder," the editor said, "or not reporting a speech or a statement by a pol-itician. Actually it's supposed to be illegal to mention the parties, but we can do some of that. It's all very civilized. I get a call from someone I know over at PID. He'll mention some trouble in Sind, for instance, and say, 'Please, we would be obliged if you would . . .' Sometimes the call is the first indication we have of how bad something really is. But it means that I am on notice that I'm playing with the future of the newspaper—and my family."

"How do you know what's going on?" I asked. "How do you get your news?"

"Real news?" he said. "I get real news the same way everybody does—the BBC."

The role of the news service of British Broadcasting Corpo-ration—and to a much lesser extent, the Voice of America, which had less reach and credibility—in a police state was a revelation to me. Day after day, in conversation after conversation, the background of what people were talking about came from the twice-daily BBC broadcasts in English and Urdu. Among the first things a foreigner was told was that neither the water nor the news in Pakistan were healthy, and friendly instructions followed on boiling the water for a half-hour and then adding "pinky" (potassium permanganate), and on how to adjust short-wave radios to get the BBC in different weather or different hours of daylight and night. One of the reliable amusements among diplomats in Islamabad was to watch the government, through newspapers, respond to BBC reports that had never been reported in the Pakistani press.

The words of Begum Nusrat Bhutto, the former prime minister's widow who periodically spoke out on Pakistani issues from exile in Europe, were rarely reported inside the country. But those statements, reported by the BBC, would produce, as if from nowhere, vague PID attacks on "certain elements." The attacks on information from outside became a little more specific, though, when demonstrations for elections began in the Sind in the summer of 1983. Anti-Zia rallies were sometimes disrupted by the tough boys of *Zia Himayat Tehriq*—an organized pro-Zia group—which one day charged a group of foreign journalists in Larkana. The gang was trying to get its many hands on Mark Tully, the Urdu-speaking BBC correspondent best known in Pakistan. Tully was not there, and police came into the crowd and took away eight foreign reporters. The reporters demanded to be let go to get back into the crowd until a bomb was thrown at them, injuring four of the police.

The controlled press—particularly, in English, *The Pakistan Times*—was used almost daily in attempts to make military rule seem legitimate. The Martial Law Administration not only pretended that the appointed advisory Federal Council, the Majlis-e-Shura, was the equivalent of an elected legislative body, but there were press campaigns to project the rump parliament as more representative than any elected one could be.

"The Federal Council though entirely nominated more often than not looks more independent than what we know of elected ones, . . ." reported the *Times*, which had seen precious little of elected ones over the years.

Then, as President Zia was planning to deliver on a promise that he had made on Independence Day, August 14, 1982—that, within a year, he would propose a plan to return the country to civilian rule—the *Times* published, on August 4, 1983, a series of articles under the headline "Sovereignty Comes Before Democracy."

"Democracy is a mere farce . . . comes the verdict with an obvious finality from a majority of people." That was the lead on what the paper called "public opinion polling [of] . . . the general run of masses." It was not scientific polling but a collection of interviews with Pakistanis who supported Zia. Men like Muhammad Shariff, president of the government-controlled Pakistan National Federation of Trade Unions, who offered the opinion that, "People opposed to the ideology of Pakistan or Islam have no right to live in this country."

"The people," the *Times* continued, "by and large believe that the president, Mohammad Zia-ul-Haq, should not rush to hand over power in a hurry and thus consign the entire nation to the winds of confrontation, polarization and uncertainty."

That was the party line, and it had been for long enough to be included in the official biography Zia had prepared to help justify or, at least, explain his *coup d'état*. "The Constitution has not been abrogated; only the operation of some of its provisions has been held in abeyance," said the biography. "In fact, President Zia remains committed to his solemn declaration that . . . 'the survival of this country lies in democracy.' But his dilemma obviously is between short-term commitment to seek the verdict of the ballot box and larger commitment to restore suitable conditions for a stable democratic order with an Islamic orientation."

His dilemma, in fact, was to find the time and a way to legitimize his rule. He had been quite resourceful about that. He managed through his years of power to maintain the acrimonious divisions between the political parties—with the minority parties more *against* the PPP than *for* elections—while attempting to create new political leaders and political structures through nonpartisan local elections and the appointed Federal Council. He won the backing or, at least, the tolerance of most of the Western world—most importantly the United States—by welcoming the millions of Afghan refugees. And he even tried his luck with the general masses; in April of 1983 he spoke at an announced rally at Gujranwala, which has a population of about 400,000, and drew

a crowd of about 100,000 people. That was not considered good
enough: the carnival spectacle of political rallies was often enough
to attract many hundreds of thousands of people in that part of
the world. During election campaigns in India—and in Pakistan
between military regimes—hundreds of thousands of people
sometimes traveled for a day or days to hear political speeches.

But as skillful as Zia was, his time seemed to be running out.
Despite their access to force, there has always been something
inherently weak about military governments. Because there was
usually very little behind the front line of guns, dictators like Zia
had to be very careful about any domestic confrontations in which
the line might be breached or confronted for too long; once it
was, soldiers tended to change sides or throw away their uniforms. Zia had been very quick to back down at the first marches
of mass movement. When Shia Muslims began demonstrating
against Islamic taxation based on Sunni Muslim interpretations,
their demands were met within days. Further, because unelected
governments could rarely trade on either the demonstrated support or the constituent pressures of their nations, they were
notoriously weak in negotiations with outsiders. Dictators generally had no voting numbers and few cheers to demonstrate that
great numbers of people would back their decisions. All they had
was the power to impose their will on great numbers, but in that
power there was inherent weakness.

"A government without a popular base can't really take a stand
against anyone else," said Mubashir Hasan, the former Finance
Minister, when he was arguing against what he sees as the restructuring of Pakistan's economy and national goals by the demands of its creditors, the United States, the International Monetary Fund and the World Bank. "Dictatorships have the power
to impose the policies demanded by outsiders in the short term.
What they don't have is the power to say 'No' to the U.S. or the
banks. The 'strong' are actually weak because they are not being
pushed by local interests and constituencies."

"The military regimes look strong, but they are weak because
of the constant uncertainty about the future," said another Pakistani, an executive in Lahore. "We have an interim, imposed
stability, and that may have been necessary. But after a while,
there was uncertainty about the future. No one knew what would

happen next. That has great impact on commerce and industry. Pakistan's capital went overseas when Bhutto began nationalizing everything, and it's still there, the money Pakistan needs to build a modern state. The time has come for a change, for a government with prospects for the future. The changeover should have happened about two years ago. But you, the United States, won't allow that. The Americans are what's sustaining Zia now."

However weak the military government actually was by 1983, and however dependent on foreign support, it had been a great deal stronger than its opposition, the politicians of Pakistan, for several years. In the beginning, after the coup of July 5, 1977, Martial Law was, for all practical purposes, welcomed by the nine parties that had formed the Pakistan National Alliance to oppose the Pakistan People's Party in the March elections. The parties—from the secularist National Democratic Party, which sought autonomy for Baluchistan and the North-West Frontier Province, to the fundamentalist Jamatt-i-Islami—embraced the enemy of their enemy, Prime Minister Bhutto. Party leaders—except for Pakistan People's Party representatives—served in Zia's cabinets until the day he officially dissolved the parties and banned all political activity in September of 1979.

It was only with the formation of the Movement for the Restoration of Democracy (MRD) in March of 1981 by eight parties, including the PPP, that some line was finally drawn between representative democracy and military rule. By the time I arrived in the summer of 1983, the military was still firmly in charge, but there was a sense of counting down the days to a crisis.

Even the Majlis-e-Shura, General Zia-ul-Haq's handpicked Federal Council, was showing signs of restlessness. Its 1983 meetings began in Islamabad on July 23, in the hall that had been the home of the old, elected Federal Assembly. Three weeks of debate were scheduled before the General and Chief Martial Law Administrator was to announce his plan for Islamized democracy, the shift of power back to elected civilians. The chairman of the council, Fida Muhammad Khan, opened the second session on July 25 by saying, rather ceremoniously, that Muhammad Ali Jinnah had founded Pakistan on the ideals of democracy and the slogan *"La Ilaha Illullah . . ."*—"There is but one God. . . ."

Before he could finish, he was interrupted by a *maulana*, Samiul Haq, who shouted, "Democracy cannot have precedence over *La Ilaha Illullah.* . . ."

The *maulana*, in turn, was shouted down by a lawyer from Karachi, Obaidur Rahman, who yelled, "How would you know? When we were fighting for Pakistan. . . ." There was pandemonium—the men in English-cut suits and ties against the men in robes and turbans and lamb's wool hats. For seven minutes the chairman called for order while lawyers and *maulanas* called each other names. The Majlis, it seemed, appointed or not, might be about to show some of the independence *The Pakistan Times* always said it had.

As much as it could, it did. The next few days were not good ones for the *maulanas*. More and more the debates began to be dominated by calls for democracy, for a return to the 1973 Constitution—*all* the provisions of the Constitution—which had established a parliamentary system with a prime minister, an elected National Assembly and an indirectly elected Senate.

By July 26, *The Muslim* was reporting: "There seems to be a consensus emerging in the Majlis-e-Shura during the debate on the future system of government that the 1973 Constitution was a sacred document that should not be touched under any circumstances." Five days after that, *Dawn* reported: "The weight of the speeches was making minimum changes in the 1973 Constitution as it was a unanimous document and had the consensus of the major political parties of the country."

The arrests began three days later, on August 3. The same newspapers, in small headlines and stories over the next eight days, reported roundups of leaders of the defunct political parties and their equally illegal alliance, the Movement to Restore Democracy (MRD): "20 Political Workers Detained" . . . "12 Political Leaders Held in Quetta" . . . "6 MRD Workers Held in NWFP" . . . "MRD Student Body Chief's Father Arrested."

The idea was to make sure that no one was out there making trouble on August 12. President Muhammad Zia-ul-Haq, Chief Martial Law Administrator of Pakistan, was about to speak to the nation on democracy.

14

HOW WE PICK
OUR FRIENDS

"It will be our endeavor, *Inshallah*, to present a positive frame-work for a Muslim state and a truly Islamic system before the nation by next Independence Day," President and Chief Martial Law Administrator Muhammad Zia-ul-Haq had said as he raised the flag of Pakistan at the country's Independence Day celebration on August 14, 1982.

One year later, on August 12, 1983, he kept that promise in an address to the Majlis-e-Shura. The flags and buntings had gone up around the old National Assembly Hall in the center of Islamabad the day before. And the tents. Islamabad is a city of great marble buildings and army tents. Soldiers guard the public buildings and embassies, and the guards pitch their tents just outside the gates or doorways of their assigned posts and just live there. Attendance at the speech was by engraved invitation only, and the small crowd of diplomats, journalists and VVIPs, about one hundred of us, were settled in place in the balcony ten minutes before the President was scheduled to appear at 4 P.M.—and he would be on time because like all the world's leaders he was subject to the tyranny of live television. The broadcast was scheduled for four o'clock and that was when it began.

The President appeared then, dressed in a long gray tunic. The two hundred and fifty Majlis members, in the many costumes of the country or in Western-style business suits, sat in eleven rows in front of him—ten rows of men and a row of women. Behind him was a huge oil portrait of the *Quaid-i-Azam*, Muhammad Ali Jinnah—in a three-piece Western suit.

After a prayer, Zia said he had been following the debates of the Majlis and the discussions of democracy in the newspapers. He had also, he said, studied and consulted with scholars but had been most impressed by the opinions and ideas of "the public." "The men who matter perhaps do not give them any importance because they are illiterate or semi-literate," he said. But he intended to, and he had determined that they wanted one thing above all others—Islamic government. He had determined that, he said, by reading letters to the editor in the newspapers.

He spoke for one hour and fifty minutes. Dictators speak for as long as they want; speeches in democracies are much shorter.

He had spoken for almost an hour on his own interpretations of Pakistan's history and his commitment to Islam and Islamic government. He emphasized, to applause, that "there is no scope for theocracy or papacy in Islam." That was the signal that there would be no direct or institutionalized religious control in government—the President's Islamic Ideology Council had proposed veto power for itself over all law-making—and on the floor of the Majlis the delegates in suits exchanged smiles, and a couple gave thumbs-up signs. The Western diplomats, sitting to my left in the balcony, were smiling, too. They had been warning Zia privately that any formal religious government would convince many foreign governments, particularly the American government, that Pakistan was going the way of Iran.

Then came the great, sustained applause of the afternoon. "After contemplation and exchanges of views with my colleagues on this subject, I have come to the conclusion that at this time there are three options open to us: first, that the 1973 Constitution be restored . . ."

The applause stopped Zia, but it was premature.

When he was able to continue, he said ". . . be restored as it is. Second, that after the abrogation of this Constitution, a new Constitution be framed and the approval of the people be sought on it. And third, that the 1973 Constitution be enforced after necessary amendments."

He picked the third option. Then he sketchily outlined the "necessary amendments"—destroying the parliamentary form of the Constitution in favor of an indirectly elected president with almost dictatorial powers and a "National Security Council" of military chiefs with the power to declare states of "emergency." The President would be chosen by elected members of the National Assembly and then would have the power to select and dismiss prime ministers and to accept or reject legislation voted by the Assembly.

"Zia," the man next to me said. "He wants to be the civilian President."

"When?" When would the elections be held? The whispering was spreading in the gallery and on the floor of the council. "At present if you hold elections"—Zia had finally said the word— "it would do nothing but endanger the security of the country. . . . I can't allow anyone to play havoc with the destiny of the country merely to hold elections."

The speech had been going on for an hour and fifteen minutes. He was listing what he called the new "rules and regulations" of the "elections." Some members of the Assembly would be appointed rather than elected to ensure that religious leaders and certain professional groups would be represented. "You should know that personal canvassing is not permissible according to Islam"; "One person, one vote," he said—but a quota of women members would be maintained, apparently one in ten.

When? When? Finally: "Local body elections this year" without political parties (the elections had, in fact, already been scheduled). "Provincial Assembly elections next year" and then "National Assembly elections, all to be completed . . . by March 23, 1985."

Eighteen months. Elections in eighteen months. A Pakistani reporter took out a pocket calculator. When Zia-ul-Haq took power he had promised elections in ninety days. That was six years, one month and seven days ago. So, based on that, Zia intended to stay in power for—*bip! bip! bip!* on the calculator— for another thirty-six years, seven months and twelve days.

"Martial law will be lifted when the democratic process is restored after this phased election program. I have given the election program. . . ." Then he warned of the "heavy hand" Islam held ready to raise against miscreants and disrupters.

" 'Oh, the believers, obey God, His Prophets and those who are in power amongst you,' " Zia quoted from the Holy Quran. Then he quoted the words of the Prophet: " 'He who obeyed me, verily obeyed the Lord, and he who disobeyed me verily disobeyed the Lord. And he who obeys his Amir' "—ruler— " 'verily obeys me and he who disobeys his Amir verily disobeys me.' "

The audience was getting a bit weary as Zia passed the hour-and-a-half mark. But they seemed pleased. The diplomats across the aisle seemed content. The Americans were smiling and nodding to each other. This was "democratization"—a plan for return to civilian rule. Better than many people had expected. Diplomatic service in a far place made one a gradualist; the Americans out there took what they thought they could get. "This isn't America . . . ," "Our personal views of human rights may be a little too esoteric . . ."—standard lines from Foreign Service officers. So our diplomats were applauding—with a certain enthusiasm.

I was making a list as Zia spoke. What did he represent to us?

Order. Order was most important to the United States. Stability—same thing. Efficiency—relative efficiency. Sovereignty. Economic Growth—some of that.

What was he against? Another list.

Change. The Rule of Law. Political Freedoms. Majority Rule. Freedom of Choice. Democracy. Hope.

Add "Bread," and a couple of other material things, and the second list could be the agenda of the illiterate masses—the ones who didn't write letters to the editor. On top of that second list I put *"Them."*

On top of the first list, I put *"Us."*

Zia was our guy. The Chief Martial Law Administrator was pursuing the American agenda as well as he could in that part of the world. "We," Mohammad Zia-ul-Haq and the Americans, were trying to find a structure of government out there that "they," the few dissidents and the many of the illiterate masses, would accept as democracy—and that the government of the United States could represent as somehow consistent with American values back home. At the operational level out there, in Pakistan, I found the Americans to be intelligent, practical people representing as well as they could what they understood to be the interests and official policies of the government of the United States of America. They admired and talked of capability and efficiency and technique, not of principles, ideas or commitments. Diplomacy in practice, after all, was not a business of abstractions. There was a job to be done, and when you work with the people you have to work with, you get along. You begin to understand their problems, perhaps a little too well.

"I tried to make it clear every day that our support was not for a man or a system, but for a country and a people," said the American ambassador, Ronald Spiers. "We made every effort to maintain contact with the opposition to Zia, although I must say I found him to be a more estimable man than most of the politicians.

"What could we do?" he said. "I asked politicians and intellectuals the same question each time; I asked it a hundred times: 'Should we refuse to give economic aid to the military government—particularly the aid that goes to rural areas—should we stop that aid? Should we stop the military aid to your country?' Only one man of the hundred answered 'yes.'

"Then they would ask me why the Americans did not support elections. Why didn't we force Zia to hold elections?

"Leaving aside the question of whether we actually had the power to do that, my answer was: 'That would be gross interference in the internal affairs of your country. Elections are your problem.' "

Spiers was a very good ambassador. I was not the only person who thought that, because in August he was appointed Under Secretary of State for Management. He had, I was told, been quietly effective in persuading President Zia to slow down his country's nuclear research and to speed up efforts toward conciliation with India. He had also organized, without public embarrassment, functioning support and weapons supply systems for the *Majahideen* fighting the Soviets inside Afghanistan. Zia, he thought, was honest and sincere and the best America could do out there. "Consultive dictator" was a phrase I was told the ambassador used privately to describe the ruler of Pakistan.

That ruler began to end his "democratization" speech by praising the youth of the country—"I am sure they will develop a keen sense of discipline among themselves and follow the right track"—and then praised the military—"They . . . rescued the country from a bloody catastrophe"—before closing with these words:

"Now let us attend to the rights of man, and save humanity, as in it lies the blessings of God, and if we are able to gain the blessings of God, then we will succeed in this world and hereafter.

"Pakistan Paindabad!" Pakistan Forever!

In Washington, the spokesman for the U.S. State Department, Alan Romberg, said: "We welcome any step toward ending Martial Law and returning Pakistan to elected government." Asked about reports of demonstrations against the delaying of elections for another year and a half, Romberg added: "I would note that there have been reports that indicate there were also demonstrations in favor of the President's plan."

"Our great ideal, the United States of America and its human rights," an important Pakistani reporter said the next morning with a mix of sarcasm and bitterness in his voice. A cynical man. We were whispering because we were in the President's house— the rambling British relic in Rawalpindi that was used before the new marble monument was built in Islamabad—waiting for him to appear for his press conference after the speech to the nation. "Then when the Americans come, they talk just like the people who are killing us. You don't have to take us too seriously, do you? We're a frightened people. I'm frightened. Someone talks here, someone gets picked up and they're beaten up. The better classes here aren't used to that. We get the message, and each of us knows we can't take it. We're too soft. If we get together to do something, they've always got new and better tear gas from the Americans. From you."

Zia-ul-Haq came in, relieving my discomfort. I didn't know what to say, and then I didn't have to say anything. There were fifty reporters in the room, almost half of them from other countries, and the questions from foreigners, in English, concentrated

on two subjects: Was Zia planning to be the new President?
Would political parties be allowed to contest elections?

The questions were repeated again and again in different forms,
but Zia, smiling easily, stuck to his two answers:

"I've never anticipated anything for myself, although I've anticipated many things for Pakistan. So, I'll leave that part out.

"We'll wait and see about the parties."

The session went on and on, for more than an hour, with fewer
questions and longer and longer answers. The President was
enjoying himself. "My only ambition in life is to complete the
process of Islamization so that there will be no turning back.
. . . The Islamization process is a lifetime job. . . . The general
society itself—you have to put their aims and objectives straight
on the path of righteousness. And that's what I call Islamization."

That was the morning, as Zia rambled on more and more
enthusiastically, that I thought the General might believe that
his next promotion would put him among the gods. The humility
and self-control I had been told about seemed to be slipping.
"He used to be sensitive to world opinion, particularly American
opinion," said my friend, the Pakistani journalist. "Bhutto was,
too. That was always one of our protections: 'The Americans want
elections. The Americans don't like torture. . . .' But Zia doesn't
have to worry about the world anymore. He thinks the Americans
will support whatever he does."

I was sure there were limits. At least, I hoped there were. But
I was getting more than a little sick of myself sitting and listening
politely as one official American after another told me I had to
understand Zia's problems. I thought it was enough that they
obviously did—empathized with him, in fact—and if I were a
more honest man, I would have jumped up and said: "Look,
there's nobody here but us Americans. We know what's going
on here. This is a police state. Our charming friend is a thug.
Maybe we do have to play ball with people like him, but we
don't have to like it. This is what we're supposed to be against."

It was easy for me to play the outraged innocent. I did not
have to represent anything larger than myself—and myself was
soon going home. Perhaps that was just as well, because except
for the occasional visitor, there did not seem to be much call

anymore for American innocence abroad. We, official America, seemed quite comfortable with what we were doing in Pakistan— and, I'm sure, in many other places. If Chief Martial Law Administrator Zia-ul-Haq decided one day that he'd just about had it with the BBC's broadcasting real news into his country and stirring up the elites and the illiterates, we might understand his problems well enough to give him the electronic gear to jam those broadcasts. Or, more likely, we would lend him the money to buy the equipment from some nice company in Southern California.

That was the elephant in the window.

That phrase came up during dinner after Zia's August 12 speech. The American reporters all repaired to the homely comforts of the United States Government Employees Association house, "The American Club," an oasis stocked with Budweiser beer, A-1 Steak Sauce, videotapes of old "M.A.S.H." episodes and reminders of home that I vowed never to make fun of again. William Stevens of *The New York Times* had come up from Delhi to cover the event and, as we ate water buffalo steaks with A-1, told of his wonder the first time he looked out his kitchen window and saw an elephant going by. "Then," he said, "you get used to it."

We began talking about writing books, and someone said to Stevens that he should write about what he had seen of ordinary life in India: "The idea is not to take what you see for granted. Don't get used to it. Remember the elephant in the window."

The conversation drifted back to Zia's speech. And to his problems. Then someone said: "He's destroyed the rule of law in this country and we're behind him. That's the elephant in the window!"

We, the Americans at that table, were hardly naïve; we were supposed to be hard-bitten, hard-drinking foreign correspondents, but we acted as if we were shocked to be considered part of what was happening in Pakistan. Americans didn't push people around; it didn't seem fair not to be loved.

"The Great American Unpopularity" was the title of a short essay writen by Mubashir Hasan, the Finance Minister under Bhutto and a former general secretary of the Pakistan People's Party, in *The Muslim* of November 12, 1982. He began by recalling what happened two years before when he told his *chowk-idar*—the servant who watched over his house—that a Pakistan International Airlines plane had crashed in Saudi Arabia:

"He hailed from the remote hills of the Hazara district. An illiterate and an introvert, he hardly knew anyone in the city. He did not even go to a mosque but said his prayers at home. He was not interested in politics at any level. But his spontaneous reaction to the news of the disaster was: 'America must have shot it down with a rocket.' "

Hasan concluded that mistrust of the United States was deep "in the very guts of our people." He wrote, then, of his days as a young Indian student in the United States at the end of World War II, of seeing the Statue of Liberty for the first time through the eyes of an angry young colonial—and of thrilling to stories of Patrick Henry and Benjamin Franklin, "the freedom fighter."

But thirty-five years later:

"Think of an unpopular and corrupt administration in a Third World Country, unabashedly violating human rights, and you find the United States patronizing it. Think of a government with a strong anti-American posture and you find the masses rallying behind it. . . .

"The great pity of it is that the people of America as individuals and in small groups are as fair and decent as they ever were. They are better educated and better able to articulate the higher values of humankind than their preceding generations. During the last four decades they made perceptible progress in their country towards integration of black people, extending social security systems, securing extension of rights for women. . . . They have perhaps the freest press in the world . . . yet for a large part of the world the freedom of Americans in America spells misery and oppression and poverty."

Whatever his own view of the world almost four decades after entering New York harbor—Hasan, I thought, was not above the temptation to kick America around because we're usually secure enough or insular enough to take it respectfully—what he wrote was objectively true. That hurt. Not because I felt a need for people everywhere to love America or to like me because I am an American. I didn't think we needed excessive affection in Pakistan. It was enough that our ideas were loved—from freedom to rampant materialism, and I didn't think there was great distance between those two. America, the very concept of our place—the ideas—was swirling within the forces of modernism that were changing Pakistan and Pakistanis. As much as modernism was American, Pakistan would become American, someday. That seemed a long time away to me, but inevitable. We only had to stand for what we have always stood for to be seen as something a little better than the people behind the rockets by illiterate *chowkidars* and the people behind the tear gas by people who wanted the freedom to assemble to demand justice.

But, in fact, we were not in their country in the interest of justice or of ideas. "U.S. Interests and Objectives Regarding Pakistan" was the title of the private briefing that the State Department and the Defense Department provided for the House Foreign Affairs Committee on March 9, 1983, and the briefers were direct and clear:

"South and Southwest Asia is a region of critical strategic importance to the United States, presently threatened by Soviet expansionism. We are committed to the search for peace and stability within the region and to the safeguarding of the supply of oil critical to U.S. and Western security."

That was the interest: the oil tankers that went through the Arabian Sea from the Persian Gulf to the West. They steamed out there somewhere beyond the shipbreakers working at Gadani Beach. Behind the beaches, the deserts of Baluchistan stretched into Iran and Afghanistan and, finally, almost one thousand miles away, to the borders of the Union of Soviet Socialist Republics.

It was our interest to control that territory—"safeguarding the sea lanes" was the term of superpower art—and, therefore, to control the people on it, even the nomads I saw through the mists of dust and time behind Gadani. But that was close to impossible. Pakistan was difficult to define, much less to control; there was too much of it, too many places, too many eras. Perhaps, somehow, it could be conquered, but the United States did not have the national will to do that. We are materialists; it is our way to buy what we want. But as rich as the United States is, we can't buy nations of 100 million people.

But we could buy the army and the air force and the navy of Pakistan. And we did that. It was not difficult to make them

financially and technologically dependent on us—for everything
from F-16s and M-48s to the tuition for the children of generals
in universities at Palo Alto, California, and Boston, Massachu-
setts. We bought control of the people who controlled the military. Therefore, it was in the American interest for the military
to rule Pakistan.

It was a bargain. The official figure for six years was $3.2 billion
in military and economic aid. The real figure might be 25 percent
higher, but most of that money would be recycled. Some of it
was loans. Most of it had to be used to buy American equipment.
And even college tuitions for generals' sons and daughters brought
those dollars back to the U.S.A.

The strategy of buying generals and doing our best to help
keep them in power seemed to have worked relatively well for
the United States over years of contesting the Soviet Union for
every strategic acre on the globe—and some not so strategic. We
managed to shore up our friends in power for as long as possible
before "losing" one country or another—as we will inevitably
"lose" Pakistan by the standards of controlling the actions of its
government—and then moving on to bases, political and military,
someplace nearby. Perhaps when we did not have such direct
influence in Pakistan, Iran would again be open to a little American persuasion—as Pakistan was open in 1980, after almost a
decade of tense relations with the United States because of our
neutrality in the Indo-Pak war of 1971. We needed Pakistan again
after we "lost" Iran.

I left Pakistan with no doubt that there would be a contest
over its poor acres. A couple of weeks in the Afghan refugee
camps and the hospitals of Peshawar were evidence enough for
me that there would be a battle—political, economic, social and
military—for those lands and that the Soviet Union would be
doing anything it could get away with in a few years to push
down on Pakistan. In ten years, when Afghanistan was forcibly
stabilized? Twenty years? The time and the firing did seem closer
than I had imagined before I sat in Chitral that night in July—
when Major Mulk, the district refugee commissioner, said: "It's
all very far away from you in America, isn't it? But it is not as
far as you think."

But when that day and that confrontation came—unless before

that, by some miracle of will and common sense, the United States and the Soviet Union rationalized their worldwide competition—Muhammad Zia-ul-Haq would not be able to mobilize the people of Pakistan to resist in his name or the name of the United States of America. Zia cannot save us. And we could not save him if his nation rose up against him and his army. The Pakistan army had been ineffective in the past; with American aid but without public support it was likely to be well equipped and ineffective.

American aid—the dollars I saw being distributed and used in Zia's Pakistan—would probably end up buying only equipment and a little time. I, at least, did not get the impression that it was either buying commitment or doing a great deal for the un-uniformed people of Pakistan, illiterate or elite.

"The people who run this country, from Zia on down, are the scared generation," said a member of the elite, a prominent but younger Pakistani. "They grew up as a minority in India, and they had reason to be frightened. All of them, like Zia, are only comfortable when they have a patron—the British, the Americans, the Russians. They do not believe Pakistan can make it on its own. Well, I've seen two wars with India, dismemberment of part of my country, two popular movements against military regimes and I'm only thirty-two years old. But I think we have become politically mature. And this country, Pakistan, is going to be taken over soon by people who are different." He smiled at what he knew he was going to say next. "I was born free."

But most of his countrymen in the nation he aspired to help lead were born prisoners of ignorance, the ignorance of generations that sometimes stretched back centuries. They were people who could not read or write and did not understand the connection between filth and disease. With good intentions or bad, foreigners could help change life for most Pakistanis only marginally—very little, very slowly. "I sometimes wonder what I'm doing here," the Canadian agricultural technician I met had said as we shared forbidden French wine on Bastille Day. "You can only teach people what they're ready to learn and what they want to learn."

What these people were ready to learn seemed pretty basic to me—to read and write, to keep their water supply clean and to wash their hands. What they wanted to learn, the lessons being brought home by the remittance workers in the oil fields, were the modern ways of convenience and pleasure that their betters decried as materialism. That was about where modernization was for most of the people of Pakistan, the illiterate masses.

Traveling in Pakistan, going back and forth in time, from Gadani Beach to Karachi, from Islamabad to Bumburet, I often found myself thinking that the United States would do better—and perhaps could do no better than—using its great wealth, which was partly my wealth, just to offer some aid that was not glorious, complicated or obviously geopolitical: such as figuring out how Pakistanis could teach each other basic sanitation and basic literacy, in any language. The shame of the United States of America was that in countries under American patronage, Pakistan for one, the illiterate masses stayed illiterate, while in countries under Soviet patronage—Cuba and Nicaragua were examples—people learned to read and write within one generation.

Why were we the ones afraid of literacy, the great carrier of modernization? I was astounded to realize that my country, the one place and people who had the most to gain materially and spiritually from the modernization of other peoples, was out there resisting the most fundamental linkage between the old and the new—literacy. If we believed in the way we lived and in what we said, in our own history and spirit, then it was in our interest for people to hear it and understand it—to know more of the ways of the modern world and the ideas that created and moved people like us, living on another level of time. Instead, we picked friends in Pakistan whose stated commitment to modernization emphasized technology over ideas, as if they could somehow use one and reject the other. Zia-ul-Haq, with perception more influenced by Machiavelli than Muhammad, understood that the more things Pakistanis knew, the worse things were going to be for the military. Mass illiteracy served the purpose of our friends in Pakistan—preservation of the *status quo* of the masses—and the United States seemed quite comfortable in going along with that. The government of Pakistan at least announced rural literacy programs, even if the programs might be run from the 350 phantom schools the British Council discovered—or, rather, didn't discover—in the rural Punjab. But the government of the United

States had specifically eliminated such programs from its $3.2 billion, five-year aid program to Pakistan.

"We were just spread too thin to bother with things like literacy," an official of the U.S. Agency for International Development told me after I returned to the United States. "Why don't you try someone over at the World Bank or the United Nations? That's more their style."

Our style, usually, was dollars for defense. But those dollars, too—at least half of the $3.2 billion total—preserved the *status quo*. In many ways it was not only that the military aid helped keep the military in power. There was also the suspicion among many American officials—angry and dismayed, in private—that after Zia and the other generals had painted crescent moons on all their new American planes and tanks, their guns would be pointed east—not north toward America's enemy Russia, but toward Pakistan's old enemy, India.

"The most discouraging thing out here," said one of those Americans, "has been trying to nudge the Pakistanis a little closer to the Indians. And vice versa for our people in Delhi. It's not only a question of preventing future wars between them and preventing a nuclear arms race between them—which, God knows, is important enough—but it's the realization that real security against Soviet expansionism in this part of the world finally depends on some sort of alliance between Pakistan and India. Pakistan alone could be vulnerable, unless you assume we are going into combat with them, which is ridiculous. But, together, Pakistan and India are too much for even a superpower to confront.

"But generals remember the last war, and with these two countries there has been more than one last war. We can't crack the old attitudes."

Preserving the *status quo* for as long as possible, holding off the future, it seemed, was the most likely historic role and purpose of the rule of Zia-ul-Haq. Talking of elections and of the transfer of power to civilians was generally seen as a trick of the trade of military dictatorship. There was a pervasive and debilitating sense while I was there that General Zia had no intention of voluntarily giving up power. Few people, Pakistani or foreign, believed that the men in uniforms intended to hold national elections they did not control, or would allow the installation of a government they did not control. So pressure was building as modern power-sharing was forcibly retarded. "Time bomb" was a cliché, but clichés come into being because they describe people, places and situations so well—and Pakistan was a time bomb, a nation and a country that might be shattered by explosions if its internal pressures were not vented into the building of a truly modern state.

From the day it was founded—or quickly put together by outsiders—there has been constant danger that Pakistan could shatter into modern feudalism. That could happen in much of the Third World as postcolonial Western models prove inadequate to governing the life of illiterate masses—with changing military or military-based regimes proclaiming central government while violence was the real arbiter of political power in the countryside. Then, for a long time, no matter what was written in constitutions and on maps, great areas of Pakistan's rural regions and urban slums would be little more than fiefdoms—going their own traditional ways under an ignored national flag and faraway superpower patronage. That disintegration beginning, perhaps, with separatist movements in Baluchistan and Khyber would be encouraged and helped along by the Soviet Union as it happened, but it has already been encouraged by American backing of the historical national domination by the military elites of the Punjab. The United States seemed blindly committed to working on Pakistan from the top down while change in the society was almost certainly coming from the bottom up.

The masses of Pakistan, reacting against the confused identification of military government and semifeudal economics with modern democratic capitalism, might effect change by moving toward socialism. It could begin with some of the excitement of overthrowing the military; celebrations in the name of bread and democracy ending with, perhaps, most of the bindings of authoritarianism, if not totalitarianism. Although it may be heresy for an American to say it, socialism might offer the most stable and most modern and modernizing future for Pakistan over the next couple of decades, at least. I could not conceive of a lot of short-term benefits in an American-model economic system for most of the people of Pakistan most of the time. American ideas of competition and free enterprise superimposed on an almost feudal economy—on the shipbreaking of Gadani Beach and the agricultural fiefdoms of the Sind and the Punjab—would be an irrational choice for the people of Pakistan at this stage of the country's development, if they actually, and ever, had a voice in their own destinies. While Pakistan struggled through the agony of modernization, some sort of socialism probably would have much more to offer the country's awakening materialists. They could get some education, maybe some land, if feudal power bases were cracked by a central government that could survive without holding back the power-sharing, materialist forces of the future.

But if there were to be a progression to socialism in Pakistan, I did not think that it would follow patterns familiar to Karl Marx, nor would it lead eventually to communism—neither the pure form he envisoned in Western industrial nations nor the totalitarian perversion practiced and propagated by the Soviet Union. Marx was wrong about the future of India when he welcomed colonialism in 1853, thinking that the British presence could only result in "the annihilation of old Asiatic society, and the laying of the material foundations of Western society in Asia . . . [and] dissolve the hereditary divisions of labor." Then, according to his theories, would come capitalism, socialism and, finally, communism.

Men and events in India—and the part of it which became Pakistan—have never managed to accommodate Western analysis and prognosis. The place and the people have never been kind to observers and visitors seeking truth or the power that comes from seeing the future. Another earnest representative of that discouraging heritage, I ended my visit believing that Pakistan would not become a Communist country—certainly the Muslims would resist communism mightily—and the Pakistani national history would probably stand Marxist theory on its head. Pakistan with intelligent help from its friends—which, I hoped, would include the United States and India—could progress fairly quickly from feudalism through the jumbled ancient and modern systems that I found, to a few generations of socialism before joining the modern world one day with a mixed economy of centralized planning and free enterprise and a democratic political system compatible with the arguments of Islam.

The next period of Pakistan's history, after almost forty years of attempting to impose Western political and economic systems on the nation with both successes and failures, will decide whether or not there will be an Islamic Republic, whether Pakistan can survive as an independent country. Three choices—or projections, since choice might not be much of a factor in what happens next—seemed obvious to me after I was there: (1) more military dictatorship, increasingly repressive; (2) the violent chaos of the shattering of the country put on maps by British arrogance and Muslim determination; (3) a fumbling, frustrating attempt to create a Pakistan that was more modern and more democratic—economically as well as politically—and more socialist than the countries usually favored by American patronage.

The third option should be the American option. Pakistan has to find its own way to the future. Generations of modernization breaking up the patterns of the past into some sort of centralized socialist (not communist) state seemed to me to be necessary to create and shape the forces—literacy and rampant materialism among them—that could bring Pakistan into the modern world with a productive economic system that was more free than slave and a democracy that existed off the pages of abrogated constitutions. Pakistanis whose materialist cravings for bread and books were satisfied would be a pretty good bet to begin moving toward abstractions like the rule of law, political freedom, majority rule, social justice and economic opportunity. Those abstractions are what America was supposed to be about—and if we are wrong in thinking that people anywhere in the world with some security and some education will choose and fight for those things for themselves and their children, then we are wrong about everything. If that is not what being an American means, then we should not worry too much about trying to make the world think and act like Americans, because we are doomed to fail in our missions in Pakistan and many other places.

I came back thinking that if the United States does fail this time in Pakistan—if we "lose" Pakistan—it will not be because American ideas and ideals were not worthy but because we didn't seem to think that illiterate masses were worthy of sharing them. Without those ideas what were we out there? Just more people with guns.

It seemed possible that we would not be there much longer. On the day after going to the Presidency for Independence Day and sipping tea with President Zia-ul-Haq, we went to Lahore for, among other things, dinner with a young lawyer and his wife. She came alone. He had been arrested that day. The police had come at two-thirty that morning, but he had already gone into hiding. Then, in the afternoon, with other attorneys, he had appeared at the Lohari Gate, volunteering to be arrested for violating orders against public assembly. "Courting arrest" was the local term. He was taken to a jail in a smaller city, a day's drive away. There would be no trial; probably he would be released in quieter times. Perhaps a few months.

"Police started mild caning to disperse the crowd at the gate," reported *Dawn*. Still, the dinner was pleasant. The woman spoke of her impressions, generally favorable, of a recent trip to the United States. When we were leaving she said: "You realize, don't you, that when Zia goes, you go?"

By the next day, four days after General Zia had announced that there would be no national elections for another year and a half, thousands of protestors were in jail. There were riots in a dozen cities.

EPILOGUE

The riots of August 1983, continued through November. More than 600 people were killed and there were about 7,000 arrests. But fortunately for the martial law administration of General Muhammad Zia-ul-Haq, almost all the demonstrations and violence were confined to one province, the Sind. Many politicians and lawyers "courted arrest" in Lahore, but the masses of Punjab did not go into the streets. The regime survived.

Zia also uncovered—and survived—a coup attempt by younger army officers who were apparently plotting his assassination. Forty officers were arrested and another 300 interrogated early in January 1984, after a false-bottomed truck carrying arms was seized in Lahore after crossing the border from India.

If such things concerned the general, he certainly didn't show it when we met again in June of that year. He assured me that he intended to honor his pledge to hold national elections before March of 1985, perhaps as early as the fall of 1984. Some sort of elections. He was, though, refusing to commit himself on when the election would be held, or who would be allowed to run, or what kind of campaigning would be permitted. Already, on May 8, the government had banned reporting of political news. The "defunct" political parties—as newspapers had been identifying them since 1979—disappeared altogether, at least journalistically.

"The Government wants a peaceful atmosphere so it can carry out its programs," announced the Press Information Department. "Excessive reporting would be likely to create political confusion."

In his den at home in Rawalpindi, a manly room of guns and swords and autographed photographs of the leaders of the world, I asked Zia about the order, and he said: "The press in Pakistan is as free as it can be under the present circumstances. . . . You can see for yourself how strong and committed journalism is today in Pakistan. Except for a little check I've introduced—of not reporting political news. I don't want people to waste their time on politics at the present time. The parties are practically dormant anyway. This is a military regime."

We talked for a while about that and Zia said he believed Pakistanis were as free as any people in the world. Then, occasionally, he would amend that to: "A man in Pakisan is as free as he can be."

What did "can be" mean?

"We have not developed the political character which the nations of the West, particularly the United States, have acquired in two hundred years," he answered. "We are only thirty-five years old. At the present time, when you talk of politics in Pakistan, you talk of polarization. People gun for each other's throats. Politics is a matter of personal vengeance.

"My experience shows that you need not only a strong man or strong men, but you need a very strong and stable structure to govern this country. Irrespective of what people think abroad, the government, the leaders, must guide the people. They must lead and not be led. The moment you start playing to street power, the moment you start playing to the gallery—well, you can't afford that here. This is not the United States of America."

So only the faces seemed to have changed in the year I was away. The United States had a new ambassador in Islamabad, Deane Hinton, a veteran of diplomatic service in El Savador, who talked in tougher tones than Ronald Spires had, but said about the same things: "When we have a choice, of course we prefer that our friends have democratic governments. We think people should participate in the process. But we have to deal with the government in power."

Then dealing with geopolitics and talking of the Soviet Union, Hinton said, "The Bear has indigestion in Afghanistan." He was smiling.

By the spring of 1984, the number of Soviet troops in Afghanistan had reached more than 125,000; the Red Army had been fighting there for longer than it fought in World War II. But they seemed willing to pay the price for a slow, humiliating victory—by then the number of Soviet dead exceeded 6,000 men with another 15,000 or so wounded. On the Afghan side, the numbers were staggering for a nation that had 15 million people in 1979: hundreds of thousands were dead and the number of refugees in Pakistan and Iran seemed to be approaching five million.

Most of the new refugees, I was told, were going into Iran as the Soviets escalated their attacks from the air on villages and farms in the western regions of Afghanistan. They were continuing to depopulate the country, terrorizing the people and destroying the food supply. Believing Mao Tse-tung's dictum that guerrilla fighters must be as fish swimming in the rivers of the people, the Soviets were trying to drain the rivers.

"The helicopters came every day in the morning and the evening, six or nine at a time," I was told by a woman named Nazirjan, a refugee who had just crossed the border into Pakistan, about 50 miles north of Peshawar. She was among 2,500 Afghans: women, old men and children, who had walked for three days and nights from areas called Kama and Gushtas, six fertile valleys near Jillalabad. There were fifty families in her village, Dehghazi, she said, and twenty-one or twenty two people had been killed by the helicopter attacks in a few weeks.

She had one son in the *Mujahideen*—one of several hundred men fighting in the mountains of Kama and Gushtas—and had crossed the border with another, an eight-year-old named Matieullah.

"What of him?" I said.

"When he is old enough," she said, making a motion with two hands to her shoulder as if hoisting a rifle. But how many Matieullahs are there? Courage and hatred must have limits.

"Recognize reality" was a new phrase I heard during my 1984

visit; it referred to the fact that more and more people were recognizing the reality that the Afghan refugees were going to be in Pakistan for a very long time, perhaps forever. "The Palestinian analogy" was another phrase, this one used by Pakistanis frightened at the implications of three million armed foreigners in their midst. There had been a few more incidents. Armed refugees had come onto university campuses in Peshawar, trying to bully students into supporting the fundamentalist candidates of the Jamatt-i-Islami in university elections.

But still, Pakistan coped—in its own ways. Cars were decorated with large decals of the Great Seal of the United States with the crescent and star of Pakistan replacing the stars and stripes on the chest of the fierce eagle under the banner, "E Pluribus Unum." And behind a car with that decal on the Khyber Road was a Suzuki truck carrying six Soviet-manufactured refrigerators, just smuggled across from Afghanistan.

Such is life along the world's front line, the border between Afghanistan and Pakistan, with Soviet helicopter gunships on one side and the first twenty American F-16s in place now on the other side.

"Are you our best friend in this part of the world?" I asked General Zia.

"I don't think I should blow my own trumpet," he said, "but we're very proud of our association with the United States of America. If we come to a stage where such things as the invasion of Afghanistan are taken for granted, I think that's the end of the human race. Of human freedom."

That is what the Americans like to hear. And, whether or not he truly speaks for the 90 million people of Pakistan, Zia seems to believe he has grown into a selfless and benevolent protector of those people. A strong guide on the straight path.

I thought I saw Zia as he sees himself on Eid-ul-Fitr. I spent a good part of that holiday, the day of thanksgiving after the Holy Month of Ramadan, June 30, 1984, with him at a beautiful old State Guesthouse and then at his home, both in Rawalpindi. He cast himself as a Moghul ruler that day, dressed in a simple white *shalwar kameez*, receiving all who came to his gate. Then he held *Khuli Kuthchery*—"open court"—hearing the complaints and pleas of a few of the thousands who had waited in line to wish him *"Eid Mubarak,"* to shake his hand, embrace him, kiss his hands, beg his favor.

The ceremony lasted seven hours. The President and his wife arrived in a black Mercedes-Benz limousine, coming through the front gate and along a driveway that wound through formal gardens built around an artificial waterfall. Begum Zia went to a side portico of the rambling Moorish building, where she began to receive women visitors, first the wives and daughters of ambassadors and Pakistani officials, then women of the masses who waited by the gate. Zia began walking along a line of men in wheelchairs—"The handicapped are the specially privileged to the President," a minister told me—listening to each one, handing each one an envelope filled with rupees. The man with the envelopes followed him all day.

After a while, Zia took his position just inside the Guesthouse's main portico and the guests began coming to him—first the ambassadors, the generals, the ministers and the deputies, then "the masses," who had lined up at a side gate. After greeting their leader, the men pushed their way through tables of curries and rice, sweets and sodas. The number of people who came seemed to be three thousand, perhaps four thousand.

"I must have a job," a young man said when he reached Zia. "I want to make money to study art."

"No," the President said. "If you want to study, we have money for that." He handed the young man over to an aide with a clipboard. I was assured a scholarship would be granted.

"Any man may come today. No one is turned away; those are the President's orders," said a deputy minister as we walked along the line in the afternoon. "It is like the bell outside the palaces of the Moghuls. Any man in the kingdom could ring the bell and the leader would come to hear his petition."

"What do you think?" the deputy said, as we reached the last man.

"It's very impressive," I said.

"What do you think of the President?"

"I think he is impressive, too," I said, pausing to choose my words with care. I had been asked the question many times and had so far avoided offense. "Intelligent. Determined. Resourceful. Courageous. Very skillful."

"It would be very dangerous for people like you to write such things," he said.

"Dangerous? Why?"

"Because Americans must not believe that this is what the people of Pakistan want."

"What do the people want?" I asked.

"I have been in a few places in the world," the deputy said. "I have seen that people are the same everywhere. Human nature is the same everywhere. People want the same things everywhere.

"What do they want?"

"We are speaking unofficially?"

"Yes, of course."

"People here are the same as people in America. The people want democracy. The people want justice. The people want freedom."

ACKNOWLEDGMENTS

The opinions in this book are mine alone, but they were shaped by many people. Because some of these opinions might displease officials of the governments of Pakistan or the United States, I decided not to list the names of many men and women to whom I am indebted. Many Pakistanis shared their homes, their intelligence and their passion for their country with me, and I am grateful. But naming them here might cause them embarrassment or worse. (In two instances in this book, I have used pseudonyms to protect the identity of friends in Pakistan.) Many American officials and representatives of international organizations were generous and candid in long conversations about their work and the workings of various governments. But there is a chance that their service or careers would be compromised if I named them publicly.

William Shawn, the editor of *The New Yorker*, helped shape my thinking on my travels both before and after I was in Pakistan. Some of our conversations involved an article on the spread of the English language around the world. I never did do a separate piece on the subject, but the research went into this book. Two men who helped me with that were Joshua A. Fishman of Yeshiva University in New York, and Robert L. Cooper of the Hebrew University in Jerusalem.

My editor at Simon and Schuster, Alice Mayhew, did even

more than usual for me on this project; without her enthusiasm and encouragement there would be no book. I am also indebted to Richard Snyder, Ann Godoff, Sally Harvey, Michael Gast, Henry Ferris, Jane Stone, and to my agent, Lynn Nesbit.

Richard Reeves
New York
May 1984

INDEX

Abbottabad, 164, 168
Abdulla Khan, 52–53, 55, 63, 72,
  85, 96, 103
  background of, 52–53
Afghanistan:
  depopulation of, 81
  land reforms in, 72
  1978 coup in, 72
  Soviet invasion of, 24, 45, 63,
    64, 67, 73, 80–81
  women in, 74
Afghan *Mujahideen*, 63, 73, 75,
  78, 80, 84, 86, 191
Afghan refugee camps, 24
  as *Mujahideen* military bases,
    75
  Shultz's visit to, 49, 62–64
Afghan refugee operation:
  corruption in, 85–86
  costs of, 84–85
  Pakistani control of, 84–85
Afghan refugees, 53, 62–63, 69–
  88
  educational programs for, 83–
    84
  independence of, 86–87

as labor resource, 79
living conditions of, 81–82
medical facilities for, 73, 74,
  75–78, 82–83
Pakistani dislike for, 87–88
wages of, 42–43
women of, 73–74, 83
Afghan Surgical Hospital, Peshawar, 76–77
Afridis, 156
Afzal Khan, Muhammad, 29, 54
Aga Khan, 98
agriculture, mechanization of, 31
Ahmad, Yasmin, 161
Ahmadis, 98
Ahmed Minto, Mahmod, 58
air conditioners, popularity of,
  121, 122
Akbar the Great, 54
alcohol:
  available to foreigners, 167
  prohibition on, 49, 152–53
Alexander the Great, 27, 69, 75,
  156
Ali, Tariq, 67
Ali Shah Kateeh, Sultan, 92

All-India Muslim League, 92
Alvi, Hamid, 91, 93
Al Zulfiqar, 176
American Express, 20
Amnesty International, on human
    rights under Zia regime,
    176–77
Among the Believers (Naipaul),
    58
amputation, as punishment for
    thievery, 59
Anwar, Shabana, 151
Arabia, 103–4
Arabic language, 26, 133, 142
    alphabet of, 51–52, 135
Arafat, Yassir, 174
Ararain tribe, 175
Asia Overland, 55
Associated Press Pakistan, 37, 50,
    135
atomic bomb, Pakistani, 66–67,
    191, 200
Aurangzeb, 94
Avicenna Balkhi hospital, 75
Awami League, 118
Azad Kashmir, 171

Babar, Farhatullah, 124
Badshahi Mosque, Lahore, 94,
    98
bakshish, 111–12, 115
Baloch language, 131, 132
Baluchistan, 30, 31, 88, 113, 131
    Local Body Elections in, 179
    Provincial Assembly of, 115
    refugees in, 72
Bangladesh, 21, 40–41, 86, 131
    malnutrition in, 40–41
    see also East Pakistan
bazaar society, 31–32
Bengali language, 131
Bhutto, Begum Nusrat, 150–51,
    182
Bhutto, Benazir, 150–51
Bhutto, Murtaza, 176

Bhutto, Zulfiqar Ali, 98, 113,
    115, 117–19, 125, 150, 185,
    193
    background of, 117–18
    elections rigged by, 114, 118,
        172
    hanging of, 38, 67, 117, 119
    Islamic reforms of, 152
    Islamic socialism of, 89, 106–7
    nationalizations of, 118, 185
    policies of, 118–19
    repression under, 118, 176
    Roti, Kapra aur Makon slogan
        of, 33, 107, 117
    Zia and, 119, 172, 174
Biharis, 86
birth-control programs, 149
black market, 108, 113, 115
body language, 50
book piracy, 101
Brahmins, Muslims and, 98
brain drain, 123–24
Brantley, David, 126
Brezhnev, Leonid, 69
British Broadcasting Corporation
    (BBC), 181–82, 194
British Council, 39, 51, 141, 199
British rule, 109–10, 202
    democratic freedom under, 176
    Hindus vs. Muslims under,
        98–99, 105
    modernization under, 110
Bumburet, 24, 26, 27–30, 54,
    132–33
bureaucracy, *see* Civil Service
Burma, 154
    English instruction in, 142
burqa, 25, 31, 145
bus accidents, 164–65
Butt, Najeeb, 52

Callebaut, Paul Jacques, 59
cannabis, 153, 158
caste system, 43, 98

China, People's Republic of, 68, 106

Chitral, 24–27, 29, 30, 47, 69–70, 132, 158, 177
  health conditions in, 27
  houses of, 26–27
  Shani Bazaar of, 24–25

Christianity, Untouchables and, 95

Churchill, Winston, 156

Civil Service, 108–13, 135
  bureaucracy of, 43, 110
  corruption in, 111–13
  coup encouraged by, 113
  military alliance with, 113–14
  nationalized industries under, 118, 119
  politicians vs., 113
  Punjabi dominance of, 113–14

civil war of 1971, 40, 86, 118, 174, 197

Close, Michael, 140–41

Cole, Simon, 51, 136, 141–42

colonialism:
  British, 98–99, 105, 176, 202
  economic, 128

communism, threat of, 202

compounders (local pharmacists), 158–59

computer technology, 47–48, 139

Constitution of the Islamic Republic of Pakistan (1973), 102, 186, 188–89

coup of 1977, 119, 172

Cromwell (film), 168

Crusades, Christian, 54–55

dacoits (bandits), 165

Darra, gun shops of, 78

Dawn, 56–57, 120, 151, 165, 173, 180, 186, 204

defecation, public, 41

Defense Department, U.S., 159, 196

democracy:

communications and, 45
  in Pakistan, 103–4, 113, 178–79, 183, 186
  of U.S., 45–46, 60, 195

divorce, Family Laws and, 148

donkeys, as means of transportation, 126

dowries, Family Laws and, 148

Doxiades, Constantine, 41

Dragoon, 21

driving, dangers of, 164–65

Drug Enforcement Administration, U.S., 160–61

Dubai, 121

dupattas, 26

Dupree, Louis, 45–46, 54–55, 59, 109

East Pakistan, 92–93
  succession of, 40, 66, 88, 95, 118, 131
  see also Bangladesh

economy:
  growth rate of, 40
  underground, 108, 113, 115

Educational Grants Commission, 39

Edwardes College, Peshawar, 140–41

Egypt, U.S. aid to, 54, 65

Eid-ul-Fitr, 90–91, 163, 179

electrification plans, 40, 122

embracing in public, 169

English language, 93, 130, 131, 133–43
  American, 138–39
  instruction in, 39, 60, 134
  as international language, 48, 129, 133–39, 137n
  as language of Pakistani elite, 133–35, 139–40
  as language of science and technology, 139
  national policy conflicts over, 136, 137–38

entertainment, lack of, 164, 166–71

examination system, corruption in, 111–12

expectations, rising, 125–26

Fadoo, Hamid, 21
Faisal, King of Saudi Arabia, 94
Family Laws of 1961, 148
farming, subsistence, 47
Farsi language, 51
Fazl-ur-Rehman, Maulana, 37, 60, 105, 176
feudalism, modern, 201
film industry, 169
films:
    censorship of, 167
    Indian, 169
flag, Pakistani, 110–11
flogging, as punishment, 59
food production, 125
For Whom the Bell Tolls (film), 167
France, 60
    English language in, 136, 138
F-16 fighters, 31, 65, 92, 197
Fukuyama, Francis, 69

Gadani Beach, 17–22, 30, 39, 110, 112, 123
    shipbreaking industry at, 17–22, 116
Gandharan Buddhist art, 130
Gandhi, Mohandas K., 92
Gandhi (film), 169
General Dynamics, 65
Genghis Khan, 69, 75, 98
Gujranwala, 34, 183–84
Gujrat, 147

Hafeez, Sabeeha, 144–45
Hafia Kardar, Abdul, 107
hajj, 109, 173
Hangu, 82, 159

Haq, Mahbubul, 39–40, 48, 115, 120, 123, 149–50
Haq, Samiul, 185–86
Hasan, Mubashir, 111, 128–29, 149, 184, 194–95
hashish, 153, 157, 161, 162, 164
hashish oil, plans exported to West for manufacture of, 158
Hebrew language, 138
Hennessey, John W., 71–72, 74, 82–83
Herald magazine, 176
Hermitage, U.S.S., 17–19, 20, 21
heroin, 153–63
    addiction treatment centers for, 161
    "Golden Triangle" production of, curtailed, 154
    Khyber region production of, 155–56
    Pakistan as major supplier of, 66, 153–54, 157–61
    Pakistani addiction to, 161–62
    seizures of, 153, 159–60
Hidzyatullah (squash player), 158
High Commissioner for Refugees, U.N. (UNHCR), 75, 79, 82–87
    educational programs of, 83–84
Hindu Kush, 24, 25, 71, 73
Hindu Raj, 24
Hindustani (Hindi) language, 131
homosexual subculture, 149
Husain, Mairaj, 158, 159–60
Hussain Sayed, Mushahid, 51, 53–54, 60

IBM, 128
illiterate masses, 32
    growing power of, 177–20
    materialism of, 33, 122–23, 126, 203
    priorities of, 120
imports, reliance on, 122
income, per capita, 31

Independence, 37, 41, 92–93, 109
India, 33, 34, 171
  conciliation encouraged with, 191, 200
  domestic industry encouraged in, 122
  intervention in 1971 civil war of, 40, 86, 118, 174, 197
Pakistani attitudes toward, 66, 95
  poverty in, 124–25
  wars with, 66, 95, 171, 174
Indian Civil Service, preparation, 48
industrial development, lack of, 122
interest, ban on, 101
International Labor Organization, 84
International Monetary Fund, 48, 128, 184
International Rescue Committee, 72, 73, 74, 82
Iqbal, Muhammad, 94
Iran, 94, 96–97, 188, 197
  Afghan refugees in, 73
  revolution in, 54, 69, 154
Iranian refugees, in Pakistan, 86
Irfani, Suroosh, 124
Islam, 30, 96–107, 108
  democracy and, 103–4
  egalitarianism in, 58–59, 94, 102–3
  family and responsibility emphasized by, 58
  fatalism of, 164
  hospitality of, 72, 86
  in Indian subcontinent, 98–99
  modernization vs., 37, 96, 104–5, 106
  Pakistani identity and, 37, 89
  progressive vs. fundamentalist perspectives in, 53, 96–98, 109
  of Saudi Arabia, 36
  Sunni vs. Shia, 60, 96–97

  as traditional values, 37–38, 91
  Untouchables and, 94, 98
  women's role in, 35–36, 59, 145–48
Islamabad, 32, 36, 41–43, 46, 170
  Sports Complex of, 44
  U.S. Embassy burned in, 66, 124
Islamization program, 35–37, 61, 89, 96, 99–101, 106, 133, 139–40, 171, 193
  cynicism of, 35, 61, 100
  oligarchy and, 115
  women and, 145–48
Ismaclis, 98
Israel:
  English language in, 137–38
  Pakistani hostility to, 137–38

Jamatt-i-Islami, 84, 106, 107, 112, 116, 185
  Afghan Surgical Hospital run by, 76, 82
Jamil, Saira, 151
Jang, 181
Japan, economic relations with, 127, 128
Jesus of Nazareth, in Islam, 97
Jhang, 32
Jinnah, Muhammad Ali, 88, 92–93, 102, 106, 109, 110, 131, 176, 185, 188
  official documentary on, 169–70
jirga (tribal council), 74, 87, 156
Jordan, 174
Jullundur, 173

"kafir," 34, 98
Kalash Kafir, 27–30, 54, 132
  religion of, 28, 29
  unsanitary conditions of, 29–30
  women of, 28, 29
Kalashwar language, 29, 132
Kamal, Anwar, 61, 95

Karachi, 30, 31, 66, 113, 144, 154
Lyari, slum of, 161
Kareem, Abdul, 76, 77
Karmal, Babrak, 73
Kashmir, territorial claims to, 66, 95, 171
katchi abadis, 42, 73
Khaleej Times, 121
Khan, Fida Muhammad, 185
Khan, Firdaus, 81–82
Khan, Mohibullah, 158
Khan, Rahlmauddin, 179
Khan, Sahabzada Yaqub, 49–50, 63
Khan, Yahya, 68, 118
Khanzada Taj, 58
Khomeini, Ayatollah Ruhollah, 54, 94, 97
Khowar language, 132
Khyber Mail, 137
Khyber Pass, 46, 66, 154
Afghan imports through, 155
smuggling at, 157
Khyber region, 31, 112, 154–59
fortress homes of, 156–57
heroin production in, 155–56
opium production in, 154, 155
Khyber Road, 76, 156
under government control, 87, 154–55, 157
Kipling, Rudyard, 27, 110
Kohat, 72, 92, 144

labor:
as export, 124
low cost of, 19, 42–46
Lahore, 30, 37, 54, 61, 99, 113, 125
Lakhti Banda refugee camp, 74
Landi Kotal, 157
black market in, 155–57, 159
opium production at, 154, 155

Underground Bazaar at, 155, 157
landowners, political role of, 108, 114–15
languages, official, 30, 130–31
Laos, 154
Larkana, 182
Liaquat Ali Khan, 38
life expectancy, 125
literacy campaigns, 39, 198–200, 203
lack of U.S. support for, 199
Little, Rich, 168
Loewenthal, Isidore, 76
Lummumba University, Moscow, 136

McNamara, Robert, 39
McPherson, Ian, 171
madrasets (religious schools), 84
Majlis-e-Shura (Federal Council), 58, 60, 92, 102, 114, 146
calls for democracy in, 185–86
equated with elected body, 182
Zia democratization speech to, 187–90, 192, 194
maliks, 63, 72, 73, 74, 85
"Man Who Would Be King, The" (Kipling), 27
marriages, arranged, 56, 148
Martial Law, 114, 150, 151, 170, 176, 182, 185, 190, 192
Marx, Karl, 43, 202
Mastuj River, 24, 69
Maududi, Hussain, 107
Maududi, Maulana Abu'l A'Ala, 107
maulanas (*mullas*), 33, 34, 36, 57, 62, 97, 101, 105, 118, 149, 168, 173, 186
Mayhew, Philip R., 65
Metropolitan Women (Hafeez), 144–45
M-48 tanks, 65, 197

Middle Ages, 104–5
middle class, lack of, 108
military, 45, 108
    civil service alliance with, 113–
    114
    losing record of, 66
    Punjabi dominance of, 113–14
    rule of, 171–86
military courts, 178
military government, weakness
    of, 184–85
modernization, 20, 34, 39–48, 54,
    91–92, 93, 101
    under British rule, 110
    capital for, 128
    Islam vs., 37, 96
    problems of, 43–48, 140
    socialism and, 202, 203
    vertical social groupings vs.,
    116–17
    women's role and, 143, 149–50
    see also Sixth Plan
Moghul rule, 98
mohajir (migrants of 1947), 93,
    131
Mohmand, Mummand, 75, 80,
    81
Moorer, Thomas, 68–69
Mormons, 105
Movement for the Restoration of
    Democracy (MRD), 185, 186
Moynihan, Daniel Patrick, 159
Muhammad the Prophet, 97, 148
Mujahideen, 63, 73, 75, 78, 80,
    84, 86, 191
Mulk, Major, 69–70, 71, 86, 88,
    197
Muslim, 44, 51, 53, 57, 60, 102,
    124, 147, 165–66, 170, 181,
    186, 194–95
Mutiny of 1857, 105, 116

Naeem, Muhammad, 92
Naeemi, Muhammad Hussain,
    103

Naipaul, V. S., 58
names, Pakistani personal, 50–52
    Western confusion over, 50–52
Narcotics Control Board, 158,
    159, 161
Nasir Bagh, 62, 68, 71, 75
National Democratic Party, 185
national identity, 92–94, 95
    linguistic diversity vs., 93
    regional identification vs., 93
Nawa-I-Wagt, 135
nepotism, 111
Ne Win, 142
Nixon, Richard, 68
Nizam-i-Mustafa, 35, 102, 146
North-West Frontier Province,
    30, 113
    labor costs in, 42–43
    refugees in, 72, 79
    tribal law in, 87
nuclear research, Pakistani, 66–
    67, 191, 200

occupational safety, 19–20
oil crisis, 54
Operation Fairplay, 119, 172
opium, 153–55, 158, 160, 161
overseas Pakistanis, 121–24, 126,
    171
    remittances from, 122, 150

paan shops, 170
Pakistan International Airlines
    (PIA), 31, 47, 48, 49, 176,
    181
Pakistan National Alliance, 185
Pakistan People's Party, 107,
    113, 117, 118, 119, 151, 183,
    185
Pakistan Times, 32–33, 129, 134,
    144, 179–80, 182–83, 186
Palestine Liberation Organiza-
    tion, 174
Palestinians, 54

partition of 1947, 37, 41, 92–93, 109
Pathans, 19, 25, 32, 41, 46, 55, 88, 140, 156
  Afghan, 72–73
  independence of, 87–88
  as laborers in Gulf States, 79–80
  as shipbreakers, 19, 22, 116
Pemref company, 129
perdah, 144
Peshawar, 46, 62, 71, 74, 75–79, 81, 113, 140, 144, 159
  Dean's Hotel in, 78
  intrigue in, 78–79
  Qissa Qahani, bazaar of, 76
  Red Cross Surgical Hospital in, 77, 171
  video game parlors in, 32, 76
  as wartime city, 75–79
pharmaceutical drugs, 158–59
pirs, worship of, 99
poligamy, 55–56, 148
politics, Pakistani:
  military repression of, 166–67
  vertical groupings in, 116
pop music, campaign against, 35, 162, 163
population, rise of, 125
Population Welfare Plan of 1981, 149
Potwar, plateau of, 41
Powers, Francis Gary, 68
Prem Tinsulanonda, 136
press, Pakistani, 31, 179–83
  censorship of, 180–81
  government financial control of, 181
  government harassment of, 179
  "self-censorship" of, 181
Press Information Department (PID), 181, 182
prison, classes of, 115–16
prosperity, sense of, 124–25
Provisional Constitutional Order of 1981, 114

Pukhtunistan issue, 88
Punjab, 30, 88
  dominance of, 113–14
  drainage problems in, 125
  refugees in, 72
Punjabi language, 129, 131, 132, 139
Punjab University professors, subject to Conduct Rules for Civil Servants, 178–79
Pushtu language, 19, 46, 129, 131, 132, 139

Quaid-i-Azam, see Jinnah, Muhammad Ali
Queen, David, 138–39, 142
Quetta, 113, 174, 179
  heroin Treatment Centre at, 161
  Pakistan Army Staff College at, 174
Quran, Holy, 35, 38, 55–56, 62, 91, 97, 102, 104, 106, 133, 150, 153, 178, 190
  Afghan guerrillas and, 77
  egalitarianism in, 102
  on women, 146–47, 150

Rachman, Gul, 156
Rahman, Obaidur, 186
Ramazan, Holy Month of, 22, 36, 90, 163, 170
  fasting during, 57–58, 77
  foreigners and, 57–58
  productivity and, 36–37, 47
rape, laws on, 36, 147
Rawal, Lake, 163
Rawalpindi, 31, 42, 99
  District Language Committee of, 129
Rawalpindi Union of Journalists, 179
Red Crescent Society, 73, 82

Red Cross, International, 73, 82, 85
in Peshawar, 77–78
Red Fort, Delhi, 98
Rehman, Maulana, 46, 53, 112
Rios Monet, Efrain, 174
rising expectations, fear of, 125–26
Riyazul Haque, Anjam, 133, 141
Romberg, Alan, 192
Rushdie, Salman, 41, 64, 140

Saeed, Shabana, 151
Safina-e-Abid, 173
Saint Stephen's College, Delhi, 140, 173
Salabuddin, Muhammad, 104
Saudi Arabia, 33, 94
Afghan *Mujahideen* supported by, 86
Afghan refugee *madrasets* sponsored by, 84
Islam of, 36, 100–101
Pakistani workers in, 79–80, 101, 129
Sayed Abdul Rahman Hashmee, 74
Schaffer, Howard B., 65
sciences, encouragement of, 105–106
Shah Faisal Masjid, 94
shalwar kamzeez, 39, 41, 55, 163
Shame (Rushdie), 64, 140
Shariat Courts, 101
Shariff, Muhammad, 183
Shia Islam, 60, 94, 96–97, 181, 184
Shinwaris, 156
shipbreaking, 17–22
in Bangladesh, 21
labor-intensive nature of, 18–20, 21–22
profits from, 20
in Taiwan, 21
Shultz, George, 49–50

Afghan refugees visited by, 49, 62–64
Siddique, Muhammad, 17, 21
sifarish, 111–12
Sind, 30, 31, 88, 113, 117, 119, 131
Sindhi language, 131, 132
Sixth Plan, 34–35, 38, 40, 120
Science and Technology section of, 106
women under, 38, 143, 144, 150
slums:
growth of, 117
narcotics addiction in, 161
Smith, William French, 159
smugglers, smuggling, 108, 113, 115
narcotics, 157–58
socialism, advantages of, 201–3
society, vertical groupings in, 116–17
Soiffer, Warren, 51
Soviet Union, 33, 34, 54, 68, 202
Afghan hatred of, 76–77
Afghanistan strategy of, 80–81, 197
expansion of, 65, 196, 197–98
invasion of Afghanistan by, 24, 45, 63, 64, 67, 73, 80–81
Pakistan supplied arms by, 68
Spiers, Ronald, 68, 191–92
State Department, U.S., 173
on Pakistan relations, 64–66, 108–9, 115, 159, 196
Policy Planning Staff of, 69
Stevens, William, 168, 194
Stone, Edward Durrell, 42, 44
Strategic Review, 69
Study Group on the Teaching of Languages, 133, 134
Sufism, 167
Sunnah-a-Muttaqi, 103
Sunni Islam, 60, 97, 116
Supreme Court, 113

Suzuki, 127
Suzuki minitruck, 123, 126

Taiwan, 21
Taj Mahal, 98, 105
Tamerlane, 98
Taxila Archeological Museum,
    130
telephone service, direct dialing,
    47–48
television, 168–69
    commercials, 23
    news programs, 168–69
Thailand, 154
    English teaching in, 136
Tharparhar, 45
Tirich Mir, 24, 26
TOKTEN program, 123
toxic weapons use in Afghanistan,
    76–77
Toyota, 127
transportation system, 45, 126
    high accident rates in, 164–65
    trucks, folk art decorations of, 92,
    163
Tully, Mark, 182
Tur Gal, Haji, 74

United Arab Emirates, Pakistani
    laborers in, 80, 121
United Nations, 128, 149, 176,
    200
    Industrial Development Orga-
        nization of, 45, 127
    refugee aid from, 71, 73
    TOKTEN program of, 123
    see also High Commissioner
        for Refugees, U.N.
        (UNHCR)
United States, 33, 34, 54, 184
    Afghan Mujahideen supported
        by, 86, 191
    Afghan refugees and, 80, 85–86
    aid from, 51, 65, 196–200
    as ambivalent about Pakistani
        democracy, 67–68, 192

commercial investment by,
    126–29
democracy of, 45–46, 60, 195
diplomacy of, 190–92
mutual-defense cooperation
    treaty with, 66
narcotics-control efforts of,
    154, 159
objectives of, 64–65, 195–97,
    203
overseas military presence of,
    68–69
Pakistan compared with, 34,
    39, 45–46, 95–96
Pakistani expatriates in, 65
Pakistani relations with, 62–70
Pakistani students in, 123–24
unpopularity of, 192, 194–95,
    197
Zia supported by, 109, 183,
    185, 190, 192–94, 198, 204
Untouchables, 94–95, 98
urbanized elite, 31
Urdu language, 51, 93, 128, 129,
    141, 143
    Hindustani and, 131
    as national language, 131–32,
        133, 134, 138–39

video cassette recorders, 121
    as entertainment industry, 123,
        167–68, 170
video-game parlors, 32, 76, 170
violence:
    daily reports of, 165–66
    official, 176–77
    against women, 147–48
Voice of America, 181

Wasak refugee camp, 75
Wazir, Muhammad Al, 104
Western culture, Pakistani views
    of, 50, 52, 54–55, 56, 59–60

women, 25–26, 38–39, 68, 143–51
   Afghan, 73–74
   ban on athletic competition for, 36, 145
   under Bhutto regime, 119
   "chador, chadiwari" and, 25–26, 147, 149
   changing role of, 38, 146
   city vs. village, 144–45
   education of, 143
   engineers, 35–36
   health of, 143–44
   in Iran, 150
   under Islam, 35–36, 146, 148, 149
   laws of evidence and, 36, 101, 146
   segregation of, 145, 149
   subjugation of, 38, 148, 149
   violence against, 147–48
World Bank, 39, 48, 128, 184, 200
World Food Program, 74, 82, 85, 86

Yawar, Altaf, 37–38, 50, 53, 145

zakat, Shia protest against, 90, 97, 184
Zia Himayat Tehriq, 182
Zia-ul-Haq, Muhammad, 42, 45, 52, 53, 58, 60, 64, 66, 93, 109, 116, 132, 144, 150–53, 168, 170, 199, 200, 204
   Afghan refugees and, 79, 85, 183
   background and personality of, 172–76
   Bhutto and, 67, 119, 172, 174
   constitutional amendments proposed by, 189
   Constitution suspended by, 102, 183
   democracy and, 103–4, 113, 178–79, 183, 186
   Eid proclamation of, 90–91
   elections promised by, 103, 172, 178, 183, 189, 193, 200
   executions under, 176, 178
   human rights under, 176–77
   Islamic advisers of, 36, 96, 188
   Islamization and, 35–37, 61, 89, 96, 99–101, 102, 140, 183, 187–90, 192, 193
   Japan visit of, 127
   narcotics banned by, 153
   Pakistani press and, 179–80
   political parties and, 119–20
   prohibition decree of, 49, 152–53
   puritanism of, 163, 166
   religious devotion of, 167, 175
   U.S. support for, 67, 100, 183, 185, 190, 192, 193–94, 198, 204
   on women, 35–36, 146, 147, 189

ABOUT THE AUTHOR

RICHARD REEVES is a writer for *The New Yorker* magazine and has been a reporter for *The New York Times* and an editor of *New York* and *Esquire*. His syndicated column appears twice weekly in more than 150 newspapers. He is the chief correspondent of "Frontline," the Public Broadcasting Service's documentary series. He is the author of six books.

DATE DUE